Contents

A 'History' play

The King of England is a unique personage. He does not achieve his position by effort and intelligence; he does not win it by power and force; and he is not elected by the people that he will rule. He is *born* to be king—chosen by God for that special purpose; and he is 'God's substitute, His deputy anointed in His right'. That quotation is from Shakespeare's play *Richard II*, and it states the official Elizabethan view of the monarchy. Such doctrine was taught in the schools, the churches—and even the theatres.

The Elizabethans were afraid of rebellion. The country was enjoying an uneasy peace under Elizabeth I, and the politicians were anxious to maintain this peace. The Queen was threatened by those (chiefly Roman Catholics) who disputed her right to the throne, so it was essential for her supporters to warn the English people of the dangers of rebelling against a divinely ordained ruler. The history of England provided plenty of examples.

Shakespeare was not the only dramatist to write plays on 'historical' subjects; but he certainly wrote *more* than anyone else, so that it is safe to infer that he was fascinated by his country's past, and that he recognized the lessons which the past might give to the future. His greatest inspiration came from the events that followed the crisis in 1399, when Henry Bolingbroke deposed King Richard II and usurped his crown. Shakespeare wrote eight plays around this subject, and they seem to form two groups of four (i.e., two 'tetralogies'), although the plays were not written in the chronological order of the reigns which they describe. The first tetralogy—the group of plays that Shakespeare wrote first—consisted of the three *Henry VI* plays with *Richard III*: the second group starts with *Richard II*, continues with the two *Henry IV* plays, and comes to a triumphant conclusion with *Henry V*.

The moral lesson that can be drawn from the eight plays is the very orthodox teaching that it is wrong to rebel against God's true king, even though he is not a good ruler; and God will punish such rebellion—but He will do so in His own time. Henry Bolingbroke wears Richard's crown, but it does not bring him happiness: he never feels secure, and he is always conscious of his guilt. At his death his son takes the crown, becoming (legitimately)

Oxford School Shakespeare

Henry IV Part I

edited by

Roma Gill, OBE
M.A. *Cantab*. B.Litt. *Oxon*

Oxford University Press
Oxford Toronto Melbourne

Oxford University Press, Walton Street, Oxford OX2 6DP

Oxford New York Athens Auckland Bangkok Bombay Calcutta Cape Town Dar es Salaam Delhi Florence Hong Kong Istanbul Karachi Kuala Lumpur Madras Madrid Melbourne Mexico City Nairobi Paris Singapore Taipei Tokyo Toronto

and associated companies in
Berlin Ibadan

Oxford is a trade mark of Oxford University Press

Reprinted 1990, 1992
Revised edition first published 1993
Reprinted 1995
Trade edition first published 1996

ISBN 0 19 831991 6 (Trade edition) 1 3 5 7 9 10 8 6 4 2
ISBN 0 19 831969 X (School edition) 3 5 7 9 10 8 6 4

Illustrations by Shirley Tourret

Cover photograph by Robbie Jack shows Michael Maloney as Prince Hal, and Robert Stephens as Falstaff, in the Royal Shakespeare Company's 1991 production of *Henry IV Part One*.

For Joanna

Oxford School Shakespeare
edited by Roma Gill

A Midsummer Night's Dream
Romeo and Juliet
As You Like It
Macbeth
Julius Caesar
The Merchant of Venice
Henry IV Part I
Twelfth Night
The Taming of the Shrew
Othello
Hamlet
King Lear
Henry V
The Winter's Tale

Printed in Great Britain at the University Press, Cambridge

Henry V; but Shakespeare still insists on the guilt of the rebellion, and before his most famous victory, at Agincourt, Henry V prays

> Not today, O Lord!
> O not today, think not upon the fault
> My father made in compassing the crown!

The 'fault' was not punished at Agincourt—nor, indeed, in the whole reign of King Henry V, whom the Elizabethans regarded as a great national hero. After the death of Henry V, however, the country endured great suffering under the weak King Henry VI and the tyrant Richard III; order and harmony were restored at the accession of Henry Tudor—King Henry VII— in 1485.

Shakespeare could assume that his sixteenth-century audiences would be familiar with some English history—even if they knew no more than the brief outline I have sketched here. To make sure that they understood the circumstances of Bolingbroke's usurpation of the English crown, he puts the details into the mouths of the rebels, who frequently seek to justify their actions by recalling the events which immediately preceded the death of Richard II.

These events were the subject of Shakespeare's play *Richard II*, which opened when the young Bolingbroke was sentenced to exile by the King. Old John of Gaunt, Bolingbroke's father, died; and the King confiscated his property—the land and goods which properly belonged to the eldest son. This theft gave Bolingbroke an excuse to break his exile and return to England. Members of the Percy family, outraged by the King's action, pledged their support to the injured heir, so long as he was trying to reclaim his own property. But the dukedom of Lancaster—his rightful heritage—was not enough for Bolingbroke, whose ambition reached to Richard's crown. Eventually Richard was compelled to resign—but he insisted that he was, and always would be, the true king:

> Not all the water in the rough, rude sea
> Can wash the balm off from an anointed king.

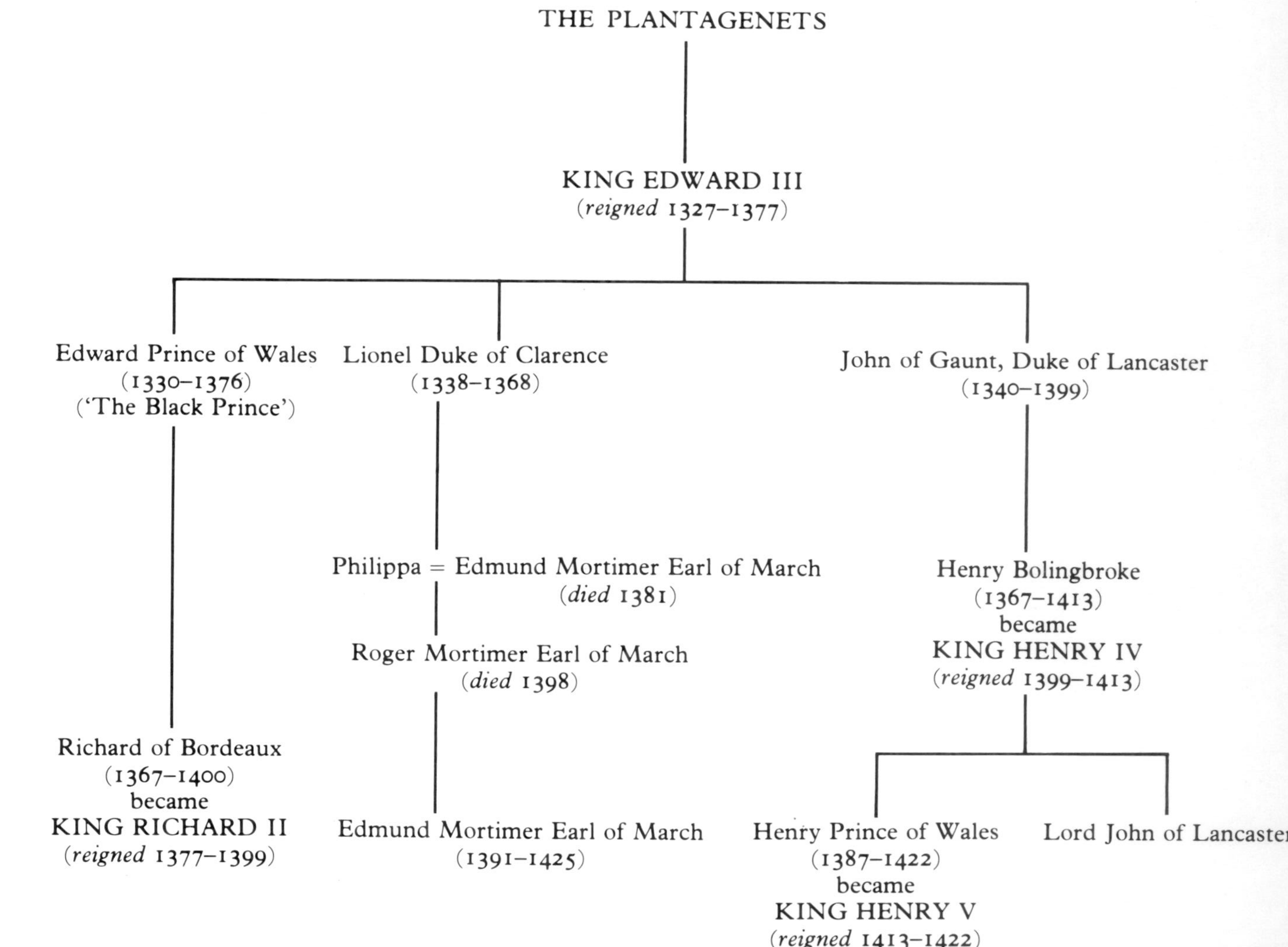
THE PLANTAGENETS
KING EDWARD III
(reigned 1327–1377)
Edward Prince of Wales
(1330–1376)
('The Black Prince')
Lionel Duke of Clarence
(1338–1368)
John of Gaunt, Duke of Lancaster
(1340–1399)
Philippa = Edmund Mortimer Earl of March
(died 1381)
Henry Bolingbroke
(1367–1413)
became
KING HENRY IV
(reigned 1399–1413)
Roger Mortimer Earl of March
(died 1398)
Richard of Bordeaux
(1367–1400)
became
KING RICHARD II
(reigned 1377–1399)
Edmund Mortimer Earl of March
(1391–1425)
Henry Prince of Wales
(1387–1422)
became
KING HENRY V
(reigned 1413–1422)
Lord John of Lancaster

The MORTIMERS and the PERCYS

Henry PERCY (Earl of Northumberland: *died* 1408)

Thomas PERCY (Earl of Worcester: *executed* 1403)

Edmund MORTIMER (Earl of March: *died* 1381)

OWEN GLENDOWER (1359–1416)

Henry PERCY ('Hotspur') (1364–1403) = Elizabeth (Lady Percy: *died* 1444)

Roger MORTIMER (Earl of March: 1374–1398)

Edmund MORTIMER (1376–1409) = Catherine (Lady Mortimer: *died* 1413)

Edmund MORTIMER (*born* 1391)

Leading characters in the play

King Henry IV This is a very worried man. When he was plain Henry Bolingbroke, he was exiled from his native country—England—but returned (after his father's death) to claim his inheritance. Soon afterwards, he deposed the King, Richard II, and usurped his throne. Now he has two great problems. He is afraid that he too may lose his throne and kingdom; and he is distressed because his elder son and heir, the Prince of Wales, seems to be a riotous, irresponsible young man.

Prince Hal The Prince of Wales is having a good time. He and his friends are usually found in taverns, and he seems to have no sense of the proper behaviour for a prince. But gradually we learn that Hal is not a mere 'playboy'.

Hotspur This is the nickname of Henry Percy, son of one of the King's chief opponents. He is young and impetuous (as the nickname suggests), but he is also a very valiant warrior who has already won a great reputation for himself. He has an exaggerated sense of military honour, which he values above everything else.

Sir John Falstaff A most complex character. He is a fat knight, who eats too much, drinks too much, and spends most of his time in the tavern. He has a great sense of humour—and makes fun of himself, as well as laughing at the other characters. He is also a liar, a thief, and a coward. Falstaff has no historical counterpart, but the original name of this character was 'Oldcastle'—which suggests that Sir John Oldcastle, a Lollard who was hanged for heresy in 1417, might have provided the inspiration for the frequent Biblical quotations and Puritan speech mannerisms which Shakespeare's character uses to comic effect.

Henry IV Part 1: commentary

Act 1

Scene 1 The play's first scene takes place in the Palace of Westminster, and we might expect to find the splendour of a royal palace combined with the vitality of the political heart of England. But the King's first speech has neither splendour nor vitality. King Henry is weary—a fact which is conveyed by the words he uses (such as 'shaken' and 'wan with care') and also by the rhythm of the lines. He speaks of the peace that has been achieved, but it is a 'frighted peace'—an insecure period waiting for the next outbreak of war, 'To be commenc'd in stronds afar remote'. The King is determined, however, that there shall be no more *civil* war—never again will England 'daub her lips with her own children's blood'. This personification of England introduces into the play an idea which was always popular with the Elizabethans: they believed that there was a similarity (or 'correspondence') between the human body and the state or country (which was the 'body politic').

Another favourite Elizabethan notion appears when King Henry compares the opposed armies to 'the meteors of a troubled heaven'. Disturbances in the universe—such as storms, thunder and lightning, or meteors—were said to reflect, or even foretell, major events happening on earth: a character in Shakespeare's *Julius Caesar* declares that 'The heavens themselves blaze forth the death of princes'. This idea recurs frequently in *1 Henry IV*.

Now that the King and his country are enjoying peace—even though it is a 'frighted peace'—it is possible for Henry to look forward to a project which is very dear to his heart: he longs to lead a crusade to the Holy Land, so that his Christian soldiers will 'chase these pagans [the Turks] in those holy fields'. This will not be a holiday but a pilgrimage, in which Henry Bolingbroke can try to atone for his sin in usurping the throne of England and causing the death of the rightful king, Richard II. He has cherished this plan for at least a year ('our purpose now is twelve month old'); but he is still frustrated.

When Westmoreland tells of the Council meeting which was

interrupted because new fighting had broken out, we (audience or readers) become more conscious of the tense political situation. In Wales 'the noble Mortimer' has suffered defeat, and further north 'the gallant Hotspur' has been doing battle with 'brave Archibald', the Earl of Douglas. This news must bring gloom—but there is fresh information: the Scots have been defeated, and Hotspur has won yet another 'gallant prize'.

When Westmoreland agrees that Hotspur has made a noble conquest, he uses an unfortunate expression: 'It is a conquest for a prince to boast of'. The word 'prince' reminds King Henry of his own son, Prince Hal, who is a great disappointment to his father. This is the first comparison of Hotspur and Prince Hal, and it should prepare us for one of the most important aspects of *1 Henry IV*: through the constant contrast of the two, Shakespeare is able to examine the personalities of both (but especially of the Prince of Wales); and he also seems to be posing the question: 'What are the qualities that make a good king?'

Scene 2

In the first scene King Henry spoke of his son's 'riot and dishonour'; the second scene shows what he means by this. In a very relaxed atmosphere (quite unlike the formality which precedes it), Prince Hal is chatting to his best friend, Sir John Falstaff. Their conversation is light-hearted, and full of jokes (especially puns—which play with the two meanings of a word). Falstaff (see p. xxv) has a very quick, inventive mind; it is usually he who begins the word-play, and the young Prince tries hard to match the older man's wit. But when Falstaff suggests an illegal action—robbing travellers on the way to London—the Prince is unwilling to join his friend. He does, however, agree to the proposal made by Poins that the two of them should waylay Falstaff after his robbery. In this way the young Prince can have the fun of law-breaking, and yet do no harm.

The scene ends with a soliloquy in which Prince Hal—who is now alone on the stage—speaks aloud his thoughts. He knows that his companions are not suitable friends for a prince, and that his own behaviour attracts serious criticism. But for the time being, he intends to have his fun and 'awhile uphold The unyok'd humour of [their] idleness'. Eventually, however, he will reform and 'throw off' his present 'loose behaviour' in such a way that he will be praised and admired for his reformation.

It is not easy to be sure how Shakespeare intends us to react to this speech. Some people regard Hal as a cold, scheming hypocrite, who has no real feeling for those whom he calls his friends and is simply making use of them until it pleases him to drop them and forget all about them. I personally feel that Hal must be a very *lonely* young man: his position as heir to the throne sets him apart from other men, and however much he wants to be like them, he can never escape from his heritage. Even when he is at ease, laughing with Falstaff, some of the jokes refer to his inescapable future: 'were it not here apparent that thou art heir apparent . . .' Prince Hal knows that he must soon reject his friends and take upon himself the responsibilities of his position—but not yet! He feels unready—and certainly unwilling—to leave his youthful, irresponsible life-style; perhaps he is trying to justify to himself the reasons for his failure to reform?

The verse of this soliloquy makes a sharp contrast with the prose in which the rest of this scene is written, and the contrast emphasizes the importance of Hal's thoughts. It is in fact the only speech of its kind in the whole play. We never again see so deeply into Hal's mind and heart—and no other character shows such depth of thought and feeling.

Scene 3 The scene and mood change again when we meet the third set of characters in the play—those who will soon show themselves as rebels against the King. As he promised at the end of Scene 1, King Henry has sent for Hotspur, and now the angry King confronts his mutinous subjects—the Earls of Northumberland and Worcester, and young Hotspur. The King reminds them that he is their ruler, 'Mighty and to be fear'd'; and in response Worcester reminds the King that he achieved his position only with their assistance. This short exchange recalls the past revolt, when Bolingbroke deposed Richard II; and it also prepares for what is to come.

The Earl of Northumberland is not so antagonistic towards the King, and both he and his son (Hotspur) try to pacify their enraged monarch. Hotspur tries to explain the circumstances of his refusal to surrender the prisoners, and his speech brings a lightness—even comedy—into a tense situation. But the King's suspicions are not so easily satisfied. He repeats his demand for the prisoners, and also, even more forcefully, his refusal 'To ransom home revolted Mortimer'. Hotspur is passionate in his defence of Mortimer as a loyal and valiant soldier who had fought nobly for the King. Tempers rise again, and Henry leaves the stage with a threat: 'Send us your prisoners, or you will hear of it'.

After the King has gone, Hotspur demonstrates the fiery spirit that has earned his nickname. Apparently the young man is ignorant of Edmund Mortimer's claims to the throne (see p. 126), and of the part played by his own uncle and his father (Worcester and Northumberland) in establishing Henry Bolingbroke as King of England. Now he refers to the deposed Richard as 'that sweet lovely rose', and contrasts the present king by referring to 'this thorn, this canker Bolingbroke'. The 'rose' imagery is significant, because in the elaborate system of 'correspondences' which the Elizabethans loved, the *rose* was held to be head of the flower hierarchy—the 'king' among flowers—and therefore an appropriate emblem for the human king.

The passionate outburst also shows Hotspur's devotion to the ideals of 'honour' (which for him means military glory), which is in complete contrast to his uncle's cold, calculated scheming. Hotspur is slow to understand Worcester's intentions, but the older man is patient: he knows that the valiant Hotspur is essential to the scheme. But at last Hotspur appears to comprehend—and of course he is eager to join in the fighting which must follow:

O, let the hours be short
Till fields, and blows, and groans applaud our sport.

Act 2

Scene 1 — In the Elizabethan theatre there were no curtains to separate the audience from the stage, and no artificial lighting; consequently there were no sudden breaks (such as we are accustomed to nowadays) in the movement of the play. So Hotspur would leave at one side of the stage, following the conspirators with his longing for *action*—and at the other side of the stage there would appear the two Carriers, yawning and scratching their flea-bites as they prepare for another day's work. When the robber Gadshill talks to the inn's Chamberlain, we hear of another conspiracy, which is also carefully plotted.

Scene 2 — This scene flows smoothly into Scene 2, where Prince Hal and Poins play tricks on their fat friend, Sir John Falstaff. The knight's anger at the loss of his horse turns to boyish delight when he can join in the robbery (although he seems to do little more than encourage the real thieves by shouting insults at their victims). When the disguised Prince and Poins attack the 'true thieves', there is no word from Falstaff, but the stage-direction in the earliest editions suggests that he is not quite so afraid as the others: '*They all run away, and Falstaff after a blow or two runs away too*'. But the best part of the joke will come when they all meet together at the tavern in Eastcheap.

Scene 3 Before we can enjoy this comedy, however, we must return to the serious business of the play. The scene changes to the north of England, where Hotspur is reading a letter. It is clear that there are problems, but Hotspur dismisses these with humorous impatience. The writer of the letter (we never learn his identity) is refusing to join the rebels. He tries to persuade Hotspur that the undertaking is dangerous—but this does not deter the fiery young revolutionary who scoffs: 'Why, that's certain; 'tis dangerous to take a cold, to sleep, to drink'. But although we laugh with Hotspur, we also become aware of the foolishness of the rebellion, and of the danger which the rebels are in. Hotspur recognizes the danger—but pretends to laugh at it: 'Hang him, let him tell the King! We are prepared'.

This sounds like bold defiance—but when we hear the words of Hotspur's wife we realize that her husband is more anxious than he will admit. Lady Percy—Kate—is distressed because her husband shows symptoms of acute depression (although of course he will not admit that he is worried). He has no appetite for food, he sleeps badly, and he has no sexual desires—for the past two weeks Kate has been 'A banish'd woman from [her] Harry's bed', but she has heard him talking in his troubled sleep. Lady Percy's tenderness for her husband suggests that there is another aspect of Hotspur's character—one that the play has not so far revealed: as well as being hot-tempered and impetuous (but not without a sense of humour) he is a man who is dearly loved by his wife.

Hotspur, however, ignores Kate's pleadings; or else he does not hear them—his mind is fixed on the business he must now deal with, and he calls for his horse. But when the Servant has left them alone, the husband and wife play a short scene of delightful intimacy, where Hotspur refuses to give serious answers to Kate's questions and she, in loving desperation, offers a lover's threat: 'I'll break thy little finger, Harry'.

Their parting shows a rather more mature Hotspur than we have seen before. He teases Kate, but explains that this is not a time to spend in making love; he loves and trusts his wife—but he believes that women are weak and may be easily tempted: 'constant you are, But yet a woman'. But he promises that she shall join him, and they will not be separated for long: 'Today will I set forth, tomorrow you'.

Scene 4

The gentle emotion of this scene gives way to some of the finest comedy in the whole play—in what is also (perhaps) the play's most serious scene. The opening is slow. Prince Hal has been drinking in the tavern cellars at Eastcheap in London, where he and Poins arranged to meet Falstaff and the other thieves after the robbery at Gad's Hill. Hal is absurdly proud that he has won the approval of the inn's apprentice-lads—the Drawers; but at the same time he realizes that this kind of behaviour is degrading, very much beneath the dignity of a future king: 'I have sounded the very base-string of humility'.

Hal has devised a trick to play on the slow-witted apprentice, Francis. It is not a very clever joke; even Poins seems unable to appreciate the fun, having to ask the Prince to explain what it is about ('come, what's the issue?'). Hal, however, seems to be almost drunk—and certainly without any serious worries. When Falstaff enters the fun begins. Pretending to ignore the Prince, the fat knight laments the state of the world, which is full of cowards who will not keep their promises. When Hal at last interrupts him, Falstaff turns his attack on the Prince. After a short verbal combat with Hal, Falstaff starts to demonstrate his greatest accomplishment: he is the master of *lies*!

The comedy increases as the number of the 'rogues in buckram' increases. All the time, Falstaff protests his honesty—if he is lying, he is 'an Ebrew Jew', 'a bunch of radish', and 'no two-legged creature'. All the time, of course, Prince Hal, with Poins (and the audience or readers), knows the real truth.

When Falstaff makes an obvious mistake, the Prince challenges his story: 'how couldst thou know these men in Kendal green when it was so dark thou couldst not see thy hand?' Anyone but Falstaff would certainly be embarrassed by such a question—but Sir John is not easily upset. By now it is very clear that he too knows what has happened: he is taking part in the joke to please the Prince, and instead of trying to hide from 'this open and apparent shame', he offers a comical reason for his behaviour: 'I was now a coward upon instinct'.

The laughter is interrupted by the arrival of the King's messenger, bringing information that war has been declared, and summoning Hal to the interview with his father when (as Falstaff knows) he will be severely reprimanded ('horribly chid') for his present conduct. There is a feeling that this is the last time the friends will be together in such a relaxed, carefree, happiness. To make the most of it, Prince Hal and Falstaff amuse themselves (and the spectators in the tavern) by acting in fun the scene which will soon become serious—the Prince's interview with King Henry IV.

First, Falstaff plays the part of the King, reproaching Hal for his unseemly conduct and unsuitable friends, but singling out for praise one 'virtuous man' who is 'A goodly portly man . . . of a cheerful look, a pleasing eye, and a most noble carriage'. This is Falstaff's defence of himself, expressed in eloquent prose which has many of the Elizabethan beauties of language (although, of course, the comedy of the situation turns these rhetorical devices into parody). But when Falstaff has finished speaking in self-defence, Hal 'deposes' him—taking from him the stool that was his 'throne' and the 'leaden dagger' that he used as a 'golden sceptre'. Now Hal speaks as though he were the King, and he makes an accusation of Falstaff—the 'old fat man'—with surprising violence. These different descriptions of Falstaff demand that we should re-consider our own views of the character. Is he simply 'old and merry'—a good companion who is always ready to share a drink and a joke? Or is he in fact a 'villainous abominable misleader of youth'?

Falstaff ends his defence of himself with a declaration which, though spoken apparently in fun, is received with the utmost seriousness. 'Banish plump Jack, and banish all the world'. The actor who plays the part of Prince Hal now has a very difficult choice to make: how shall he speak the Prince's next words? Whatever intonation he chooses, I think there should be a pause after 'I will'. The other characters wait in embarrassed silence to hear how Falstaff will turn *this* situation into comedy. And Falstaff himself (for the first—and only—time in the play) does not have a ready answer. He knows that with these words, Hal has pronounced a sentence of banishment on 'old Jack Falstaff'.

Before Falstaff can make any response, the tension of the situation is broken by the knocking at the door. The sheriff has come to charge Falstaff with the Gad's Hill robbery. For the time being, everything returns to its normal state: Falstaff hides; Hal protects his friend, and promises to settle the damage—and more: 'The money shall be paid back again with advantage'.

But there is a sense that, 'betimes in the morning', things will be very different.

Act 3

Scene 1 Whilst we have been laughing in the tavern, the King's enemies have been gathering forces; now their leaders have met together in Wales.

Owen Glendower makes his first appearance in the play. The references to him in earlier scenes should have prepared us for a rather unusual character—he was described as 'irregular and wild' in the play's first scene (line 40); and at another time King Henry spoke of 'that great magician, damn'd Glendower' (*1*, 3, 82). The man himself believes that he has magic powers, and tries to impress Hotspur by telling of the mysteries that surrounded his birth, and of his wonderful skills: 'I can call spirits from the vasty deep'. He uses 'call' in a technical sense (meaning 'conjure up'), but Hotspur refuses to be impressed and responds with humorous commonsense, pretending that 'call' has its usual meaning:

> Why, so can I, or can any man;
> But will they come when you do call for them?

This amusing interlude is the preface to some very serious business.

The rebels plan to divide between them the united kingdom of England and Wales so that (after they have defeated King Henry IV) each of the three leaders (Mortimer, Hotspur, and Glendower) will rule over one-third of the land. An Elizabethan audience would know immediately that it is very wrong to make any such division—and the argument between Hotspur and Glendower gives a hint of the kind of territorial disputes that would inevitably follow any partition. But for the moment the dispute is not serious, and the two are easily calmed.

Glendower goes to find the ladies, leaving Mortimer and Worcester to reprove Hotspur for his lack of respect. The scene ends with music, and the teasing tenderness of Hotspur and his wife, Kate.

Scene 2 Meanwhile in London the King has been making *his* preparations for war; and this is the day for the interview with his elder son, the Prince of Wales. Remembering the comedy of the mock-interview with Falstaff, we become even more sensitive to the solemnity of the present scene.

King Henry speaks more in sorrow than anger as he reproaches Hal for his wild behaviour; his distress and disappointment in his son make him believe that God is angry with him, and perhaps using Hal as a means of punishing the 'mistreadings' of the past (i.e. his usurpation of the throne of England). Hal humbly asks for his father's forgiveness, confessing that there is *some* truth in the accusations made against him. The King grants pardon ('God pardon thee!'), but insists upon giving a lecture to Hal, pointing out the difference between his own conduct as a young man, and the present conduct of his son. He compares Prince Hal to the foolish Richard II, whose crown Henry now wears: this should be a warning to the Prince, who will inherit the crown and must develop the sense of responsibility which will make him fit to wear it. Henry finally speaks of Hotspur, whose fine military career (like that of the King himself) seems to entitle him—rather than Prince Hal—to be the next heir to the throne:

> He hath more worthy interest to the state
> Than thou the shadow of succession.

This comparison seems to hurt Hal, especially when his father speaks of the advance of the rebels and of his feeling that Prince Hal, more than the Percy family, is his 'nearest and dearest enemy'. Hal reassures his father; and we can see that the time has come when (as he promised at the end of *Act 1*, Scene 2) he will 'throw off' his 'loose behaviour' and present himself as he really is—a worthy successor to Henry IV.

The King trusts his son at last; and the scene ends as he gives marching orders to meet the rebels at Shrewsbury.

Scene 3 At the Boar's Head tavern, Falstaff is examining his life and (like Prince Hal) vowing to repent. But we cannot believe *him* as we believe the Prince: Falstaff's repentance is due to his 'hangover' after the heavy drinking of the previous night, and Bardolph observes that he is 'fretful'. Yet Falstaff is still in command of his inventive wit, and he cheers up when he starts abusing the red-faced Bardolph with amazing insults. For a short time Falstaff is in control of the situation, as he insults Bardolph and argues with the Hostess; but all the characters have to become sober again when Prince Hal enters with Peto. A stage-direction in the early editions describes how Falstaff should greet the Prince—'*playing upon his truncheon like a fife*'. This direction may have been written by Shakespeare himself, and it shows yet another quick move on the part of Falstaff. Just before the Prince's entrance, Falstaff was threatening to beat Hal: 'and he were here I would cudgel him like a dog'. Presumably he raised his 'truncheon' as he spoke the line; but on the arrival of the Prince he turns the weapon into an imagined musical instrument.

The same stage-direction instructs the Prince that he is to enter '*marching*'; and Falstaff immediately realizes what this means; 'Is the wind in that door, i'faith? Must we all march?'. Very quickly (but still with comedy) all the problems created by the Gad's Hill robbery are sorted out; the episode is finished. Arrangements are made for the next, more serious, engagement; then Prince Hal leaves the tavern with the heroic words:

> The land is burning, Percy stands on high,
> And either we or they must lower lie.

It is a fine battle-cry, and Falstaff applauds it. But he will not follow the Prince until he has eaten his breakfast.

Act 4

Scene 1 The Fourth Act is an Act of *preparation*, in which we witness all the different characters making their plans for war. The first scene is set in the rebel camp, where Hotspur and the Earl of Douglas are exchanging compliments. In the first scene of the play we heard how Hotspur encountered Douglas as an enemy and defeated him at the battle of Holmedon—but now the enmity is forgotten as the two warriors join forces against King Henry. Hotspur's pleasure in his new ally soon gives way to disappointment when he hears—by letter—that his father is 'grievous sick' and cannot join in the fighting. At first Hotspur is angry, thinking of the effect his father's absence will have; but he quickly decides how to turn this apparent loss of support into a positive advantage to the rebels.

He maintains his confidence when news is brought of the King's approaching army, although this sounds very much more powerful than his own forces. He asks scornfully about Prince Hal, 'The nimble-footed madcap Prince of Wales'. Vernon replies, giving a brief description of the splendid appearance of the King's army; and then he speaks about 'young Harry'. He seems to describe a very different character from the one we are already familiar with: this is the *new*, reformed, Prince of Wales—a glamorous knight in glittering armour, who seems more like a Greek god ('feather'd Mercury') than a human being.

If he is dismayed by this account, Hotspur tries to hide his feelings and urge his supporters to fight. But there is one more piece of bad news: the Welsh Glendower will not be fighting with the rebels because he is still unprepared for war—'He cannot draw his power this fourteen days'.

Hotspur speaks brave words as he leaves the stage, but it is already clear to him (and to us) that the rebellion is doomed to failure. Douglas tells him to 'Talk not of dying'; but Hotspur makes no reply.

Scene 2 The gloom of Scene 1 is quickly lightened at the start of Scene 2 when Falstaff gives an account of his conscription techniques, confessing at once that he has 'misused the King's press damnably'. The King's authority allowed him to conscript into his regiment any man he chose; and Falstaff chose only those men who were willing and able to bribe him so that he would release them from the service. Consequently his regiment now consists only of miserable wretches who are not even properly clothed. When Prince Hal sees them, he is horrified: 'I did never see such pitiful rascals'. But Falstaff has no pity, dismissing them contemptuously as 'food for powder'.

It seems probable (since there is no stage-direction for them) that these poor 'scarecrows' do not appear on the stage. If the audience were to *see* them, the scene would lose much of its comedy—and Falstaff would lose some of the audience's sympathy. But the scene changes quickly; and we are back in the rebel camp again.

Scene 3 Whilst the rebels are arguing about the best time to start fighting, they are interrupted by the arrival of Sir Walter Blunt with a final offer of peace from the King. King Henry has asked for a full statement of their grievances, so once again we are reminded of the historical circumstances: the usurping of the crown by Henry Bolingbroke, and the murder of Richard II. The battle is postponed.

The Archbishop of York is also one of the rebel 'confederacy', and in this short scene we learn from him that many of the King's opponents have not presented themselves on the battlefield at Shrewsbury. This is a very useful scene. The Archbishop and Sir Michael are not important characters, and so our attention is not at all distracted from what they say. They repeat the names of those who have joined Hotspur and the other rebels to fight against the King; and the Archbishop names the different leaders of King Henry's forces.

In addition to this useful roll-call of the opposing sides, the Archbishop voices a fear for the future:

> if Lord Percy thrive not, ere the King
> Dismiss his power he means to visit us.

The fighting at Shrewsbury will bring *1 Henry IV* to an end; but this will not be the end of his troubles for King Henry IV: Shakespeare is in possession of enough material for *2 Henry IV*.

Act 5

Scene 1

Now we are ready for the battle at Shrewsbury, where even the weather seems to be disturbed by the preparations for war. But before the fighting starts the King makes yet another offer of peace, and Worcester re-states the grievances of the rebels. In the hope of avoiding total war Prince Hal suggests a token combat, in which he alone will fight with Hotspur; but the King can see that this would not be an adequate solution. He makes his final peace offer.

Both the King and his son are shown to good advantage in this debate with Worcester. Henry IV seems ready to forgive and forget all the faults of the rebels who have created this terrible situation 'Of pellmell havoc and confusion'. Prince Hal is noble and modest in praising Hotspur; he shows compassion when he refers to the soldiers, in both armies, who will suffer if the fighting starts; and his challenge to Hotspur is brave without being boastful. He speaks wisely after the King's offer of peace, knowing that 'It will not be accepted'. Falstaff tries to detain the Prince as he is leaving the stage, but Hal refuses to waste time. After a quick joke, he is gone.

Falstaff is now left alone on the stage, contemplating the thought of the battle which must soon be fought. During the course of this play a great deal has been spoken about 'honour'—

the kind that is won by courage and strength in fighting. Hotspur, of course, is the chief authority on the subject: the first time he appeared in the play he extolled the subject with exaggerated terms of praise:

> By heaven, methinks it were an easy leap
> To pluck bright honour from the pale-fac'd moon . . .
> (*1*, 3, 199 ff.)

Now Falstaff is going to say a few words on the matter, but he speaks in prose. His language is simple and colloquial, contrasting sharply with Hotspur's passionate rhetoric; and in the same way, Falstaff's ideas about 'honour' are very different from those of the young man. Hotspur will give all for 'honour'—but Falstaff can find no practical value 'in that word "honour"' and so he dismisses the whole concept: 'Therefore I'll none of it'.

Scene 2 As well as lightening the atmosphere, Falstaff's speech has allowed the Earl of Worcester and his companion, Vernon, to cross the battlefield from the King's camp. We meet them again as they are approaching the tents of the rebels.

Worcester and Vernon are still discussing the King's 'liberal and kind offer' of peace, but Worcester does not trust King Henry. Perhaps he is right to be suspicious—but he is wrong not to tell the truth when he reports on his mission. He lies to them: 'The King will bid you battle presently'. When he tells Hotspur of the challenge to single combat with Prince Hal, it is clear that he intends to make Hotspur even more angry—and he almost succeeds in doing this. Hotspur wants to know *how* the challenge was made: 'How show'd his tasking? Seem'd it in contempt?'. But Worcester is prevented from answering by Vernon's quick interruption, and Vernon describes exactly how Prince Hal spoke his challenge: 'I never in my life Did hear a challenge urg'd more modestly'. He continues in his praise of the Prince, and his words seem to foretell not only the noble reformation of the Prince of Wales, but also his future greatness as King Henry V.

Hotspur is not worried by this praise of Hal; indeed, he seems almost amused at Vernon's enthusiasm, and he looks forward to the time when he will 'embrace [Prince Hal] with a soldier's arm'—and kill him. Now the battle must commence. Hotspur speaks a few words to the assembled troops, insisting that he does not have 'the gift of tongue'; at last he draws his sword, and with his family's war-cry of 'Esperance! Percy!' he leads the rebels into battle.

Scene 3 We now witness the honourable (and dishonourable) deeds that are done in war. Blunt is protecting his King by his disguise, as well as by his fighting; Hotspur recognizes and praises the valour of an old enemy (Douglas) and a new one ('A gallant knight he was, his name was Blunt'); and Prince Hal will make a fresh charge against the 'vaunting enemies'. But Falstaff has 'led [his] ragamuffins where they are peppered', and he is proud of it! This was a fairly common practice: a corrupt captain would take his men into a dangerous situation and leave them there to be killed—and then keep their wages for himself.

Falstaff can still make us laugh, however; and we are once again compelled to question the ideal of military honour when Falstaff contemplates the dead body of the valiant Blunt, with the words 'I like not such grinning honour as Sir Walter hath. Give me life . . .'

Scene 4 The division of the play into 'scenes' can sometimes be misleading. The stage-direction here (*Alarum. Excursions.*) shows that there is no real break between Scenes Three and Four; the fighting is continuous, and in the theatre the actors, flourishing their swords, cross constantly from one side of the stage to the other. When the conversation starts once more, we find that the King and a few of his supporters have come together for a brief moment.

Both the sons of the King—Prince Hal and Lord John—have been fighting bravely, and their father is proud and delighted. He fails to persuade Hal to retire to his tent, even though the Prince is wounded and bleeding. It is in this scene that the Prince of Wales will show his true worth—as a son (when he rescues his father from the Earl of Douglas); as a knight (in his encounter with Hotspur); and as a friend (in his treatment of Falstaff).

In the interview with Prince Hal (*Act 3*, Scene 2) the King admitted his fear that his son might even join the rebels and fight against him:

> Thou . . . art like enough, through vassal fear,
> Base inclination, and the start of spleen,
> To fight against me under Percy's pay. (124–6)

At that time, the Prince could use only *words* to express his loyalty to his father; but now his *sword* speaks even more powerfully for him. It is the complete reconciliation of father and son.

Now Prince Hal must meet Hotspur. At first the two are cautiously polite—like two tigers, circling round each other before they start to fight. It is certainly a fight for mastery: much is at stake in this duel, as both the combatants know:

> Two stars keep not the motion in one sphere,
> Nor can one England brook a double reign
> Of Harry Percy and the Prince of Wales.

Soon the time for courtesy is past, and Hotspur attacks Hal. Whilst they are fighting, Falstaff arrives on the scene and—as though he were the spectator at a prize-fight—proceeds to shout encouragement to the Prince until he is himself surprised by a sudden attack from the Earl of Douglas. At almost the same moment, both Falstaff and Hotspur, mortally wounded, fall to the ground.

Hotspur speaks a few last words, lamenting the loss of his honour—'those proud titles'—more than the loss of his life. In the middle of a sentence, his voice breaks off and he dies. Prince Hal completes the sentence, clearly moved by the death of this 'great heart'. He does not triumph over his dead enemy, but instead shows tender magnanimity as he covers Hotspur's face with the 'favours'—the silks or plumes—which he wears on his own helmet.

As he turns away from the dead Hotspur, Hal sees another body lying on the ground. His reaction is very interesting: 'could not all this flesh Keep in a little life?' He makes one of his usual jokes about Falstaff's size, but the laughter has turned to grief. Yet Hal can find few words to speak of his friend; he has spoken so much—with deep feeling—about his enemy. His speech is rich with puns (on 'heavy', 'deer', and 'in blood') which suggests that he is trying to conceal, rather than express, his sorrow.

But there is no need for sorrow! An audience watching the play (if not the readers of the book) can experience joyful surprise when the fat knight waits until the stage is empty, and then lumbers to his feet with words that (in Falstaff's usual manner) seize upon the Prince's puns and extend them: 'If thou embowel me today, I'll give you leave to powder me and eat me too tomorrow'. Once again, Falstaff turns a scene that would otherwise have been heroic—or even tragic—into comedy. He has a few words to say on the subject of 'valour' and these, together with his treatment of the dead Hotspur, insist that we make a comparison between Falstaff and the Prince of Wales, and examine our ideas of 'valour'.

Falstaff has already explained to the audience how he

managed to extricate himself from a difficult situation when he was attacked by 'that hot termagant Scot', the Earl of Douglas. Characteristically, he escaped by means of falsehood—by *acting* a lie and pretending to be dead. Now, when he encounters Prince Hal and Lord John, he exaggerates the lie to monstrous proportions when he claims to have been merely resting, so that he could rise refreshed to fight for 'a long hour by Shrewsbury clock', killing Hotspur at the end of the hour. Lord John is astounded, but the Prince seems to be amused: he can still share a joke with Falstaff, even though he is now no longer the same 'lad of mettle' that he was in the tavern in Eastcheap (*2*, 4, 12).

A serious note returns as the play ends. King Henry IV confronts the defeated rebels, reproaching Worcester and condemning him to death. Prince Hal once more shows his great generosity of spirit when he requests life and freedom for the Earl of Douglas. The fighting is over: but the war is not yet won. King Henry must now divide the troops, sending one detachment northwards to York whilst he and the Prince Hal lead the other soldiers into Wales. The success at Shrewsbury has given the King confidence, so that he can at last promise

> Rebellion in this land shall lose his sway,
> Meeting the check of such another day.

Sir John Falstaff

This is the character who has always attracted more attention than any of Shakespeare's creations: even Queen Elizabeth I, it is reported, was so entertained by him that she demanded another play, in which she could see the fat knight in love. Shakespeare satisfied her by writing *The Merry Wives of Windsor*. All the great critics have written about Falstaff, but none has shown more sympathetic appreciation than Dr Samuel Johnson, the eighteenth-century editor of Shakespeare's plays, and his account of Falstaff is printed on page xxix of this edition.

Falstaff is a very complex character, and a different aspect is shown every time he appears. His quick wit, however, is constant: he never ceases to provoke laughter—which is very often directed at himself, and especially at his bulk. The first impression (when he appears in *Act 1*, Scene 2) is of a great, carefree, jester, who cares nothing for the dreary routine of everyday life. Prince Hal seems almost envious when he asks, 'What a devil hast thou to do with the time of day?' Falstaff's relationship with the Prince is relaxed and easy; he seems to have an almost *fatherly* regard for the young man when he addresses him as 'sweet wag', and plays verbal games with him—which he allows Hal to win, conceding victory with 'Thou hast the most unsavouriest similes, and art indeed the most comparative, rascalliest, sweet young prince'.

This admission of affection is speedily followed by a mock-reproach, when Falstaff chooses to see *himself* in the role of the young innocent, led astray by the 'sweet young prince' who is now 'able to corrupt a saint'. Here Falstaff demonstrates another of his peculiar skills as he adopts a religious manner of speech (with frequent reference to the Bible). The comedy lies not only in the words, but in the contrast between the speech (full of sham piety) and the speaker (full of real mischief).

The lighthearted tone of this scene draws attention away from the faults, crimes, and sins of Falstaff. His gluttony and drunkenness are subjects for witty amusement; and his thieving activities are dismissed as the work of 'Diana's foresters, gentlemen of the shade'. To Falstaff, villainy is merely excitement—although he does seem rather sensitive when Hal introduces the subject of prison-clothes: 'What a plague have I to do with a buff jerkin?'

The robbers' conspiracy is planned with the enthusiasm of boys who play at being highwaymen; and when Falstaff abuses the victims at Gad's Hill, it is impossible to feel sympathy for the defrauded travellers. Here the comedy resides in Falstaff's wonderfully inventive insults—'whoreson caterpillars, bacon-fed knaves'—and also in the contrast of speech and speaker as the old man declares 'They hate us youth'.

Before the actual robbery, Falstaff speaks out to the audience, cursing Prince Hal for having stolen his horse, thus compelling him to shift his enormous weight on foot. Falstaff frequently delivers such speeches: they are not soliloquies in the usual sense, because the character is not speaking aloud his inner thoughts. Falstaff knows that he is being listened to, and his speech is intended to create an effect on the audience: it has much more in common with the 'patter' of a modern comedian (on stage or television) than with the sensitive broodings of a character like Hamlet—or Prince Hal when he murmurs to himself 'I know you all . . .' (*1*, 2, 197 ff.).

After the 'real' robbery, the Prince and Poins attack the robbers, who offer no serious resistance before they run away. In the Eastcheap tavern we wait to share in the grand joke that Poins has promised:

> The virtue of this jest will be the incomprehensible lies that this same fat rogue will tell us when we meet at supper: how thirty at least he fought with; what wards, what blows, what extremities he endured; and in the reproof of this lies the jest.
> (*1*, 2, 187–92)

Everything happens as Poins promised. Falstaff pours out lies, excuses, explanations and insults, in an apparently endless explosion of invention whose climax comes when the Prince at last accuses him of cowardice. Hal, having given a brief account of the attack on the would-be robbers—two against four—charges Falstaff with having 'roared for mercy, and still run and roared'. He waits for an explanation—and it is quickly given: 'By the Lord, I knew ye as well as he that made ye'. And Falstaff wriggles (verbally) out of another dilemma with the grand defence that he was 'a coward on instinct'.

The episode can, I think, be taken in one of two ways. Perhaps Falstaff, like Bardolph and the others, *was* deceived on

Gad's Hill when the disguised Hal and Poins attacked them; and perhaps he is boasting about his valour in the encounter with the 'buckram men' and the 'knaves in Kendal green'. Certainly Bardolph and Peto were genuinely afraid of their attackers, and they ran away in fear. But neither of these is particularly intelligent, and they do what they are told to do: Bardolph admits freely, 'I ran when I saw others run'. But was *Falstaff* so easily deceived?

Perhaps he recognized the Prince and Poins (despite their 'vizards' and their 'cases of buckram'), and joined in the joke?

At Gad's Hill no one was seriously hurt: but this is not the case at Shrewsbury. Falstaff callously admits—again in a speech addressed to the theatre audience—that he has 'led [his] ragamuffins where they are peppered', so that of his original conscripts 'there's not three of my hundred and fifty left alive', and these are so badly wounded that they can have no hopes for the future—'they are for the town's end, to beg during life'. And Falstaff will pocket the money intended for the soldier's pay.

This is not a *sudden* change in Falstaff. Gradually, throughout the play, we have been shown that there is indeed an unpleasant side to his character: he can be selfish, and cruel. He tries to cheat the Hostess at Eastcheap, who laments 'you owe me money, Sir John, and now you pick a quarrel to beguile me of it' (*3*, 3, 68–9). He boasts of his cleverness in conscripting (initially) only those men who were able to buy themselves out of his army, acknowledging—without any shame—that he has 'misused the King's press damnably', making more than three hundred pounds profit for himself.

Such a man—dishonest, selfish, and with no thought for the welfare, or even the lives, of those for whom he should be responsible—is not a very suitable companion for the Prince of Wales, the future King of England. But Hal is perhaps thinking most of all about Falstaff when he muses at the end of *Act 1*, Scene 2

> I know you all, and will awhile uphold
> The unyok'd humour of your idleness.

In the hilarious scene in the tavern at Eastcheap, the Prince shows that he understands what he has to do when he promises that he will indeed 'Banish plump Jack, and banish all the world'.

In this scene the Prince, when he speaks in the person of his father and denounces the 'old fat man', refers to Falstaff as 'that reverend vice'. This description should make Falstaff's role perfectly clear—to an Elizabethan audience!

Before the drama became commercialized, with the building of theatres in London and the rise of the new profession of playwrights, the people of England got much of their dramatic entertainment from groups of strolling actors. These wandered around the country, carrying their costumes and properties, and performing a small repertoire of short pieces often known as 'Morality Plays'. As the name implies, these plays were didactic, teaching some kind of moral; and most frequently they told of a young man (perhaps even called 'Youth') who had to make a choice between right and wrong—between a good life, which would lead to heaven, and a bad one, which became the pathway to hell. His choice was always made more difficult by the presence in the play of a figure called 'The Vice', whose function was to tempt the young man and lead him away from the life of virtue. Audiences would never have had any difficulty in identifying the Vice character (whatever his name in the play) because he always carried a short, cheap dagger, usually made of wood. The Vice was in fact a 'villainous abominable misleader of youth'; and these are the words used to describe Falstaff in *Act 2*, Scene 4.

Sir John Falstaff: an appreciation by Dr Samuel Johnson

But Falstaff, unimitated, inimitable Falstaff, how shall I describe thee? Thou compound of sense and vice; of sense which may be admired but not esteemed, of vice which may be despised but hardly detested.

Falstaff is a character loaded with faults, and with those faults which naturally produce contempt. He is a thief, and a glutton, a coward, and a boaster, always ready to cheat the weak, and prey upon the poor; to terrify the timorous and insult the defenceless. At once obsequious and malignant, he satirizes in their absence those whom he lives by flattering. He is familiar with the Prince only as an agent of vice, but of this familiarity he is so proud as not only to be supercilious and haughty with common men, but to think his interest of importance to the Duke of Lancaster.

Yet the man thus corrupt, thus despicable, makes himself necessary to the Prince that despises him, by the most pleasing of all qualities, perpetual gaiety, by an unfailing power of exciting laughter, which is the more freely indulged, as his wit is not of the splendid or ambitious kind, but consists in easy escapes and sallies of levity, which make sport but raise no envy.

It must be observed that he is stained with no enormous or sanguinary crimes, so that his licentiousness is not so offensive but that it may be borne for his mirth.

[1765]

Shakespeare's Verse

Shakespeare's plays are mainly written in 'blank verse', the form preferred by most dramatists in the sixteenth and early seventeenth centuries. It is a very flexible medium, which is capable—like the human speaking voice—of a wide range of tones. Basically the lines, which are unrhymed, are ten syllables long. The syllables have alternating stresses, just like normal English speech; and they divide into five 'feet'. The technical name for this is 'iambic pentameter'.

King

So sháken ás we áre, so wán with cáre,
Find ẃe a tiḿe for fŕighted péace to pánt,
And bréathe short-wińded áccents óf new bŕoils
To bé comménc'd in strónds afár remóte:
No móre the thiŕsty éntrance óf this sóil
Shall dáub her lips with hér own chíldren's blóod;
No móre shall ťrenching wár channél her fiélds,
Nor brúise her flów'rets wíth the aŕmed hóofs
Of hóstile páces.

Here the King speaks a verse which is completely regular, expressing his command of the situation and his personal dignity. The verse line sometimes contains the grammatical unit of meaning, thus allowing for a pause at the end of the line before a new idea is started: 'No more shall trenching war channel her fields'. At other times, the sense runs on from one line to the next—'the armed hoofs/Of hostile paces'. This makes for the natural fluidity of speech, avoiding monotony but still maintaining the iambic rhythm.

Date and Text

The first part of *Henry IV* was entered in the Stationers' Register in 1598, and printed soon afterwards. The play was probably written and performed a year or two earlier. It may well have been revised by Shakespeare, perhaps in 1597, when he changed the name of the fat knight from 'Oldcastle' to 'Falstaff' because the Lord Chamberlain, the patron of Shakespeare's company of actors, was descended from the historical Oldcastle and objected to Shakespeare's portrayal of his ancestor. A trace of the earlier version can possibly be seen in *Act 1*, Scene 2, where Prince Hal addresses his friend as 'my old lad of the castle' (line 44).

The Quarto edition of 1598 is a well printed text on which all modern editions are based.

Characters in the Play

THE KING

Henry IV	*formerly* Henry Bolingbroke

THE KING'S SONS

Prince Hal	Henry Prince of Wales, *heir to the throne*
Lord John of Lancaster	

THE KING'S ALLIES

Earl of Westmoreland
Sir Walter Blunt

REBELS AGAINST THE KING

Earl of Worcester	Thomas Percy
Earl of Northumberland	Henry Percy, Worcester's *brother*
Hotspur	Henry (Harry) Percy, Northumberland's *son*
Edmund Mortimer	Earl of March
Owen Glendower	
Earl of Douglas	Archibald
Archbishop of York	Richard Scroop
Sir Michael	*the* Archbishop's *friend*
Sir Richard Vernon	

Lady Percy (Kate)	Mortimer's *sister*, Hotspur's *wife*
Lady Mortimer	Mortimer's *wife*, *daughter of* Glendower

PRINCE HAL'S FRIENDS

Sir John Falstaff
Poins
Peto
Bardolph

AT THE TAVERN IN EASTCHEAP

Mistress Quickly	*Hostess of the tavern*
Francis	*Drawer*
Vintner	

IN THE INN AT ROCHESTER

Gadshill	*A robber*
Two Carriers	
Chamberlain	
Ostler	

Sheriff, Officers, Messengers, Travellers, Lords, Attendants

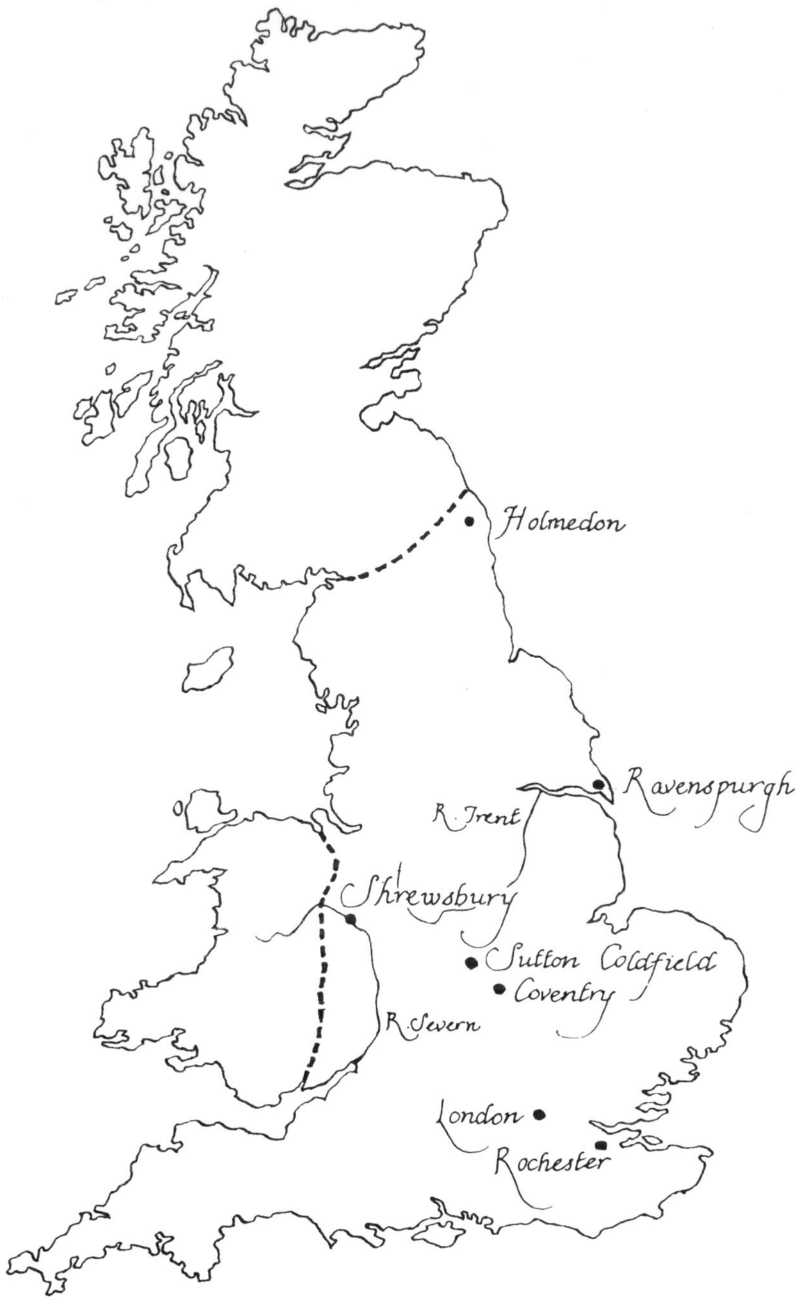

Holmedon
Ravenspurgh
R. Trent
Shrewsbury
Sutton Coldfield
Coventry
R. Severn
London
Rochester

Act I

Act I Scene I

King Henry is addressing his supporters. He hopes that England will continue to be peaceful, free from the horrors of civil war. He intends now to lead an army in a Crusade to Jerusalem, to fight the pagans (Turks) who are in possession of the Christian Holy Land. Westmoreland, however, has brought bad news of fresh aggression: the Welsh and the Scots are now attacking the English – and so the Crusade must be postponed. The King's nephew, Hotspur, is being difficult; but Henry wishes that his own son were like Hotspur in bravery.

1 *shaken*: upset.
wan: pale.

2 *frighted*: frightened.
pant: pause for breath.

3 *breathe . . . accents*: speak breathlessly.
broils: quarrels.

4 *stronds*: shores.

5–6 The King hopes that the blood of Englishmen will never again be shed in their own motherland.

7 *trenching*: digging trenches (channels).

8 *flow'rets*: little flowers.
armed: iron-shod.

9 *opposed eyes*: i.e. the eyes of opposing armies.

11 All of the same sort and nationality.

12 *intestine*: internal.

13 *close*: meeting (in battle).

14 *mutual*: united.
well-beseeming: suitable.
ranks: military order.

Scene I *London: the Palace of Westminster*

Enter the King, Lord John of Lancaster, Earl of Westmoreland, Sir Walter Blunt, *with others*

King

So shaken as we are, so wan with care,
Find we a time for frighted peace to pant,
And breathe short-winded accents of new broils
To be commenc'd in stronds afar remote:
No more the thirsty entrance of this soil
Shall daub her lips with her own children's blood;
No more shall trenching war channel her fields,
Nor bruise her flow'rets with the armed hoofs
Of hostile paces. Those opposed eyes
Which, like the meteors of a troubled heaven,
All of one nature, of one substance bred,
Did lately meet in the intestine shock
And furious close of civil butchery,
Shall now, in mutual well-beseeming ranks,

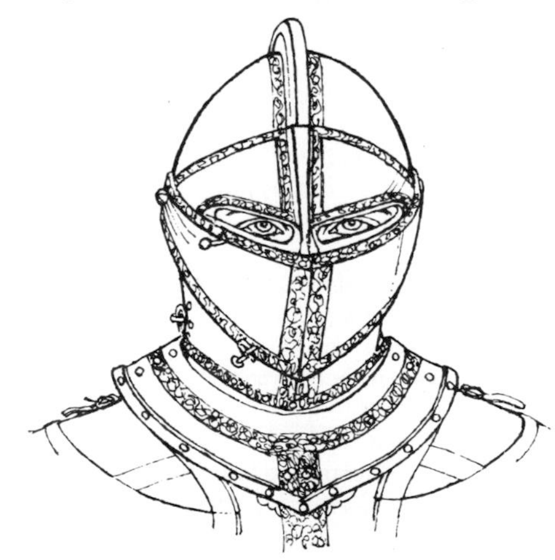

March all one way, and be no more oppos'd
Against acquaintance, kindred, and allies.
The edge of war, like an ill-sheathed knife,
No more shall cut his master. Therefore, friends,
As far as to the sepulchre of Christ—
Whose soldier now, under whose blessed cross
We are impressed and engag'd to fight—
Forthwith a power of English shall we levy,
Whose arms were moulded in their mothers' womb
To chase these pagans in those holy fields
Over whose acres walk'd those blessed feet
Which fourteen hundred years ago were nail'd
For our advantage on the bitter cross.
But this our purpose now is twelve month old,
And bootless 'tis to tell you we will go;
Therefor we meet not now. Then let me hear
Of you, my gentle cousin Westmoreland,
What yesternight our Council did decree
In forwarding this dear expedience.

Westmoreland

My liege, this haste was hot in question,
And many limits of the charge set down
But yesternight, when all athwart there came
A post from Wales, loaden with heavy news,
Whose worst was that the noble Mortimer,
Leading the men of Herefordshire to fight
Against the irregular and wild Glendower,
Was by the rude hands of that Welshman taken,
A thousand of his people butchered,
Upon whose dead corpse there was such misuse,
Such beastly shameless transformation,
By those Welshwomen done, as may not be
Without much shame retold or spoken of.

King

It seems then that the tidings of this broil
Brake off our business for the Holy Land.

Westmoreland

This match'd with other did, my gracious lord,
For more uneven and unwelcome news
Came from the north, and thus it did import:
On Holy-rood day, the gallant Hotspur there,
Young Harry Percy, and brave Archibald,

15 *all one way*: in the same direction.

16 *acquaintance*: friends.

17 *edge*: sword.

19–22 The King intends to recruit ('levy') an army ('power') of English soldiers and lead them as far as Jerusalem (to the tomb where Christ was buried).

20–21 Henry sees himself as a soldier of Christ, conscripted ('impressed') to fight under the sign of the cross (as soldiers marched behind the banners of their commanders).

27 *for our advantage*: Christians believe that Christ was crucified for the salvation of mankind.
bitter: cruel.

28 'We have intended to do this for the past year'.

29 *bootless*: unnecessary.

30 *Therefor . . . now*: that is not why we are meeting now.

31 *Of*: from.
gentle cousin: noble relation (Shakespeare uses the word 'cousin' to refer to any close relation: Westmoreland was in fact married to Henry's half-sister.)

32 *yesternight*: last night.

33 *expedience*: undertaking (which is important – 'dear' – to Henry's heart).

That ever valiant and approved Scot,
At Holmedon met, where they did spend
A sad and bloody hour;
As by discharge of their artillery,
And shape of likelihood, the news was told;
For he that brought them, in the very heat
And pride of their contention did take horse,
Uncertain of the issue any way.

King

Here is a dear, a true industrious friend,
Sir Walter Blunt, new lighted from his horse,
Stain'd with the variation of each soil
Betwixt that Holmedon and this seat of ours;
And he hath brought us smooth and welcome news.
The Earl of Douglas is discomfited;
Ten thousand bold Scots, two and twenty knights,
Balk'd in their own blood, did Sir Walter see
On Holmedon's plains; of prisoners Hotspur took
Mordake, Earl of Fife and eldest son
To beaten Douglas, and the Earl of Athol,
Of Murray, Angus, and Menteith:

34 *liege*: lord.
haste: urgent business.
hot in question: being seriously discussed.

35 We had already decided ('set down') who should have the responsibility (limit) for many of the duties ('charge').

36 *all athwart*: interrupting, upsetting.

37 *post*: messenger.
heavy: serious, worrying.

38 *Whose worst*: the worst of which.

40 *irregular*: lawless; Glendower was fighting guerrilla warfare.

43 *Whose . . . corpse*: i.e. the bodies of the thousand soldiers.

44 *transformation*: atrocity.

48 *Brake*: broke.

49 *match'd with other*: together with other bad news.

50 *uneven*: unpleasant, disturbing.

51 *thus it did import*: this is what it said.

52 *Holy-rood Day*: 14 September, the day of the Christian festival celebrating the Cross (rood) of Christ.

54 *approved*: of proven worth.

55 *Holmedon*: see map, p. xxxiv.

56–7 'So far as we could tell from the way they were firing ('artillery' means arrows and other missiles, as well as guns) and from the way things seemed likely to happen'.

59 *them*: i.e. the news.

60 *pride of their contention*: height of their battle.

61 *issue*: outcome.

63 *lighted*: alighted.

64–5 Sir Walter's mud-stained clothes seem to show all the different soils that he has ridden through to get to London and the King's palace ('this seat of ours').

66 *smooth*: pleasant.

67 *discomfited*: defeated.

69 *Balk'd*: overthrown; a 'balk' is the ridge between two furrows of a ploughed field—the bodies were piled in heaps, making furrows through which their blood drained away.

74 *spoil*: prize.
75 *In faith*: indeed.
80 'A son who is always the subject when men are talking about honour'.
82 *minion*: darling, favourite.
86–7 There was a popular superstition that the fairies would sometimes steal a beautiful human baby from its cradle, leaving in its place a weak or ugly child (a changeling).
90 *let . . . thoughts*: forget about him.
coz: the abbreviation of 'cousin'.
92 *surpris'd*: captured.
93 *To . . . use*: for his own advantage (i.e. so that Hotspur can keep the ransom money instead of giving it to the King).
94 *Mordake*: the earl was of royal blood, so Hotspur was obliged to surrender him to the King.
96 Worcester is spoken of as a planet which, however it appears ('in all aspects') is always hostile ('Malevolent').
97–8 Taught by his uncle, Hotspur is proud and disdainful: he is like a cock, which will preen ('prune') its feathers and erect its comb ('crest') when it intends to fight.

103 *so . . . lords*: inform the Council of these facts.
106 'Than I can say in my present anger'.

And is not this an honourable spoil?
A gallant prize? ha, cousin, is it not?

Westmoreland In faith,
It is a conquest for a prince to boast of.

King
Yea, there thou mak'st me sad, and mak'st me sin
In envy that my Lord Northumberland
Should be the father to so blest a son;
A son who is the theme of honour's tongue,
Amongst a grove the very straightest plant,
Who is sweet Fortune's minion and her pride;
Whilst I, by looking on the praise of him,
See riot and dishonour stain the brow
Of my young Harry. O that it could be prov'd
That some night-tripping fairy had exchang'd
In cradle-clothes our children where they lay,
And call'd mine Percy, his Plantagenet!
Then would I have his Harry, and he mine:
But let him from my thoughts. What think you, coz,
Of this young Percy's pride? The prisoners
Which he in this adventure hath surpris'd
To his own use he keeps, and sends me word
I shall have none but Mordake, Earl of Fife.

Westmoreland
This is his uncle's teaching, this is Worcester,
Malevolent to you in all aspects,
Which makes him prune himself and bristle up
The crest of youth against your dignity.

King
But I have sent for him to answer this;
And for this cause awhile we must neglect
Our holy purpose to Jerusalem.
Cousin, on Wednesday next our Council we
Will hold at Windsor, so inform the lords:
But come yourself with speed to us again,
For more is to be said and to be done
Than out of anger can be uttered.

Westmoreland
I will, my liege. [*Exeunt*

Act 1 Scene 2
Whilst his father worries about the safety of the country, Prince Hal amuses himself by teasing his friend, Sir John Falstaff. They are joined by another friend, Poins, who tells them he is planning a robbery. When he is alone, Prince Hal offers an explanation for his conduct.

2 *fat-witted*: stupid, slow-minded.
3 *sack*: Spanish white wine.
unbuttoning thee: loosening your clothes (because he has eaten so much).
4–5 *that . . . know*: that you have forgotten how to ask properly for what you really want to know.
5–12 Hal observes that Falstaff is interested only in food, drink, and women.
8 *capons*: chickens.
9 *leaping-houses*: brothels.
10 *hot*: lustful.
11 *taffeta*: prostitutes were recognized by their taffeta (stiff silk) petticoats.
12 *superfluous*: unnecessary (also 'self-indulgent').

Scene 2 *London: an Apartment of the Prince's in the Royal Palace*

Enter Prince of Wales *and* Sir John Falstaff

Falstaff
Now, Hal, what time of day is it, lad?

Prince
Thou art so fat-witted with drinking of old sack, and unbuttoning thee after supper, and sleeping upon benches after noon, that thou hast forgotten to demand that truly which thou wouldst truly know. What a devil has thou to do with the time of the day? Unless hours were cups of sack, and minutes capons, and clocks the tongues of bawds, and dials the signs of leaping-houses, and the blessed sun himself a fair hot wench in flame-coloured taffeta, I see no reason why thou shouldst be so superfluous to demand the time of the day.

Falstaff

Indeed, you come near me now, Hal, for we that take purses go by the moon and the seven stars, and not 'by Phœbus, he that wand'ring knight so fair'. And I prithee sweet wag, when thou art king, as God save thy Grace—Majesty, I should say, for grace thou wilt have none—

Prince

What, none?

Falstaff

No, by my troth, not so much as will serve to be prologue to an egg and butter.

Prince

Well, how then? Come, roundly, roundly.

Falstaff

Marry then sweet wag, when thou art king, let not us that are squires of the night's body be called thieves of the day's beauty: let us be Diana's foresters, gentlemen of the shade, minions of the moon; and let men say we be men of good government, being governed as the sea is, by our noble and chaste mistress the moon, under whose countenance we steal.

13 *you . . . me*: you've hit the mark (you show that you understand me).

14 *take purses*: are thieves.
go by the moon: walk by the light of the moon (i.e. work at night); and 'tell the time by the moon' (not the sun).
the seven stars: the stars that form the constellation Pleiades.

15 *Phœbus . . . fair*: Falstaff is probably quoting the words of a popular song: Phœbus Apollo was the Greek god of the sun.

16 *prithee*: pray you.
wag: fool, joker.

17 *grace*: Falstaff plays with three senses of the word: he addresses Hal properly as 'Your Highness'; refers to his lack of spiritual grace; and (in line 20) puns on 'grace' as a prayer before a meal.

20 *troth*: truth, faith.

21 *egg and butter*: a light meal (Falstaff implies that this needs only a short grace).

22 *Come, roundly*: come to the point (explain what you mean).

23 *Marry*: by (the Virgin) Mary (a very mild oath).

23–5 'Don't let those of us who work by night be called thieves in the daytime'. A nobleman's personal attendants were called 'squires of the body'; Falstaff makes a pun here with 'night' and 'knight'—also with 'beauty' and 'booty'.

25 *Diana's foresters*: hunters who serve Diana—who was goddess of hunting and of the moon.

26 *gentlemen*: servants of the royal household were often called 'Gentlemen'.

27 *good government*: *both* 'serving a good ruler'; *and* 'law-abiding'.

29 *under whose countenance*: *both* 'by the light of the moon'; *and* 'with the approval of'.

30 *steal*: walk secretly; *and* thieve.

31 *it holds well*: it is a good comparison (i.e. Falstaff's comparison of robbers and the sea: Hal now explains the similarities).

34 *proof*: demonstration.

37 *Lay by*: the demand of highwaymen that the travellers should drop their weapons.

38 *Bring in*: the order that they should be served with food and drink in the inn.

39 *the ladder*: the condemned thief had to climb a ladder in order to be hanged (death by hanging was the punishment for theft).

43 *Hybla*: a mountain in Sicily where the best-quality honey was made.

old lad of the castle: rioter. It is possible that, in an early version of this play, Falstaff was called Sir John Oldcastle.

44 *a buff . . . durance*: Hal refers obliquely to the possibility of arrest. The Elizabethan constable wore a leather ('buff') jerkin, and Hal is able to make a pun on the two senses of 'durance'—'hard-wearing'; *and* 'imprisonment'.

46–7 *What . . . quiddities*: 'You are full of jokes and quibbles'.

47–9 Both the plague (bubonic) and the pox (venereal disease) provided the Elizabethans with mild oaths (a modern equivalent might be 'What the devil').

51 *called . . . reckoning*; asked her to give an account of herself; *and* asked her for the bill.

55–7 Hal has paid the bills whenever he had money; and on other occasions he has been able to obtain goods 'on credit' (i.e. with a promise to pay later).

58–9 *were it . . . apparent*: Falstaff begins to make an old joke which depends upon the similarity in sound between 'here' and 'heir'.

61 *resolution*: boldness.

fubbed: restrained.

62 *old father Antic*: that old fool (see also p. viii).

Prince

Thou sayest well, and it holds well too: for the fortune of us that are the moon's men doth ebb and flow like the sea, being governed as the sea is, by the moon—as for proof now, a purse of gold most resolutely snatched on Monday night, and most dissolutely spent on Tuesday morning; got with swearing 'Lay by!', and spent with crying 'Bring in!'; now in as low an ebb as the foot of the ladder, and by and by in as high a flow as the ridge of the gallows.

Falstaff

By the Lord thou say'st true, lad; and is not my hostess of the tavern a most sweet wench?

Prince

As the honey of Hybla, my old lad of the castle; and is not a buff jerkin a most sweet robe of durance?

Falstaff

How now, how now, mad wag? What, in thy quips and thy quiddities? What a plague have I to do with a buff jerkin?

Prince

Why, what a pox have I to do with my hostess of the tavern?

Falstaff

Well, thou hast called her to a reckoning many a time and oft.

Prince

Did I ever call for thee to pay thy part?

Falstaff

No. I'll give thee thy due, thou hast paid all there.

Prince

Yea, and elsewhere, so far as my coin would stretch; and where it would not I have used my credit.

Falstaff

Yea, and so used it that were it not here apparent that thou art heir apparent—But I prithee sweet wag, shall there be gallows standing in England when thou art king? And resolution thus fubbed as it is with the rusty curb of old father Antic the law? Do not thou, when thou art king, hang a thief.

Prince

No; thou shalt.

Falstaff

Shall I? O rare! By the Lord, I'll be a brave judge!

Prince

Thou judgest false already. I mean—thou shalt have the hanging of the thieves, and so become a rare hangman.

Falstaff

Well, Hal, well; and in some sort it jumps with my humour as well as waiting in the court, I can tell you.

Prince

For obtaining of suits?

Falstaff

Yea, for obtaining of suits, whereof the hangman hath no lean wardrobe. 'Sblood, I am as melancholy as a gib cat, or a lugged bear.

Prince

Or an old lion, or a lover's lute.

Falstaff

Yea, or the drone of a Lincolnshire bagpipe.

Prince

What sayest thou to a hare, or the melancholy of Moorditch?

Falstaff

Thou hast the most unsavoury similes, and art indeed the most comparative, rascalliest, sweet young prince. But Hal, I prithee trouble me no more with vanity. I would to God thou and I knew where a commodity of good names were to be bought: an old lord of the Council rated me the other day in the street about you, sir, but I marked him not; and yet he talked very wisely, but I regarded him not; and yet he talked wisely, and in the street too.

Prince

Thou didst well, for wisdom cries out in the streets and no man regards it.

66 *rare*: splendid.
brave: fine.

70 *in some sort*: in a way.

70–1 *jumps . . . humour*: suits my nature.

73 *suits*: Hal speaks of 'suits' with reference to legal petitions (in a court of law) or requests for preferment (in the royal court). But Falstaff speaks of the clothes worn by a hanged man; these were always given to the executioner.

75 *lean*: thin.
'Sblood: an oath (by God's blood).

76 *gib cat*: tomcat.
lugged: baited; in the Elizabethan sport of bear-baiting, the bear was fastened to a post and tormented by dogs.

78 *drone . . . bagpipe*: a continuous low note on the bagpipes, which were as popular in England as they now are in Scotland.

79 *hare*: this animal was proverbially melancholy.

80 *Moorditch*: one of the main open sewers in London.

82 *comparative*: rich in comparisons.
rascalliest: the biggest rascal.

83–99 Falstaff begins to speak (comically) in the style of the Puritans—a religious sect (particularly opposed to the pleasures of the flesh) whose speech was modelled on the Bible. Hal follows his example.
85 *commodity*: supply.
86 *rated*: reproached.
87 *marked him not*: paid no attention to him.
89 *regarded him not*: took no notice of him.
91–2 *wisdom . . . it*: Hal's words are quoted from the Bible (*Book of Proverbs*, 1:20, 24).
93 *iteration*: habit of quoting.
95 *upon me*: to me.
99 *and*: if.
102 *take*: steal.
103 *'Zounds*: by God's wounds.
make one: join the gang [of thieves].
an: if.
104 *baffle me*: hang me upside down (Falstaff refers to the treatment given to a knight who had dishonoured himself).
109–10 *set a match*: planned a robbery.
110 *saved*: i.e. from eternal damnation.
by merit: by their deeds. Theologians argue about whether a man is saved by his good works, or by his faith in God.
112 *omnipotent*: Hal speaks humorously, using the word to mean 'unequalled'.
113 *true*: honest.
116 *Sack-and-Sugar*: sugar was sometimes used to sweeten the wine (sack); in *Act 2*, Scene 4 (line 23) Hal speaks of a gift of sugar.
118 *Good Friday*: the day on which Christ was crucified; a strict fast was kept on this day in the sixteenth century.
120 *stands to*: keeps.
122 The expression 'Give the devil his due' usually means 'Give even the worst person the praise he deserves'.

Falstaff
O, thou hast damnable iteration, and art indeed able to corrupt a saint! Thou hast done much harm upon me, Hal—God forgive thee for it! Before I knew thee, Hal, I knew nothing; and now am I, if a man should speak truly, little better than one of the wicked. I must give over this life, and I will give it over: by the Lord, and I do not I am a villain! I'll be damned for never a king's son in Christendom.

Prince
Where shall we take a purse tomorrow, Jack?

Falstaff
'Zounds, where thou wilt, lad, I'll make one—an I do not, call me villain and baffle me.

Prince
I see a good amendment of life in thee—from praying to purse-taking.

Falstaff
Why, Hal, 'tis my vocation, Hal; 'tis no sin for a man to labour in his vocation.

Enter Poins

Poins!—Now shall we know if Gadshill have set a match. O, if men were to be saved by merit, what hole in hell were hot enough for him? This is the most omnipotent villain that ever cried 'Stand!' to a true man.

Prince
Good morrow, Ned.

Poins
Good morrow, sweet Hal. What says Monsieur Remorse? What says Sir John Sack-and-Sugar? Jack, how agrees the devil and thee about thy soul, that thou soldest him on Good Friday last for a cup of Madeira and a cold capon's leg?

Prince
Sir John stands to his word, the devil shall have his bargain; for he was never yet a breaker of proverbs: he will give the devil his due.

Poins
Then art thou damned for keeping thy word with the devil.

125 *Else*: otherwise.
cozening: cheating.
127 *Gad's Hill*: on the road between London and Canterbury, Gad's Hill (near Rochester) is about 30 miles from London.
127–8 *pilgrims . . . offerings*: the pilgrims (like those of Chaucer's *Canterbury Tales*) were going to visit the shrine of St. Thomas à Becket.
130 *vizards*: masks.
131 *Gadshill*: the character in the play takes his name from the place which is the scene of his crimes.
lies: stays at the inn.
bespoke: ordered.
132 *Eastcheap*: a district of London.
134 *tarry*: stay.
136 *Yedward*: a form of 'Edward'.
138 *chops*: fat cheeks, 'fat-face'.
139 *make one*: come with us, join the party.
142–3 *cam'st . . . royal*: are not of royal birth. Falstaff now makes a pun on 'royal' (= a coin worth 50p).
143 *stand for*: fight for; *and* be worth.
144 *once in my days*: for once in my life.
146 *come what will*: whatever happens.
151 *lay him down*: present him with.
153–5 Falstaff again speaks in the manner of a Puritan.

Prince
Else he had been damned for cozening the devil.

Poins
But my lads, my lads, tomorrow morning, by four o'clock early at Gad's Hill, there are pilgrims going to Canterbury with rich offerings, and traders riding to London with fat purses. I have vizards for you all; you have horses for yourselves. Gadshill lies tonight in Rochester. I have bespoke supper tomorrow night in Eastcheap. We may do it as secure as sleep. If you will go, I will stuff your purses full of crowns: if you will not, tarry at home and be hanged.

Falstaff
Hear ye, Yedward, if I tarry at home and go not, I'll hang you for going.

Poins
You will, chops?

Falstaff
Hal, wilt thou make one?

Prince
Who, I rob? I a thief? Not I, by my faith.

Falstaff
There's neither honesty, manhood, nor good fellowship in thee, nor thou cam'st not of the blood royal, if thou darest not stand for ten shillings.

Prince
Well then, once in my days I'll be a madcap.

Falstaff
Why, that's well said.

Prince
Well, come what will, I'll tarry at home.

Falstaff
By the Lord, I'll be a traitor then, when thou art king.

Prince
I care not.

Poins
Sir John, I prithee leave the Prince and me alone: I will lay him down such reasons for this adventure that he shall go.

Falstaff
Well, God give thee the spirit of persuasion, and

him the ears of profiting, that what thou speakest may move, and what he hears may be believed, that the true prince may (for recreation sake) prove a false thief, for the poor abuses of the time want countenance. Farewell, you shall find me in Eastcheap.

Prince

Farewell, the latter spring! Farewell, All-hallown summer! [*Exit* Falstaff

Poins

Now, my good sweet honey lord, ride with us tomorrow. I have a jest to execute that I cannot manage alone. Falstaff, Bardolph, Peto, and Gadshill shall rob those men that we have already waylaid—yourself and I will not be there: and when they have the booty, if you and I do not rob them, cut this head off from my shoulders.

Prince

How shall we part with them in setting forth?

Poins

Why, we will set forth before or after them, and appoint them a place of meeting, wherein it is at our pleasure to fail; and then will they adventure upon the exploit themselves, which they shall have no sooner achieved but we'll set upon them.

Prince

Yea, but 'tis like that they will know us by our horses, by our habits, and by every other appointment, to be ourselves.

Poins

Tut, our horses they shall not see—I'll tie them in the wood; our vizards we will change after we leave them; and sirrah, I have cases of buckram for the nonce, to immask our noted outward garments.

Prince

Yea, but I doubt they will be too hard for us.

Poins

Well, for two of them, I know them to be as true-bred cowards as ever turned back; and for the third, if he fight longer than he sees reason, I'll forswear arms. The virtue of this jest will be the incomprehensible lies that this same fat rogue will

---

154 *ears of profiting*: the ability to learn (profit) from what he hears.

156 *recreation*: amusement.

157 *poor abuses*: petty crimes.
want countenance: need protection.

160 *latter spring*: second-late-spring; Hal seems to be implying that Falstaff is in his second childhood.
All-hallown summer: England sometimes enjoys a period of late summer weather in autumn; the feast of All Saints (hallows) is celebrated on 1 November.

163 *execute*: perform.

166 *waylaid*: ambushed, set a trap for.

169 *part with*: get away from.

171–2 *wherein . . . fail*: and we can choose not to appear.

175 *'tis like*: it is likely, probably.

176 *habits*: clothes.
appointment: pieces of equipment (such as swords).

179 *vizards*: masks.

180 *sirrah*: sir.
cases of buckram: suits of rough cloth.

181 *nonce*: purpose.
inmask: conceal.
noted: well-known.

183 *I doubt*: I'm afraid that.
hard: strong.

185 *turned back*: ran away.

187 *forswear arms*: stop carrying (and using) weapons.
virtue: force.
incomprehensible: endless, beyond all comprehension.

tell us when we meet at supper: how thirty at least he fought with; what wards, what blows, what extremities he endured; and in the reproof of this lives the jest.

Prince

Well, I'll go with thee. Provide us all things necessary, and meet me tomorrow night in Eastcheap; there I'll sup. Farewell.

Poins

Farewell, my lord. [*Exit*

Prince

I know you all, and will awhile uphold
The unyok'd humour of your idleness.
Yet herein will I imitate the sun,
Who doth permit the base contagious clouds
To smother up his beauty from the world,
That, when he please again to be himself,
Being wanted he may be more wonder'd at
By breaking through the foul and ugly mists
Of vapours that did seem to strangle him.
If all the year were playing holidays,
To sport would be as tedious as to work;
But when they seldom come, they wish'd-for come,
And nothing pleaseth but rare accidents:
So when this loose behaviour I throw off,
And pay the debt I never promised,
By how much better than my word I am,
By so much shall I falsify men's hopes;
And like bright metal on a sullen ground,
My reformation, glitt'ring o'er my fault,
Shall show more goodly, and attract more eyes
Than that which hath no foil to set it off.
I'll so offend, to make offence a skill,
Redeeming time when men think least I will.
[*Exit*

190 *wards*: fighting positions (a technical term in fencing).

191 *extremities*: sufferings.
reproof: disproof (they will make Falstaff confess that he is lying).

194 *tomorrow night*: either Shakespeare or Hal has forgotten that the robbery at God's Hill is to take place *before* the supper in Eastcheap.

197 *know*: understand.
awhile: for a time.
uphold: agree with, share.

198 *unyok'd*: unrestrained.
humour: mood, nature.

199 *the sun*: this was traditionally a symbol of kingship.

200 *contagious clouds*: the Elizabethans believed that infectious diseases were bred in the clouds.

202 *that . . . himself*: when the sun chooses to shine again.

205 *vapours*: fogs.
strangle: eclipse.

207 *to sport*: to be on holiday.

208 'When holidays are rare, they are more welcome'.

209 *rare accidents*: unusual events.
loose behaviour: wild conduct.

210 *pay the debt*: fulfil the obligations.

211 *never promised*: showed no signs of paying.

213 *falsify*: prove wrong.
hopes: expectations (fears as well as hopes).

214 *sullen ground*: dull background.

216 *goodly*: precious.

218 *Redeeming time*: making up for lost time.

Act 1 Scene 3
King Henry confronts the rebels. He argues chiefly with his nephew, Henry Percy (Hotspur), who has refused to surrender his prisoners to the King. Hotspur explains the reason for his refusal: he will give up his prisoners if King Henry will pay the ransom money for Mortimer, whom Henry hates. After the King, in great anger, has left the stage, we are told why he hates Mortimer so much: Mortimer has a stronger claim than Henry to be King of England. Now Hotspur is angry; he urges his father and his uncle to revolt, reminding them of King Henry's ingratitude. The scene ends with a decision to fight against the King.

1 *blood*: nature.
2 'Unwilling to be excited about these insults'.
3 *found me*: realized this.
4 *tread upon*: take advantage of.
5 *be myself*: be the King I am.
6 *condition*: natural disposition.
7 *down*: the small feathers on a bird.
8 *title of respect*: claim to be respected.
10 *house*: family (the Percy family, who were Henry's first supporters).
11 *scourge*: whip (i.e. Henry's threat to show his power).
13 *holp*: helped.
portly: powerful.
16 *presence*: appearance.
peremptory: insolent.
17 *majesty*: a king (he means himself).
18 *moody*: bad-tempered.
frontier: forehead.
servant brow: the frown of a subject.
19 *good leave*: permission.
20 *use and counsel*: help and advice.
23 *took*: captured.
24 *deny'd*: refused.
25 *deliver'd*: reported.
26 *misprision*: misunderstanding.

Scene 3 *Windsor: the Council Chamber*

Enter the King, Northumberland, Worcester, Hotspur, Sir Walter Blunt, *with others*

King
My blood hath been too cold and temperate,
Unapt to stir at these indignities,
And you have found me—for accordingly
You tread upon my patience: but be sure
I will from henceforth rather be myself,
Mighty and to be fear'd, than my condition,
Which hath been smooth as oil, soft as young down,
And therefore lost that title of respect
Which the proud soul ne'er pays but to the proud.

Worcester
Our house, my sovereign liege, little deserves
The scourge of greatness to be us'd on it—
And that same greatness too which our own hands
Have holp to make so portly.

Northumberland My lord—

King
Worcester, get thee gone, for I do see
Danger and disobedience in thine eye:
O sir, your presence is too bold and peremptory,
And majesty might never yet endure
The moody frontier of a servant brow.
You have good leave to leave us; when we need
Your use and counsel we shall send for you.
[*Exit* Worcester
[*To* Northumberland] You were about to speak.

Northumberland Yea, my good lord.
Those prisoners in your Highness' name demanded,
Which Harry Percy here at Holmedon took,
Were, as he says, not with such strength deny'd
As is deliver'd to your Majesty.
Either envy, therefore, or misprision,
Is guilty of this fault, and not my son.

Hotspur
My liege, I did deny no prisoners.
But I remember, when the fight was done,

30 *dry*: thirsty.
33 *his chin new reap'd*: his freshly-trimmed beard.
34 'Looked like a corn-field after the corn has been harvested'.
35 *milliner*: the goods sold by milliners (e.g. gloves) were always highly scented.
36 *'twixt*: between.
37 *pouncet-box*: snuff-box—a small box containing perfumed powder.
ever and anon: from time to time.
39 *Who*: i.e. the lord's nose; the perfumed snuff was intended to take away the smell of the dead bodies on the battlefield.
40 *Took it in snuff*: sniffed it up; the phrase 'to take in snuff' also meant 'to be angry'.
still: always.
43 *corse*: corpse.
44 *his nobility*: his noble self (Hotspur is ironic).
45 'Using a lot of fancy, lady-like language'.
46 *amongst the rest*: among other things.

When I was dry with rage and extreme toil,
Breathless and faint, leaning upon my sword,
Came there a certain lord, neat and trimly dress'd,
Fresh as a bridegroom, and his chin new reap'd
Show'd like a stubble-land at harvest-home.
He was perfumed like a milliner,
And 'twixt his finger and his thumb he held
A pouncet-box, which ever and anon
He gave his nose, and took't away again—
Who therewith angry, when it next came there,
Took it in snuff—and still he smil'd and talk'd;
And as the soldiers bore dead bodies by,
He call'd them untaught knaves, unmannerly,
To bring a slovenly unhandsome corse
Betwixt the wind and his nobility.
With many holiday and lady terms
He question'd me, amongst the rest demanded
My prisoners in your Majesty's behalf.
I then, all smarting with my wounds being cold,
To be so pester'd with a popinjay,
Out of my grief and my impatience
Answer'd neglectingly, I know not what—
He should, or he should not; for he made me mad

48 *all . . . cold*: very sore because my wounds were feeling cold.
49 *popinjay*: parrot.
50 *grief*: pain.
51 *neglectingly*: without thinking, carelessly.
53 *shine so brisk*: look so smart.
54 *waiting-gentlewoman*: lady-in-waiting (a lady of noble birth attending one of even higher rank).
55 *God . . . mark*: God preserve us (an exclamation of contempt).
56 *sovereignest thing*: most healing medicine.
57 *parmacity*: an ointment or liniment.
58–62 Hotspur tries to imitate the lord's effeminate speech.
59 *saltpetre*: a mineral used for making gunpowder.
61 *tall*: brave.
64 *bald unjointed*: empty and disconnected.
65 *indirectly*: without thinking.
67 *Come current for*: be accepted as money.
72 *retold*: recounted.
73 *die*: be forgotten.
74 *wrong*: harm.
74–5 *impeach . . . said*: prove that he was disloyal in what he said.
75 *so*: provided that.
unsay: contradict.
76 *yet*: still.
77 *with . . . exception*: on condition.
78 *charge*: expense.
straight: immediately.
79 *his brother-in-law*: see p. 126.
80 *on my soul*: an oath.
82 *magician*: Glendower's belief in his magic powers is described in *Act 3*, Scene 1.
84 *coffers*: treasury.
86 *indent with*: make a bargain with.
fears: cowards *and* causes for fear.
87 'When they (the cowards) have given themselves up'.
89 *hold*: consider.

To see him shine so brisk, and smell so sweet,
And talk so like a waiting-gentlewoman
Of guns, and drums, and wounds, God save the mark!
And telling me the sovereignest thing on earth
Was parmacity for an inward bruise;
And that it was great pity, so it was,
This villainous saltpetre should be digg'd
Out of the bowels of the harmless earth,
Which many a good tall fellow had destroy'd
So cowardly; and but for these vile guns
He would himself have been a soldier.
This bald unjointed chat of his, my lord,
I answer'd indirectly, as I said,
And I beseech you, let not his report
Come current for an accusation
Betwixt my love and your high Majesty.

Blunt

The circumstance consider'd, good my lord,
Whate'er Lord Harry Percy then had said
To such a person, and in such a place,
At such a time, with all the rest retold,
May reasonably die, and never rise
To do him wrong, or any way impeach
What then he said, so he unsay it now.

King

Why, yet he doth deny his prisoners,
But with proviso and exception
That we at our own charge shall ransom straight
His brother-in-law, the foolish Mortimer—
Who, on my soul, hath wilfully betray'd
The lives of those that he did lead to fight
Against that great magician, damn'd Glendower
(Whose daughter, as we hear, the Earl of March
Hath lately marry'd). Shall our coffers then
Be empty'd to redeem a traitor home?
Shall we buy treason, and indent with fears,
When they have lost and forfeited themselves?
No, on the barren mountains let him starve;
For I shall never hold that man my friend
Whose tongue shall ask me for one penny cost
To ransom home revolted Mortimer.

93 *fall off*: lose his allegiance to the King.
95 *no more but one*: only.
96 *mouthed wounds*: wounds which speak for him.
took: received.
97 *sedgy*: grassy (sedge is a small, grass-like plant).
98 Only these two men were fighting, at close quarters.
99 *confound . . . hour*: spend almost an hour.
100 *changing hardiment*: matching strength.
101 *breath'd*: paused for breath.
101–2 *three . . . flood*: they agreed to drink three times from the river.
102 *flood*: waters.
103 *Who*: i.e. the river.
affrighted: frightened.
105 *crisp*: rippled (with small waves).
107 *bare*: miserable.
108 *Colour*: justify, make excuses for (*also* stain).
111 *with revolt*: with the accusation of rebellion.
112 *belie*: tell lies about.
113 *encounter with*: fight.
114 *durst*: dare.
118 *with the speediest means*: as quickly as possible.
119 *kind*: way
121 *license*: permit.
123 *And if*: even if.
124 *will*: will follow.
straight: at once.
125 *ease my heart*: set my heart at rest (by expressing his feelings).
126 'Although I risk having my head cut off'.

Hotspur
Revolted Mortimer!
He never did fall off, my sovereign liege,
But by the chance of war: to prove that true
Needs no more but one tongue for all those wounds,
Those mouthed wounds, which valiantly he took
When on the gentle Severn's sedgy bank,
In single opposition hand to hand,
He did confound the best part of an hour
In changing hardiment with great Glendower.
Three times they breath'd, and three times did they drink
Upon agreement of swift Severn's flood;
Who then affrighted with their bloody looks
Ran fearfully among the trembling reeds,
And hid his crisp head in the hollow bank,
Bloodstained with these valiant combatants.
Never did bare and rotten policy
Colour her working with such deadly wounds,
Nor never could the noble Mortimer
Receive so many, and all willingly.
Then let not him be slander'd with revolt.

King
Thou dost belie him, Percy, thou dost belie him.
He never did encounter with Glendower.
I tell thee, he durst as well have met the devil alone
As Owen Glendower for an enemy.
Art thou not asham'd? But sirrah, henceforth
Let me not hear you speak of Mortimer.
Send me your prisoners with the speediest means,
Or you shall hear in such a kind from me
As will displease you. My Lord Northumberland:
We license your departure with your son.
Send us your prisoners, or you will hear of it.
[*Exit* King, *with* Blunt *and other lords*

Hotspur
And if the devil come and roar for them
I will not send them. I will after straight
And tell him so, for I will ease my heart,
Albeit I make a hazard of my head.

Northumberland
What, drunk with choler? Stay, and pause awhile.
Here comes your uncle.

Enter Worcester

Hotspur Speak of Mortimer?
'Zounds, I will speak of him, and let my soul
Want mercy if I do not join with him:
Yea, on his part I'll empty all these veins,
And shed my dear blood drop by drop in the dust,
But I will lift the down-trod Mortimer
As high in the air as this unthankful king,
As this ingrate and canker'd Bolingbroke.

Northumberland
Brother, the King hath made your nephew mad.

Worcester
Who struck this heat up after I was gone?

Hotspur
He will forsooth have all my prisoners.
And when I urg'd the ransom once again
Of my wife's brother, then his cheek look'd pale,
And on my face he turn'd an eye of death,
Trembling even at the name of Mortimer.

Worcester
I cannot blame him: was not he proclaim'd,
By Richard that dead is, the next of blood?

Northumberland
He was, I heard the proclamation.
And then it was, when the unhappy king
(Whose wrongs in us God pardon!) did set forth
Upon his Irish expedition;
From whence he, intercepted, did return
To be depos'd, and shortly murdered.

Worcester
And for whose death we in the world's wide mouth
Live scandaliz'd and foully spoken of.

Hotspur
But soft, I pray you! Did King Richard then
Proclaim my brother, Edmund Mortimer,
Heir to the crown?

Northumberland He did, myself did hear it.

Hotspur
Nay, then I cannot blame his cousin king,

127 *choler*: anger.

129–30 *let . . . mercy*: damn me.

131 *on his part*: for his sake.

133 *down-trod*: dejected.

135 *ingrate*: ungrateful.
canker'd: thoroughly rotten.

137 *struck . . . up*: excited this passion.

138 *forsooth*: indeed.

139 *urg'd*: argued for.

141 *an eye of death*: a look which threatened death; *or* a look which showed the king in fear of death.

144 *that dead is*: who is dead.
the next of blood: i.e. the heir to the throne; see p. 126.

147 *Whose . . . pardon*: may God forgive the wrong we did to Richard.

148 *his Irish expedition*: see p. v.

149 *intercepted*: interrupted.

151–2 *in . . . spoken of*: throughout the whole wide world we are abused and slandered.

153 *soft*: wait a minute.

159 *forgetful*: Hotspur accuses the King of having forgotten how he was supported by the Percy family.

160 *wear . . . subornation*: suffer the terrible disgrace of having aided and abetted murder.

163 *base second means*: inferior instruments.

165–6 Hotspur asks pardon for speaking so plainly when he told Worcester and Northumberland that they had been only the instruments used in murder—they are of the same rank and category ('the line and the predicament') as the ropes ('cords') and ladder needed to hang a man.

167 *range*: rank.
subtle: cunning.

168 *in these days*: at the present time.

169 'Be written in the history books ('chronicles') of the future'.

171 *gage them both*: pawn both the nobility and their power.
behalf: cause.

173 *rose*: Richard II belonged to the house of Lancaster, whose emblem was a red rose.

174 *canker*: wild rose (or even 'canker-worm', the disease which kills roses).

175 *in more shame*: to your even greater shame.
be further spoken: be said in addition.

176 *fool'd*: deceived.

178 *time serves*: there is time.

180 *thoughts*: opinions.

181 *disdain'd*: disdainful.

183 *To answer*: how he can repay.

That wish'd him on the barren mountains starve.
But shall it be that you, that set the crown
Upon the head of this forgetful man,
And for his sake wear the detested blot
Of murderous subornation—shall it be
That you a world of curses undergo,
Being the agents, or base second means,
The cords, the ladder, or the hangman rather?
O, pardon me, that I descend so low,
To show the line and the predicament
Wherein you range under this subtle king!
Shall it for shame be spoken in these days,
Or fill up chronicles in time to come,
That men of your nobility and power
Did gage them both in an unjust behalf
(As both of you, God pardon it, have done)
To put down Richard, that sweet lovely rose,
And plant this thorn, this canker Bolingbroke?
And shall it in more shame be further spoken,
That you are fool'd, discarded, and shook off
By him for whom these shames ye underwent?
No, yet time serves wherein you may redeem
Your banish'd honours, and restore yourselves
Into the good thoughts of the world again:
Revenge the jeering and disdain'd contempt
Of this proud king, who studies day and night
To answer all the debt he owes to you
Even with the bloody payment of your deaths.
Therefore I say—

Worcester Peace, cousin, say no more.
And now I will unclasp a secret book,
And to your quick-conceiving discontents

185 *Peace*: be quiet.
186 *unclasp*: unfasten, open (some very precious books were kept shut with locks and keys).
187 *quick-conceiving discontents*: discontented minds, which are quick to understand).
190–91 Worcester's example of a dangerous exploit is taken from medieval tales where a knight had to cross ('o'er-walk') a river ('current'), using a spear for a bridge.
191 *unsteadfast*: insecure.

192 'If he falls in the river, that is the end—whether he sinks or swims'. Even if he can swim, the man has failed the trial.
194 *So*: provided that.
195–6 'It is more exciting ('the blood more stirs') to begin a lion-hunt than to chase a hare'. Hotspur uses the correct hunting terms—'rouse' and 'start'—for the different animals.
199 *methinks*: I think.
were: would be.
201 *deep*: ocean.
202 *fathom-line*: a line which sailors dropped into the sea to find how deep it was.
203 *locks*: hair; Hotspur now imagines 'honour' in the person of a woman.
204 *redeem*: rescue.
205 *corrival*: partner.
dignities: trophies.
206 'But I have no patience ('out upon') with this practice of sharing honour'.
207–8 Worcester comments that Hotspur has a rich imagination but he will not pay attention to the real business.
apprehends: catches (imaginatively).
a world: a great many.
figures: fancies, rhetorical devices of speech.
form: substance.
210 *I cry you mercy*: I am sorry.

I'll read you matter deep and dangerous,
As full of peril and adventurous spirit
As to o'er-walk a current roaring loud
On the unsteadfast footing of a spear.

Hotspur
If he fall in, good night—or sink, or swim!
Send danger from the east unto the west,
So honour cross it from the north to south,
And let them grapple: O, the blood more stirs
To rouse a lion than to start a hare!

Northumberland
Imagination of some great exploit
Drives him beyond the bounds of patience.

Hotspur
By heaven, methinks it were an easy leap
To pluck bright honour from the pale-fac'd moon,
Or dive into the bottom of the deep,
Where fathom-line could never touch the ground,
And pluck up drowned honour by the locks,
So he that doth redeem her thence might wear
Without corrival all her dignities.
But out upon this half-fac'd fellowship!

Worcester
He apprehends a world of figures here,
But not the form of what he should attend.
Good cousin, give me audience for a while.

Hotspur
I cry you mercy.

212 *a Scot*: Hotspur makes a pun with 'scot' = a very small payment.
214 *start*: jump.
215 *lend . . . purposes*: do not listen to my plans.
216 *that's flat*: that is certain.
220 *holla*: shout.
221 *starling*: many Elizabethan texts refer to starlings (wild brown birds) which had been taught to speak.

223 *still in motion*: always alive.
225 *defy*: reject.
226 *gall and pinch*: irritate (as a tight saddle rubs and pinches a horse).
227 *sword-and-buckler*: swashbuckling, playboy.
229 *mischance*: accident.
232 *better temper'd*: more controlled.
233 *wasp-stung*: irritable (as though stung by a wasp).
234 *to break . . . mood*: to burst into these feminine tantrums.
235 *Tying thine ear*: listening.

237 *pismires*: ants.
238 *politician*: scheming villain.

241 *kept*: lived.
242 *bow'd my knee*: affirmed my loyalty.

Worcester Those same noble Scots
That are your prisoners—
Hotspur I'll keep them all;
By God he shall not have a Scot of them!
No, if a Scot would save his soul he shall not.
I'll keep them, by this hand!
Worcester You start away,
And lend no ear unto my purposes.
Those prisoners you shall keep—
Hotspur Nay, I will: that's flat!
He said he would not ransom Mortimer,
Forbade my tongue to speak of Mortimer;
But I will find him when he lies asleep,
And in his ear I'll holla 'Mortimer!'
Nay, I'll have a starling shall be taught to speak
Nothing but 'Mortimer', and give it him
To keep his anger still in motion.
Worcester
Hear you, cousin, a word—
Hotspur
All studies here I solemnly defy,
Save how to gall and pinch this Bolingbroke.
And that same sword-and-buckler Prince of Wales—
But that I think his father loves him not,
And would be glad he met with some mischance—
I would have him poison'd with a pot of ale!
Worcester
Farewell, kinsman: I'll talk to you
When you are better temper'd to attend.
Northumberland
Why, what a wasp-stung and impatient fool
Art thou to break into this woman's mood,
Tying thine ear to no tongue but thine own!
Hotspur
Why, look you, I am whipp'd and scourg'd with rods,
Nettled, and stung with pismires, when I hear
Of this vile politician Bolingbroke.
In Richard's time—what do you call the place?
A plague upon it, it is in Gloucestershire—
'Twas where the mad-cap duke his uncle kept,
His uncle York—where I first bow'd my knee

Unto this king of smiles, this Bolingbroke—
'Sblood! when you and he came back from Ravenspurgh.

Northumberland

At Berkeley castle.

Hotspur

You say true.
Why, what a candy deal of courtesy
This fawning greyhound then did proffer me!
'Look when his infant fortune came to age',
And 'gentle Harry Percy', and 'kind cousin':
O, the devil take such cozeners!—God forgive me!
Good uncle, tell your tale; I have done.

Worcester

Nay, if you have not, to it again,
We will stay your leisure.

Hotspur I have done, i'faith.

Worcester

Then once more to your Scottish prisoners:
Deliver them up without their ransom straight,
And make the Douglas' son your only mean
For powers in Scotland—which, for divers reasons
Which I shall send you written, be assur'd
Will easily be granted. [*To* Northumberland] You, my lord,
Your son in Scotland being thus employ'd,
Shall secretly into the bosom creep
Of that same noble prelate well-belov'd,
The Archbishop.

Hotspur Of York, is it not?

Worcester True, who bears hard
His brother's death at Bristow, the Lord Scroop.
I speak not this in estimation,
As what I think might be, but what I know
Is ruminated, plotted, and set down,
And only stays but to behold the face
Of that occasion that shall bring it on.

Hotspur

I smell it. Upon my life it will do well!

244 *'Sblood*: an oath (by God's blood).
Ravenspurgh: in Yorkshire, where Bolingbroke landed when he returned from exile in 1399.
247 *candy deal*: sugary load.
248 *proffer*: hold out (as though offering sweets to a child).
249 *Look when*: as soon as.
his infant fortune: Bolingbroke's kingship was newly-born.
came to age: matured.
251 *cozeners*: cheats (with a pun on 'cousin').
253 *to it again*: go on with it.
254 *stay*: wait.
255 *once more*: let us return to the subject of.
256 *Deliver them up*: let them go free.
straight: at once.
257 *the Douglas' son*: the son of the Earl of Douglas. It is correct to speak of the head of a Scottish family by using the definite article; Shakespeare is, however, mistaken about the parentage of Mordake, who is the prisoner referred to (see *1*, 1, 94).
257–8 *your . . . Scotland*: your only way of raising an army ('powers') in Scotland.
258 *divers*: various.
262 *bosom*: confidence.
263 *prelate*: important man in the church hierarchy.
269–70 'And only waits to see an opportunity for action'.
271 *I smell it*: 'I can guess what you are talking about'.

272 'You always ('still') release the hounds ('let'st slip') before the hare ('game') is running ('afoot').

273 *choose but be*: be anything other than.

276 *aim'd*: directed, planned.

277 *'tis . . . reason*: i.e. it is a very good reason.
speed: hurry.

278 'To save our own lives ('heads') by calling up an army ('head')'.

279 'However well we behave ('bear ourselves')'.

284 *strangers to*: unfamiliar with.

288 *ripe*: ready.

289 *steal*: go secretly.
suddenly: very soon.

291 *fashion*: arrange.
happily: with luck.

292–3 They will themselves have control over what happens to them (their 'fortunes') instead of being insecure ('at much uncertainty') because they are dependent on the King.

294 *thrive*: do well.

296 *sport*: performance on the battlefield.

Northumberland
Before the game is afoot thou still let'st slip.
Hotspur
Why, it cannot choose but be a noble plot;
And then the power of Scotland and of York,
To join with Mortimer, ha?
Worcester And so they shall.
Hotspur
In faith it is exceedingly well aim'd.
Worcester
And 'tis no little reason bids us speed
To save our heads by raising of a head;
For, bear ourselves as even as we can,
The King will always think him in our debt,
And think we think ourselves unsatisfy'd,
Till he hath found a time to pay us home:
And see already how he doth begin
To make us strangers to his looks of love.
Hotspur
He does, he does! We'll be reveng'd on him.
Worcester
Cousin, farewell. No further go in this
Than I by letters shall direct your course.
When time is ripe, which will be suddenly,
I'll steal to Glendower and Lord Mortimer,
Where you, and Douglas, and our powers at once—
As I will fashion it—shall happily meet,
To bear our fortunes in our own strong arms,
Which now we hold at much uncertainty.
Northumberland
Farewell, good brother; we shall thrive, I trust.
Hotspur
Uncle, adieu: O, let the hours be short
Till fields, and blows, and groans applaud our sport!

[*Exeunt*

Act 2

Scene 1 *Rochester : an Inn Yard*

Enter a Carrier *with a lantern in his hand*

First Carrier
Heigh-ho! An it be not four by the day I'll be hanged; Charles' wain is over the new chimney, and yet our horse not packed. What, ostler!

Ostler
[*Within*] Anon, anon.

First Carrier
I prithee, Tom, beat Cut's saddle, put a few flocks in the point; poor jade is wrung in the withers out of all cess.

Enter another Carrier

Second Carrier
Peas and beans are as dank here as a dog, and that is the next way to give poor jades the bots. This house is turned upside down since Robin Ostler died.

First Carrier
Poor fellow never joyed since the price of oats rose; it was the death of him.

Act 2 Scene 1
It is early morning at Rochester, and the Carriers are preparing to start their journey. The robber Gadshill is also awake, and when the Carriers have departed we see how the thief and the Chamberlain are working together to plot the robbery.

1 *by the day*: in the morning.

2 *Charles' wain*: the Plough, or Great Bear: a constellation in the northern sky (the Carrier can tell the time by the position of the stars).

3 *packed*: loaded.
ostler: inn-servant in charge of the stables.

4 *Anon*: at once (the usual reply of an inn-servant).

5 *beat Cut's saddle*: i.e. to soften it. 'Cut' was a common name for a working-horse.
a few flocks: some stuffing.

6 *point*: pommel (the front of a saddle).
poor jade: the absence of the definite article indicates the rustic, uneducated, speech idiom; a 'jade' is a poor quality horse.
wrung in the withers: rubbed on the shoulders.

7 *out of all cess*: excessively.

8–9 *Peas . . . bots*: the Carriers are complaining that the food provided for the horses is damp ('dank'), and will cause worms in the animals.

9 *next*: quickest.

10–11 *This . . . died*: this inn has been completely disorganized since the death of the stableman, Robin.

12 *never joyed*: he was never happy.

14–15 'There must be more fleas here than at any other inn ('house') on the road to London'.

15 *stung*: bitten.

tench: a fish whose speckled markings look like flea-bites.

16 *By the mass*: an old-fashioned oath.

a king christen: a Christian king. Kings have the best (and most) of everything, and the Carrier assumes that they must therefore have more and better flea-bites.

Second Carrier

I think this be the most villainous house in all London road for fleas; I am stung like a tench.

First Carrier

Like a tench! By the mass, there is ne'er a king christen could be better bit than I have been since the first cock.

18 *the first cock*: midnight (it was generally agreed that the first cock-crow—marking the beginning of a new day—should be at midnight.)

19 *allow . . . jordan*: they won't even give us chamber-pot, and so we urinate ('leak') in the fireplace ('chimney'), and urine encourages the fleas to breed.
loach: a small fish reputed to breed fleas.

22 *Come away*: hurry up.

24 *gammon*: almost half a pig (the best portion).
razes: roots (ginger was imported from the East, and this would be a valuable commodity).

25 *Charing Cross*: a village on the opposite side of London.

26 *pannier*: the large basket holding the Carrier's merchandise.

27 *hast . . . head*: can't you see what needs to be done (i.e. the turkeys should have been fed).

29 *as . . . drink*: a proverbial saying. The Carrier seems to be saying that it is necessary to hit the ostler over his head ('break the pate on thee') in order to make him do anything.

31 *Hast . . . thee*: can you not be trusted.

32 *Good morrow*: Good morning.
what's o'clock: what time is it.

34 *gelding*: horse (the castrated male, used for most working purposes).

36 *I know . . . that*: I'm not such a fool—you can't catch me that way.

39 *Ay . . . tell*: words uttered to deride, or refuse, a request.
quoth he: says he (the speaker mocks Gadshill).

Second Carrier
Why, they will allow us ne'er a jordan, and then we leak in your chimney, and your chamber-lye breeds fleas like a loach.

First Carrier
What, ostler! Come away, and be hanged! Come away!

Second Carrier
I have a gammon of bacon and two razes of ginger, to be delivered as far as Charing Cross.

First Carrier
God's body! The turkeys in my pannier are quite starved. What, ostler! A plague on thee, hast thou never an eye in thy head? Canst not hear? And 'twere not as good deed as drink to break the pate on thee, I am a very villain. Come, and be hanged! Hast no faith in thee?

Enter Gadshill

Gadshill
Good morrow, carriers, what's o'clock?

First Carrier
I think it be two o'clock.

Gadshill
I prithee lend me thy lantern, to see my gelding in the stable.

First Carrier
Nay, by God, soft! I know a trick worth two of that, i'faith.

Gadshill
I pray thee lend me thine.

Second Carrier
Ay, when? Canst tell? Lend me thy lantern, quoth he! Marry, I'll see thee hanged first.

Gadshill

Sirrah carrier, what time do you mean to come to London?

Second Carrier

Time enough to go to bed with a candle, I warrant thee. Come, neighbour Mugs, we'll call up the gentlemen; they will along with company, for they have great charge. [*Exeunt* Carriers

Gadshill

What ho! Chamberlain!

Enter Chamberlain

Chamberlain

'At hand, quoth pick-purse.'

Gadshill

That's even as fair as 'At hand, quoth the chamberlain': for thou variest no more from picking of purses than giving direction doth from labouring—thou layest the plot how.

Chamberlain

Good morrow, master Gadshill. It holds current that I told you yesternight: there's a franklin in the Wild of Kent hath brought three hundred marks with him in gold; I heard him tell it to one of his company last night at supper—a kind of auditor, one that hath abundance of charge too, God knows what. They are up already, and call for eggs and butter—they will away presently.

Gadshill

Sirrah, if they meet not with Saint Nicholas' clerks, I'll give thee this neck.

Chamberlain

No, I'll none of it; I pray thee keep that for the hangman, for I know thou worshippest Saint Nicholas as truly as a man of falsehood may.

Gadshill

What talkest thou to me of the hangman? If I hang, I'll make a fat pair of gallows: for if I hang, old Sir John hangs with me, and thou knowest he is no starveling. Tut, there are other Troyans that thou dream'st not of, the which for sport sake are content to do the profession some grace; that would (if matters should be looked into) for their

---

41 *mean*: intend.

43 *Time enough*: with plenty of time.
to go . . . candle: to go to bed with a candle (the Carriers are refusing to give information to Gadshill).

44 *call up*: rouse, awaken.

45 *will along*: want to go along with us.

46 *great charge*: a lot to look after.

48 *At hand . . . pickpurse*: I'm here, says the thief; the Chamberlain speaks a common catchphrase.

49 *fair*: true.

50–51 Telling people to steal is just as bad as the actual theft.

52 *thou . . . how*: you say how it (the robbery) is to be done.

53 *holds current*: is still true.

54 *franklin*: a land-owning farmer.

55 *Wild*: Weald: a rich part of the county of Kent.
marks: gold coins.

57 *auditor*: an official of the Royal Exchequer.

58 *abundance of charge*: a lot to look after.

59 *eggs and butter*: i.e. for breakfast.

60 *will away*: will leave.
presently: immediately.

61 *Saint Nicholas' clerks*: highwaymen, robbers; St Nicholas was the patron saint of travellers—and therefore of highwaymen.

62 *give . . . neck*: be hanged.

63 *I'll . . . it*: I don't want it.

67 *fat . . . gallows*: there will be a fat (or 'rich') pair of us on the gallows.

69 *starveling*: thin, starved creature.
Troyans: mates, companions (the Trojans were great heroes who fought against the Greeks in classical mythology). Gadshill is referring to Prince Hal—but he dare not name him.

70 *the which*: who.
for sport sake: for their own amusement.

71 *to do . . . grace*: to honour the profession (of robbers).

71–3 'Who, if any questions are asked, would make everything all right for the sake of their own reputations ('credit')'.

own credit sake make all whole. I am joined with no foot-landrakers, no long-staff sixpenny strikers, none of these mad mustachio purple-hued maltworms, but with nobility and tranquillity, burgomasters and great oneyers, such as can hold in, such as will strike sooner than speak, and speak sooner than drink, and drink sooner than pray—and yet, 'zounds, I lie, for they pray continually to their saint the commonwealth—or rather not pray to her, but prey on her, for they ride up and down on her and make her their boots.

Chamberlain

What, the commonwealth their boots? Will she hold out water in foul way?

Gadshill

She will, she will; justice hath liquored her. We steal as in a castle, cock-sure: we have the receipt of fern-seed, we walk invisible.

73 *joined with*: accompanied by.

foot-landrakers: robbers wandering around on foot.

74 *long . . . strikers*: thieves who used long poles to knock the riders from their horses in order to steal amounts which were often paltry (worth no more than sixpence).

75–6 *mad . . . maltworms*: crazy drunken revellers with their whiskers and purple faces. The 'mustachio' (moustache) was thought by such men to be a sign of virility; their faces were red as a result of heavy drinking of strong liquor (brewed from 'malt').

76 *nobility*: noble men (both 'men of high rank' and 'men of good character').

tranquillity: peaceful men (in contrast to the riotous 'maltworms').

77 *burgomasters*: important men in the town.

great oneyers: great men; the noun seems to be Gadshill's own invention.

78 *can hold in*: are self-disciplined (they can keep secrets; stay together; and concentrate on the job they are doing).

78–80 *will strike . . . pray*: they will hit a man (or rob him) before they speak to him; and challenge ('speak'—calling 'Lay by') rather than drink; and drink rather than pray.

81 *commonwealth*: the state (and also 'wealth', which the thieves believe to be 'common'—free for all).

83 *boots*: spoil, booty.

84–5 Will the boots keep you dry in muddy roads; *and* Will the state protect you in a time of trouble.

86 *justice . . . her*: Those who operate the laws have been given bribes.

87 *as in a castle*: with complete safety.

cocksure: confidently.

receipt of: recipe for.

88 *fernseed*: fernseed was believed to appear only on 23 June (Midsummer Eve); any man who wore it became invisible.

89 *more beholding to*: owe more to.

93 *purchase*: the goods we steal.
true: honest.

95 *Go to . . . men*: Gadshill resents being called thief and argues that he has a right to be called a man. He quotes from a Latin text-book which explains the difference between 'proper' and 'common' nouns with the example that *homo* is the common noun for 'man'.

97 *muddy*: stupid.

Chamberlain
Nay, by my faith, I think you are more beholding to the night than to fern-seed for your walking invisible.

Gadshill
Give me thy hand. Thou shalt have a share in our purchase, as I am a true man.

Chamberlain
Nay, rather let me have it, as you are a false thief.

Gadshill
Go to, 'homo' is a common name to all men. Bid the ostler bring my gelding out of the stable. Farewell, you muddy knave. [*Exeunt*

Act 2 Scene 2
The thieves are assembling at their meeting-place, ready to waylay the travellers on the road to London. Prince Hal, Poins and Peto have played a trick on Falstaff by hiding his horse, so that the fat knight has to walk. The Prince and Poins hide (as they had planned to do in *Act 1*, Scene 2). After the robbery, Hal and Poins return (in disguise) and attack the robbers.

2 *frets*: is irritated, worries.
a gummed velvet: velvet was treated with gum to make it shine, but the gum irritated the wearer's skin and was said to 'fret' or chafe.

3 *Stand close*: hide.

5 *fat-kidneyed*: the kidneys are always enclosed in fat, but Falstaff's must have more fat than normal kidneys.

6 'What a terrible noise you are making'.

8 *is walked*: has walked.

12–13 *If I . . . afoot*: If I go another four feet on foot ('afoot'); a 'squier' is a measuring-rod.

13 *break my wind*: burst my lungs.

13–14 *I doubt . . . this*: I am sure I shall die a good Christian death as a result of all this suffering.

Scene 2 *Gad's Hill: the Highway*

Enter Prince, Poins, *and* Peto

Poins
Come, shelter, shelter! I have removed Falstaff's horse, and he frets like a gummed velvet.

Prince
Stand close! [*They hide themselves*

Enter Falstaff

Falstaff
Poins! Poins, and be hanged! Poins!

Prince
[*Comes forward*] Peace, ye fat-kidneyed rascal! What a brawling dost thou keep!

Falstaff
Where's Poins, Hal?

Prince
He is walked up to the top of the hill; I'll go seek him. [*Exit*

Falstaff
I am accursed to rob in that thief's company! The rascal hath removed my horse and tied him I know not where. If I travel but four foot by the squier further afoot, I shall break my wind. Well, I doubt not but to die a fair death for all this, if I scape

14 *scape hanging*: avoid being hanged.
15 *forsworn his company*: sworn not to be in his company.
16 *hourly . . . years*: every hour for the past 22 years.
18 *medicines*: love-potions.
20 *else*: otherwise (there is no other explanation).
21 *starve*: die.
22 *rob . . . further*: do any more robbing (especially on foot).
and: if.
22–3 *as good . . . man*: as sensible to become honest as it is to drink.
24 *veriest varlet*: biggest villain.
25–6 *eight . . . with me*: to walk eight yards over uneven ground is worse for me than for other men to go 70 miles.

hanging for killing that rogue. I have forsworn his company hourly any time this two and twenty years, and yet I am bewitched with the rogue's company. If the rascal have not given me medicines to make me love him, I'll be hanged. It could not be else: I have drunk medicines. Poins! Hal! A plague upon you both! Bardolph! Peto! I'll starve ere I'll rob a foot further—and 'twere not as good a deed as drink to turn true man and to leave these rogues, I am the veriest varlet that ever chewed with a tooth. Eight yards of uneven ground is threescore and ten miles afoot with me, and the stony-hearted villains know it well enough. A plague upon it when thieves cannot be true one to another! [*They whistle*] Whew! A plague upon you all! Give me my horse, you rogues, give me my horse and be hanged!

33 *list*: listen.
35 *being down*: when I am lying down.
36–7 *bear . . . afoot*: carry my own body on foot.
37 *coin*: money.
38 *colt*: trick.
39 *uncolted*: unhorsed; the Prince makes a pun on 'colt' = to trick, and 'colt' = a young horse.
42 The Prince pretends to think that Falstaff is speaking to him as though he were a stableboy.
43 'Hang yourself in your own garters' was a popular expression; Falstaff adapts it slightly, playing on the fact that as heir apparent to the throne the Prince is a member of the Order of the Garter.
44 *ta'en*: taken, caught.
peach: impeach, inform on you.
and I have not: if I do not have.

45 *ballads*: songs (to be sung to well-known tunes) which were printed on sheets of paper and sold in the streets. They were the equivalent of newspapers, describing current events; and they could also be used (as Falstaff now threatens) to ridicule enemies.
on: about.
filthy tunes: tunes associated with unpleasant songs (so that the ballads would be even more hurtful).
46 *let . . . poison*: let me be poisoned with a glass of wine.
46–7 *is so forward*: goes so far (is taken to such extremes).

Prince
[*Comes forward*] Peace, ye fat guts! Lie down; lay thine ear close to the ground, and list if thou canst hear the tread of travellers.

Falstaff
Have you any levers to lift me up again, being down? 'Sblood, I'll not bear my own flesh so far afoot again for all the coin in thy father's exchequer. What a plague mean ye to colt me thus?

Prince
Thou liest: thou art not colted, thou art uncolted.

Falstaff
I prithee good Prince Hal, help me to my horse, good king's son.

Prince
Out, ye rogue, shall I be your ostler?

Falstaff
Hang thyself in thine own heir-apparent garters! If I be ta'en, I'll peach for this. And I have not ballads made on you all, and sung to filthy tunes, let a cup of sack be my poison—when a jest is so forward, and afoot too! I hate it.

Enter Gadshill *and* Bardolph

Gadshill
Stand!

Falstaff
So I do, against my will.

Poins
O, 'tis our setter; I know his voice. [*Comes forward with* Peto] Bardolph, what news?

Bardolph
Case ye, case ye, on with your vizards! There's money of the King's coming down the hill; 'tis going to the King's exchequer.

Falstaff
You lie, ye rogue, 'tis going to the King's tavern.

Gadshill
There's enough to make us all.

Falstaff
To be hanged.

50 *setter*: a word used by thieves, meaning 'informant'.
52 *Case ye*: disguise yourselves.
vizards: masks.
56 *make us all*: make all our fortunes.
58 *front*: confront.
59 *scape*: escape.
60 *light on*: meet.
61 *be*: are.
62 *Some*: about.

64 *Paunch*: the Prince speaks playfully of Falstaff's belly.

65 *John of Gaunt*: Hal's grandfather took his name from the town of Gaunt (now Ghent); he was a brave soldier—and he was also thin.
67 *to the proof*: to be tested.

70 *fast*: firm (do not run away).

73 *hard by*: near by.
stand close: hide.

74 *happy . . . dole*: good luck, everybody ('dole' = fortune).
75 'Let everyone do his job'.

Prince
Sirs, you four shall front them in the narrow lane: Ned Poins and I will walk lower—if they scape from your encounter, then they light on us.

Peto
How many be there of them?

Gadshill
Some eight or ten.

Falstaff
'Zounds, will they not rob us?

Prince
What, a coward, Sir John Paunch?

Falstaff
Indeed, I am not John of Gaunt your grandfather, but yet no coward, Hal.

Prince
Well, we leave that to the proof.

Poins
Sirrah Jack, thy horse stands behind the hedge; when thou need'st him, there thou shalt find him. Farewell, and stand fast.

Falstaff
Now cannot I strike him, if I should be hanged.

Prince
[*to* Poins] Ned, where are our disguises?

Poins
Here, hard by, stand close.

[*Exeunt* Prince *and* Poins

Falstaff
Now, my masters, happy man be his dole, say I. Every man to his business.

Enter the Travellers

First Traveller
Come, neighbour, the boy shall lead our horses down the hill; we'll walk afoot awhile and ease our legs.

Thieves
Stand!

Second Traveller
Jesus bless us!

Falstaff
Strike! Down with them! Cut the villains' throats!

Ah, whoreson caterpillars! Bacon-fed knaves! They hate us youth! Down with them, fleece them!

First Traveller

O, we are undone, both we and ours for ever!

Falstaff

Hang ye, gorbellied knaves, are ye undone? No, ye fat chuffs; I would your store were here! On bacons, on! What, ye knaves! Young men must live. You are grandjurors, are ye? We'll jure ye, faith.

[*They rob them and bind them. Exeunt*

Enter the Prince *and* Poins, *disguised*

Prince

The thieves have bound the true men. Now could thou and I rob the thieves and go merrily to London, it would be argument for a week, laughter for a month, and a good jest for ever.

Poins

Stand close, I hear them coming

[*They stand back*

82 *whoreson caterpillars*: idle parasites.
bacon-fed: well-fed.

83 *us youth*: us young men.
fleece them: rob them.

85 *undone*: ruined.
ours: our families.

86 *gorbellied*: fat-bellied.

87 *chuffs*: misers.
your store: all you possess.

89 *grandjurors*: great jurymen (only the rich could serve on a grand jury).
jure: the word has no special meaning; Falstaff is uttering vague threats such as 'We'll show you'.

91–2 *could . . . rob*: if you and I could rob.

93 *argument*: something to talk about.
laughter: something to laugh at.

96 *share*: i.e. what they have stolen.
to horse . . . day: ride away before it is light.
97 *And*: if.
98 *arrant*: total.
no . . . stirring: no judgement alive.

105 Each one thinks that the other is an officer of the law (they cannot recognize each other in the dark).
106 *lards*: drips fat (as a cook bastes a lean joint of meat).
107 *Were't . . . laughing*: if I were not laughing so much.

Enter Falstaff, Gadshill, Bardolph *and* Peto

Falstaff
Come, my masters, let us share, and then to horse before day. And the Prince and Poins be not two arrant cowards there's no equity stirring; there's no more valour in that Poins than in a wild duck.

[*As they are sharing, the* Prince *and* Poins *attack them*

Prince
Your money!

Poins
Villains!

[*They all run away, and* Falstaff *after a blow or two runs away too, leaving the booty behind them*

Prince
Got with much ease. Now merrily to horse! The thieves are all scatter'd and possess'd with fear so strongly that they dare not meet each other: each takes his fellow for an officer! Away, good Ned—Falstaff sweats to death, and lards the lean earth as he walks along. Were't not for laughing I should pity him.

Poins
How the fat rogue roared. [*Exeunt*

Act 2 Scene 3
Hotspur is reading a letter. The writer (we never learn his identity) is unable to join the rebellion, and he warns Hotspur not to go ahead with his plans. The warnings, however, only make Hotspur more determined. Kate, Hotspur's wife, tries to find out what is worrying her husband, but he refuses to tell his secrets. He calls for his horse, and prepares to ride away.
1 *for mine own part*: to speak for myself.
2 *there*: i.e. with Hotspur and the rebels, fighting against the King.
4 *in respect of*: because of.

Scene 3 *Warkworth Castle*

Enter Hotspur *reading a letter*

Hotspur
'*But, for mine own part, my lord, I could be well contented to be there, in respect of the love I bear your house.*' He could be contented: why is he not then? In respect of the love he bears our house! He shows in this, he loves his own barn better than he loves our house. Let me see some more. '*The purpose you undertake is dangerous*'—Why, that's certain; 'tis dangerous to take a cold, to sleep, to drink; but I tell you, my lord fool, out of this nettle, danger, we pluck this flower, safety. '*The*

4 *house*: family; in line 6 Hotspur deliberately misunderstands, making word-play with the sense of 'house' = a building.
8 *take a cold*: catch a cold.
9 *my lord fool*: my foolish lord.
nettle: a wild plant whose leaves sting when touched.
12 *uncertain*: unreliable.
unsorted: badly chosen.
13 *light*: weak.
for . . . of: to be balanced against.
15 *hind*: peasant.
16 *lack-brain*: idiot.
19 *expectation*: hope.
20 *frosty-spirited*: faint-hearted, cowardly.
21 *my Lord of York*: i.e. the Archbishop of York.
22 *course of the action*: plan of campaign.
Zounds: by God's wounds.
23 *by*: near.
brain: knock out his brains.
28 *to meet me*: promising to meet me.
in arms: ready to fight.
29 *set forward*: started.
30 *pagan*: unbelieving (he does not believe that Hotspur will succeed).
infidel: faithless.
31–2 *in very . . . heart*: perfect honesty caused by fear and cowardice.
32 *will he*: he will go.
lay open: reveal.
33 *proceedings*: plans.
33–4 *I could . . . buffets*: I wish I could split myself in two and let the two parts fight each other.
34 *moving*: persuading.
dish . . . milk: weakling (Hotspur compares the writer to milk which has lost its cream).
36 *set forward*: start out.

purpose you undertake is dangerous, the friends you have named uncertain, the time itself unsorted, and your whole plot too light, for the counterpoise of so great an opposition.' Say you so, say you so? I say unto you again, you are a shallow cowardly hind, and you lie. What a lack-brain is this! By the Lord, our plot is a good plot, as ever was laid, our friends true and constant: a good plot, good friends, and full of expectation; an excellent plot, very good friends. What a frosty-spirited rogue is this! Why, my Lord of York commends the plot, and the general course of the action. 'Zounds, and I were now by this rascal, I could brain him with his lady's fan. Is there not my father, my uncle, and myself? Lord Edmund Mortimer, my Lord of York, and Owen Glendower? Is there not, besides, the Douglas? Have I not all their letters to meet me in arms by the ninth of the next month, and are they not some of them set forward already? What a pagan rascal is this, an infidel! Ha! You shall see now—in very sincerity of fear and cold heart will he to the King, and lay open all our proceedings! O, I could divide myself, and go to buffets, for moving such a dish of skim milk with so honourable an action! Hang him, let him tell the King! We are prepared. I will set forward tonight.

Enter Lady Percy

How now, Kate? I must leave you within these two hours.

Lady Percy

O my good lord, why are you thus alone?
For what offence have I this fortnight been

A banish'd woman from my Harry's bed?
Tell me, sweet lord, what is't that takes from thee
Thy stomach, pleasure, and thy golden sleep?
Why dost thou bend thine eyes upon the earth,
And start so often when thou sit'st alone?
Why hast thou lost the fresh blood in thy cheeks,
And given my treasures and my rights of thee
To thick-ey'd musing and curst melancholy?
In thy faint slumbers I by thee have watch'd,
And heard thee murmur tales of iron wars,
Speak terms of manage to thy bounding steed,
Cry 'Courage! To the field!' And thou hast talk'd
Of sallies and retires, of trenches, tents,
Of palisadoes, frontiers, parapets,
Of basilisks, of cannon, culverin,
Of prisoners' ransom, and of soldiers slain,
And all the currents of a heady fight.
Thy spirit within thee hath been so at war,
And thus hath so bestirr'd thee in thy sleep,
That beads of sweat have stood upon thy brow
Like bubbles in a late-disturbed stream;
And in thy face strange motions have appear'd,
Such as we see when men restrain their breath
On some great sudden hest. O, what portents are
these?
Some heavy business hath my lord in hand,
And I must know it, else he loves me not.

Hotspur

What ho!

Enter a Servant

Is Gilliams with the packet gone?

Servant

He is, my lord, an hour ago.

43 *stomach*: appetite.
44 *bend . . . earth*: stare at the ground.
45 *start*: stir (as though startled).
46 *Why . . . cheeks*: why are you so pale.
47–8 *given . . . melancholy*: exchanged my pleasure and marital rights for dull-eyed thoughtfulness and miserable depression.
49 *faint slumbers*: disturbed sleep.
watch'd: been awake.
51 *Speak . . . manage*: use the language of horsemanship.
53 *sallies and retires*: advances and retreats.
54 *palisadoes*: defences made with pointed iron stakes in the ground.
frontiers, parapets: fortifications.
55 *basilisks . . . cannon . . . culverin*: different kinds of cannon.
57 *currents*: movements.
heady: violent.
58 *at war*: distressed.
59 *bestirr'd*: disturbed.
61 *late-disturbed*: recently disturbed.
62 *motions*: movements.
64 *hest*: command.
what . . . these: what do these things mean.
65 *heavy*: important.
66 *else*: otherwise (i.e. if he does not tell me).
68 *packet*: parcel of letters.

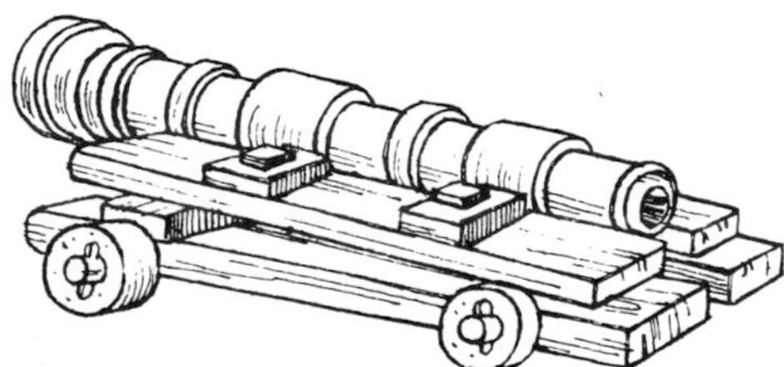

72 *even now*: just now.

73 *a roan, a crop-ear*: in a 'roan' horse the main colour (perhaps chestnut) is mixed with grey or white; horses' ears were sometimes cut (cropped) to make the animal look more alert.

75 *back him*: mount him.

straight: immediately.

Esperance: hope; the Percy family motto was 'Esperance ma comforte'.

77 *hear you*: listen.

79 'What is the business that takes you away from home'.

80 Hotspur wilfully misunderstands his wife.

82–3 *A weasel . . . toss'd with*: a weasel has not such an excitable temper as you are troubled with. Weasels are very savage, reddish-brown little animals, sometimes used to kill rabbits. The Elizabethans believed that the spleen was the source of irritable emotions.

85 *stir*: make trouble.

86 *About his title*: see p. 128.

87 *line*: strengthen (as the lining strengthens a coat).

88 *afoot*: on foot.

89 *paraquito*: talking parrot.

89–90 *answer me directly*: give me a straight answer.

91 *little finger*: only lovers would twist each other's little fingers (as Kate and Hotspur seem to be doing here).

And if: if.

96 *mammets*: dolls (feminine things).

tilt with lips: fight with lips—i.e. kiss.

97 *crowns*: skulls; in the next line Hotspur speaks of 'crowns' as coins.

Hotspur

Hath Butler brought those horses from the sheriff?

Servant

One horse, my lord, he brought even now.

Hotspur

What horse? A roan, a crop-ear, is it not?

Servant

It is, my lord.

Hotspur That roan shall be my throne.

Well, I will back him straight: O Esperance!
Bid Butler lead him forth into the park.

[*Exit* Servant

Lady Percy

But hear you, my lord.

Hotspur

What say'st thou, my lady?

Lady Percy

What is it carries you away?

Hotspur

Why, my horse, my love, my horse.

Lady Percy

Out, you mad-headed ape!
A weasel hath not such a deal of spleen
As you are toss'd with. In faith,
I'll know your business, Harry, that I will!
I fear my brother Mortimer doth stir
About his title, and hath sent for you
To line his enterprise. But if you go—

Hotspur

So far afoot I shall be weary, love.

Lady Percy

Come, come, you paraquito, answer me directly unto this question that I ask; in faith, I'll break thy little finger, Harry, and if thou wilt not tell me all things true.

Hotspur

Away,
Away, you trifler! Love! I love thee not;
I care not for thee, Kate. This is no world
To play with mammets, and to tilt with lips;
We must have bloody noses, and crack'd crowns,

98 *pass them current*: exchange them as though they were good (cracked coins were not acceptable currency). *God's me*: God save me (an exclamation of impatience).

99 *What . . . me*: what do you want from me.

103 'Tell me if you are joking or not'.

105 *a-horseback*: mounted on my horse.

108 *reason whereabout*: wonder where I am (*or* what I am doing).

109 *I must*: I must go.

111 *no farther wise*: no more wise.

112 *constant*: faithful.

114 *closer*: more able to keep secrets.

115 'You will not talk about what you do not know'.

116 *so far*: i.e. not at all (he has told her nothing).

121 *of force*: of necessity.

And pass them current too. God's me, my horse!
What say'st thou, Kate? What wouldst thou have
with me?

Lady Percy

Do you not love me? Do you not indeed?
Well, do not then; for since you love me not
I will not love myself. Do you not love me?
Nay, tell me if you speak in jest or no.

Hotspur

Come, wilt thou see me ride?
And when I am a-horseback, I will swear
I love thee infinitely. But hark you, Kate,
I must not have you henceforth question me
Whither I go, nor reason whereabout:
Whither I must, I must; and, to conclude,
This evening must I leave you, gentle Kate.
I know you wise, but yet no farther wise
Than Harry Percy's wife; constant you are,
But yet a woman; and for secrecy,
No lady closer, for I well believe
Thou wilt not utter what thou dost not know;
And so far will I trust thee, gentle Kate.

Lady Percy

How? So far?

Hotspur

Not an inch further. But hark you, Kate:
Whither I go, thither shall you go too;
Today will I set forth, tomorrow you.
Will this content you, Kate?

Lady Percy It must, of force. [*Exeunt*

Act 2 Scene 4
At the Boar's Head Tavern in Eastcheap, Prince Hal and Poins are waiting for Falstaff. To amuse themselves, they play a trick on Francis, one of the Drawers in the tavern. Falstaff and the other thieves arrive. Falstaff gives an account of what happened at Gad's Hill, telling enormous lies until the Prince

Scene 4 *Eastcheap: the Boar's Head Tavern*

Enter Prince *and* Poins

Prince

Ned, prithee come out of that fat room, and lend me thy hand to laugh a little.

Poins

Where hast been, Hal?

interrupts and confronts Falstaff with the truth. A message arrives for Prince Hal: he is commanded to go to the royal palace for an interview with his father. The friends then hold two 'rehearsals' for the interview: in the first, Falstaff plays the part of King Henry IV; in the second 'rehearsal' Prince Hal speaks for his father. The laughter ceases when the Sheriff comes to arrest Falstaff. Hal protects his friend.

1 *fat*: stuffy.
4 *loggerheads*: thickheads, fools.
5 *hogsheads*: large barrels; the Prince has been in the cellars of the tavern (inn-servants invited favourite customers to drink there).
sounded . . . string: reached the very lowest level (the base-string plays the lowest notes on a stringed instrument).
6 *I am . . . brother*: I have promised to be a brother (according to the rules of chivalry).
7 *leash*: set of three (especially hounds).
drawers: waiters, tapsters.
8 *christen*: Christian (christened).
9 *take . . . salvation*: are already prepared to swear by their hopes of eternal salvation.
10 *king of courtesy*: the most courteous (polite) man (in this respect Hal is a king, although in fact he is only a prince).
11 *flatly*: without hesitation.
Jack: fellow.
12 *a Corinthian*: a wild fellow (Corinth was famous for riotous living).
a good boy: one of us.
15 *the good lads*: i.e. their mates, the other drawers.
drinking deep: drinking heavily, emptying the cup.
16 *dyeing scarlet*: because heavy drinkers usually have red faces.
breathe . . . watering: pause for breath whilst drinking.
17 *Play it off*: get on with it.
18 *proficient*: expert.

Prince
With three or four loggerheads, amongst three or fourscore hogsheads. I have sounded the very base-string of humility. Sirrah, I am sworn brother to a leash of drawers, and can call them all by their christen names, as Tom, Dick, and Francis. They take it already upon their salvation, that though I be but Prince of Wales, yet I am the king of courtesy, and tell me flatly I am no proud Jack like Falstaff, but a Corinthian, a lad of mettle, a good boy (by the Lord, so they call me!), and when I am King of England I shall command all the good lads in Eastcheap. They call drinking deep, 'dyeing scarlet'; and when you breathe in your watering, they cry 'Hem!' and bid you 'Play it off!' To conclude, I am so good a proficient in one quarter of an hour that I can drink with any tinker in his own language during my life. I tell thee, Ned, thou hast lost much honour that thou wert not with me in this action. But, sweet Ned—to sweeten which name of Ned I give thee this pennyworth of sugar, clapped even now into my hand by an underskinker, one that never spake other English in his life than 'Eight shillings and sixpence', and 'You are welcome', with this shrill addition, 'Anon, anon, sir! Score a pint of bastard in the Half-moon', or so. But Ned, to drive away the time till Falstaff come—I prithee do thou stand in some by-room, while I question my puny drawer to what end he gave me the sugar, and do

18–19 'For the rest of my life I shall be able to drink with tinkers (notoriously heavy drinkers) and use their own language (which he has just learned)'.

20–21 The Prince speaks of his meeting with the drawers as though it were a military battle ('action').

24 *sugar*: this was sold in taverns to sweeten the sack.

even now: just now.

clapped: thrust.

25 *underskinker*: under-tapster, tapster's assistant.

25–7 The Prince comments that the tapster's vocabulary is limited to the words he uses in his job.

28 *Anon*: at once, I'm coming.

Score: note the price of; as the tapster served the drinks, he called to the tavern-keeper who made out the bills.

bastard: sweet Spanish wine.

29 *the Half-moon*: names were given to the different inn-rooms.

or so: or something like that.

drive away: pass.

31 *by-room*: side room, leading out of a larger one.

puny: young, inexperienced.

32 *to what end*: for what purpose, why.

32–3 *do thou never leave*: don't ever stop.

thou never leave calling 'Francis!', that his tale to me may be nothing but 'Anon'. Step aside, and I'll show thee a precedent. [*Exit* Poins

Poins

[*Within*] Francis!

Prince

Thou art perfect.

Poins

[*Within*] Francis!

Enter Francis, *a Drawer*

Francis

Anon, anon, sir. Look down into the Pomgarnet, Ralph.

Prince

Come hither, Francis.

Francis

My lord?

Prince

How long hast thou to serve, Francis?

Francis

Forsooth, five years, and as much as to—

Poins

[*Within*] Francis!

Francis

Anon, anon, sir.

Prince

Five year! By'r lady, a long lease for the clinking of pewter. But Francis, darest thou be so valiant as to play the coward with thy indenture, and show it a fair pair of heels, and run from it?

Francis

O lord, sir, I'll be sworn upon all the books in England, I could find in my heart—

Poins

[*Within*] Francis!

Francis

Anon, sir.

Prince

How old art thou, Francis?

Francis

Let me see, about Michaelmas next I shall be—

33–4 'So that all he answers to my questions is "I'm coming"'.

35 *show . . . precedent*: show you what I mean.

39 *Pomgarnet*: Pomegranate (another of the inn-rooms).

43 *to serve*: i.e. as an apprentice; an apprenticeship was for seven years.

47 *By'r lady*: by Our Lady.

47–8 *long . . . .pewter*: a long time to spend clashing pewter mugs (cheap drinking vessels were made of pewter).

49 *indenture*: apprentice's contract.

51 *books*: Bibles (anyone making a formal oath must place his right hand on a Bible).

52 *I could . . . heart*: I would like to.

56 *Michaelmas*: Michaelmas (St Michael's) Day is 29 September.

61 *would*: wish.
67 *a-Thursday*: on Thursday.
70–73 The Prince describes the innkeeper.
leathern-jerkin: leather tunic.
crystal-button: glass buttoned.
not-pated: short-haired (a gentleman's hair was long).
agate-ring: signet-ring with an agate stone.
puke-stocking: 'puke' was a dark woollen material.
caddis-garter: 'caddis' was a coarse material used for garters.
smooth-tongue: fast talking.
Spanish pouch: the innkeeper wore on his belt a purse of soft Spanish leather.

74–7 The Prince now seems to be talking complete nonsense; he perhaps means to imply that Francis should not think about changing his trade.
brown bastard: very sweet wine.
your only: the best.
look you: be careful.
your white . . . sully: your apron will get dirty.

Poins
[*Within*] Francis!

Francis
Anon, sir—pray stay a little, my lord.

Prince
Nay—but hark you, Francis; for the sugar thou gavest me—'twas a pennyworth, was't not?

Francis
O Lord! I would it had been two!

Prince
I will give thee for it a thousand pound—ask me when thou wilt, and thou shalt have it.

Poins
[*Within*] Francis!

Francis
Anon, anon.

Prince
Anon, Francis? No, Francis, but tomorrow, Francis; or, Francis, a-Thursday; or indeed, Francis, when thou wilt. But Francis!

Francis
My lord?

Prince
Wilt thou rob this leathern-jerkin, crystal-button, not-pated, agate-ring, puke-stocking, caddis-garter, smooth-tongue Spanish pouch?

Francis
O Lord, sir, who do you mean?

Prince
Why then your brown bastard is your only drink: for look you, Francis, your white canvas doublet will sully. In Barbary, sir, it cannot come to so much.

Francis
What, sir?

Poins
[*Within*] Francis!

Prince
Away, you rogue, dost thou not hear them call?

[*Here they both call him; the* Drawer *stands amazed, not knowing which way to go*

Enter Vintner

Vintner

What, stand'st thou still and hear'st such a calling? Look to the guests within. [*Exit* Francis] My lord, old Sir John with half-a-dozen more are at the door—shall I let them in?

Prince

Let them alone awhile, and then open the door. [*Exit* Vintner] Poins!

Enter Poins

Poins

Anon, anon, sir.

Prince

Sirrah, Falstaff and the rest of the thieves are at the door; shall we be merry?

Poins

As merry as crickets, my lad; but hark ye, what cunning match have you made with this jest of the drawer: come, what's the issue?

Prince

I am now of all humours that have showed themselves humours since the old days of goodman Adam to the pupil age of this present twelve o'clock at midnight.

Enter Francis

What's o'clock, Francis?

Francis

Anon, anon, sir. [*Exit*

Prince

That ever this fellow should have fewer words than a parrot, and yet the son of a woman! His industry is up-stairs and down-stairs, his eloquence the parcel of a reckoning. I am not yet of Percy's mind, the Hotspur of the north—he that kills me some six or seven dozen of Scots at a breakfast, washes his hands, and says to his wife, 'Fie upon this quiet life, I want work'. 'O my sweet Harry', says she, 'how many hast thou killed today?' 'Give my roan horse a drench', says he, and answers, 'Some fourteen', an hour after, 'a trifle, a trifle'. I prithee call in Falstaff; I'll play Percy, and that damned brawn shall play Dame

82 *Look to*: attend to.

90 *merry as crickets*: the comparison is proverbial; crickets are little insects which make a continuous chirping sound.

90–92 *what . . . drawer*: what clever trick have you been playing with this joke on the drawer.

92 *what's the issue*: what is happening.

93–6 The Prince is ready for anything: *humours*: moods. *showed themselves*: been recognized. *goodman Adam*: old Father Adam (the first human being). *pupil age*: youth.

99 *That ever*: how odd.

101–102 *His industry . . . down stairs*: all his work is running up and down stairs.

102 *his eloquence . . . reckoning*: all his conversation consists of the parts of a bill.

103 *of Percy's mind*: like Percy (i.e. Hotspur).

105 *at a breakfast*: for a beginning.

106 *Fie upon*: I'm bored with. *work*: something to do.

108 *drench*: dose of medicine.

109 *Some*: about.

110 *a trifle*: nothing much.

111 *brawn*: fat pig.

Mortimer his wife. 'Rivo!' says the drunkard. Call in Ribs, call in Tallow.

Enter Falstaff, Gadshill, Bardolph, *and* Peto; *followed by* Francis, *with wine*

Poins

Welcome, Jack; where hast thou been?

Falstaff

A plague of all cowards, I say, and a vengeance too, marry and amen! Give me a cup of sack, boy. Ere I lead this life long. I'll sew nether-stocks, and mend them and foot them too. A plague of all cowards! Give me a cup of sack, rogue; is there no virtue extant? [*He drinks*

Prince

Didst thou never see Titan kiss a dish of butter (pitiful-hearted Titan!), that melted at the sweet tale of the sun's? If thou didst, then behold that compound.

Falstaff

You rogue, here's lime in this sack too! There is nothing but roguery to be found in villainous man, yet a coward is worse than a cup of sack with lime in it. A villainous coward! Go thy ways, old Jack, die when thou wilt—if manhood, good manhood, be not forgot upon the face of the earth, then am I a shotten herring: there lives not three good men unhanged in England, and one of them is fat, and grows old. God help the while! A bad world, I say. I would I were a weaver; I could sing psalms, or anything. A plague of all cowards, I say still.

Prince

How now, wool-sack, what mutter you?

Falstaff

A king's son! If I do not beat thee out of thy kingdom with a dagger of lath, and drive all thy subjects afore thee like a flock of wild geese, I'll never wear hair on my face more. You, Prince of Wales!

Prince

Why, you whoreson round man, what's the matter?

112 *Rivo*: a (meaningless) word used by drinkers: a modern equivalent is 'Cheers'.

113 *Tallow*: dripping (the fat melted from roasted meat).

117 *nether-stocks*: stockings.

118 *foot them*: put feet in the stockings.

120 *virtue*: courage.
extant: living.

121–4 The exact sense of these lines is not clear. Falstaff's red face is bent over the cup of sack, and the Prince is reminded of a hot sun ('Titan' was a name for the sun-god) shining on and melting a dish of butter.

124 *compound*: combination (Falstaff and the wine).

125 *lime*: lime was used to make poor quality sack seem more sparkling and dry.

131 *shotten herring*: a common simile for extreme thinness: after the herring (a fish) has shot its roe (released its eggs) it is very thin.
lives: a singular verb with plural subject is quite common at this time.

132 *one of them*: Falstaff means himself.

133 *God . . . while*: God help these times.

134 *I would*: I wish.
weaver . . . psalms: weavers were often Puritans, and the songs they sang as they worked were the religious psalms.

136 *wool-sack*: Falstaff is as fat and shapeless as a sack of wool.

138 *dagger of lath*: a wooden dagger; see p. xxviii.

139 *afore*: before.

140 *hair on my face*: a beard.

142 *whoreson*: disgusting.

146 *and*: if.

151–2 *sees your back*: i.e. as you run away.

152 *call . . . backing*: is that what you call supporting (the pun is on 'back').

158 *All . . . that*: that doesn't matter.

165 *poor*: merely.

167 *at half-sword*: fighting very closely—only the length of half a sword from his opponents.

170 *buckler*: shield.

172 *ecce signum*: behold the sign (Falstaff displays his battered sword).
dealt: fought.

173 *all . . . do*: it was not enough (to save the money they had stolen).

Falstaff
Are not you a coward? Answer me to that—and Poins there?

Poins
'Zounds, ye fat paunch. And ye call me coward, by the Lord I'll stab thee.

Falstaff
I call thee coward? I'll see thee damned ere I call thee coward; but I would give a thousand pound I could run as fast as thou canst. You are straight enough in the shoulders, you care not who sees your back: call you that backing of your friends? A plague upon such backing, give me them that will face me! Give me a cup of sack: I am a rogue if I drunk today.

Prince
O villain! Thy lips are scarce wiped since thou drunk'st last.

Falstaff
All is one for that. [*He drinks*] A plague of all cowards, still say I.

Prince
What's the matter?

Falstaff
What's the matter? There be four of us here have ta'en a thousand pound this day morning.

Prince
Where is it, Jack, where is it?

Falstaff
Where is it? Taken from us it is. A hundred upon poor four of us.

Prince
What, a hundred, man?

Falstaff
I am a rogue if I were not at half-sword with a dozen of them two hours together. I have scaped by miracle. I am eight times thrust through the doublet, four through the hose, my buckler cut through and through, my sword hacked like a handsaw—*ecce signum*! I never dealt better since I was a man: all would not do. A plague of all cowards! Let them speak—if they speak more or

175 *sons of darkness*: damned (the phrase is from the Bible).

177 *set upon*: attacked.

183 *an Ebrew Jew*: a Hebrew (Jewish) Jew.

184 *sharing*: i.e. the stolen goods.
fresh: different.

186 *other*: others (the men they had first attacked).

189 *radish*: thin root vegetables.

191 *no two-legged creature*: not a man.

193 *that's . . . for*: it is too late to pray for that.
peppered: killed.

194 *paid*: finished.

195 *buckram suits*: the 'cases of buckram' (disguises made of coarse fabric) that Poins promised to obtain in *Act 1*, Scene 2.

197 *old ward*: usual fighting position.
here . . . point: this is how I placed myself, and this is how I held my sword.

198 *let drive*: thrust their swords.

199 *Thou . . . now*: just now you said there were only two of them.

less than truth, they are villains, and the sons of darkness.

Prince
Speak, sirs, how was it?

Gadshill
We four set upon some dozen—

Falstaff
Sixteen at least, my lord.

Gadshill
And bound them.

Peto
No, no, they were not bound.

Falstaff
You rogue, they were bound, every man of them, or I am a Jew else: an Ebrew Jew.

Gadshill
As we were sharing, some six or seven fresh men set upon us—

Falstaff
And unbound the rest, and then come in the other.

Prince
What, fought you with them all?

Falstaff
All? I know not what you call all, but if I fought not with fifty of them I am a bunch of radish: if there were not two or three and fifty upon poor old Jack, then am I no two-legged creature.

Prince
Pray God you have not murdered some of them.

Falstaff
Nay, that's past praying for: I have peppered two of them. Two I am sure I have paid, two rogues in buckram suits. I tell thee what, Hal, if I tell thee a lie, spit in my face, call me horse. Thou knowest my old ward—here I lay, and thus I bore my point. Four rogues in buckram let drive at me—

Prince
What, four? Thou saidst but two even now.

Falstaff
Four, Hal; I told thee four.

Poins
Ay, ay, he said four.

202 *afront*: abreast.
mainly: violently.

203 *I . . . ado*: I myself made no more fuss.

203–4 *took . . . target*: received all seven sword-points in my shield.

208 *hilts*: the handle of his sword (in the form of a cross—see illustration).

209 *let him alone*: don't argue with him.

212 *mark*: pay attention to.

216–17 Falstaff speaks of the points of the swords; but Poins pretends to understand 'points' as the laces which fastened doublet and hose together.

218 *give me ground*: give way (yield) to me.
followed me close: quickly seized my advantage.

219 *came . . . hand*: advanced, with my feet and my sword.
with a thought: quick as a thought.

220 *paid*: killed.

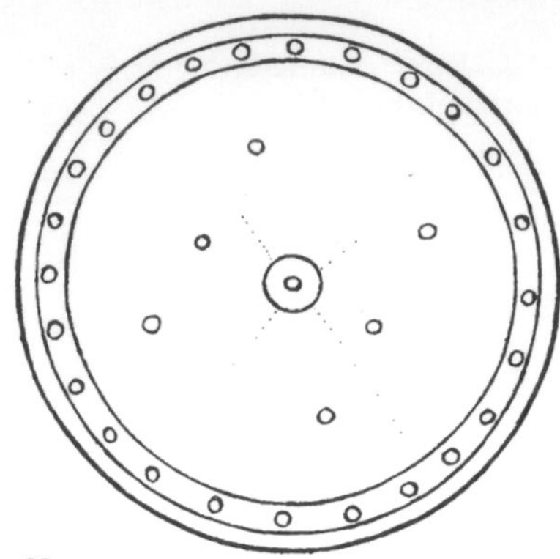

Falstaff
These four came all afront, and mainly thrust at me; I made me no more ado, but took all their seven points in my target, thus!

Prince
Seven? Why, there were but four even now.

Falstaff
In buckram?

Poins
Ay, four, in buckram suits.

Falstaff
Seven, by these hilts, or I am a villain else.

Prince
[*To* Poins] Prithee let him alone; we shall have more anon.

Falstaff
Dost thou hear me, Hal?

Prince
Ay, and mark thee too, Jack.

Falstaff
Do so, for it is worth the listening to. These nine in buckram that I told thee of—

Prince
So, two more already.

Falstaff
Their points being broken—

Poins
Down fell their hose.

Falstaff
Began to give me ground; but I followed me close, came in, foot and hand—and, with a thought, seven of the eleven I paid..

223 *misbegotten*: cursed.
Kendal green: coarse green cloth, worn by peasants.
229 *knotty-pated*: block-headed.
230 *whoreson*: bastardly.
tallow-catch: lump of fat.
238 *and*: if.
239 *strappado*: a form of torture (which pulled the victim's joints apart).
racks: this torture stretched the man's body until he died (or confessed).
241 *reasons*: the pronunciation of this word allows Falstaff to make a pun with 'raisins'—which had to be imported into England, unlike the 'blackberries', which grow wild.
244 *this sin*: i.e. of appearing to believe Falstaff's story.
sanguine: ruddy-faced (cowards are usually pale).
247 *starveling*: skinny creature.
eel-skin: eels are long, snakelike fishes.
248 *neat's-tongue*: cow's tongue.
bull's-pizzle: bull's penis (when dried, it was used as a whip).
stock-fish: dried cod-fish (stored in long strips to be eaten in winter).
250 *yard*: measuring-stick (it was one yard long).
sheath: in which the sword was kept.
bow-case: the long, narrow cover for an archer's bow.
251–2 *standing tuck*: rapier (a long thin sword) standing on its end.
252 *breathe awhile*: stop for a moment to get your breath back.
to it again: continue to insult me.

Prince

O monstrous! Eleven buckram men grown out of two!

Falstaff

But as the devil would have it, three misbegotten knaves in Kendal green came at my back and let drive at me; for it was so dark, Hal, that thou couldst not see thy hand.

Prince

These lies are like their father that begets them: gross as a mountain, open, palpable. Why, thou clay-brained guts, thou knotty-pated fool, thou whoreson obscene greasy tallow-catch,—

Falstaff

What, art thou mad? Art thou mad? Is not the truth the truth?

Prince

Why, how couldst thou know these men in Kendal green when it was so dark thou couldst not see thy hand? Come, tell us your reason. What sayest thou to this?

Poins

Come, your reason, Jack, your reason.

Falstaff

What, upon compulsion? 'Zounds, and I were at the strappado, or all the racks in the world, I would not tell you on compulsion. Give you a reason on compulsion? If reasons were as plentiful as blackberries, I would give no man a reason upon compulsion, I.

Prince

I'll be no longer guilty of this sin. This sanguine coward, this bed-presser, this horse-back-breaker, this huge hill of flesh,—

Falstaff

'Sblood, you starveling, you eel-skin, you dried neat's-tongue, you bull's pizzle, you stock-fish—O for breath to utter what is like thee!—you tailor's-yard, you sheath, you bow-case, you vile standing tuck!

Prince

Well, breathe awhile, and then to it again, and

253 'When you are tired of making these wretched comparisons'.
254 'Let me say just this'.
255 *Mark*: take notice.
257 *were . . . of*: took possession.
258 *put you down*: beat you.
259 *with a word*: quite simply.
outfaced: defeated.
264 *slave*: wretch.
267 *starting-hole*: hiding-place.
268 *apparent*: obvious.
269 *trick*: excuse.
270 *he . . . ye*: i.e. God.
272 *turn upon*: attack.
274 *Hercules*: the super-man of classical mythology.
beware: take notice of.
274–5 *the lion . . . prince*: this was a very old belief.

276–7 *think the better*: have a higher opinion.
277 *during my life*: for as long as I live.
280 *clap to*: shut.
Watch: stay awake. The Bible instructs Christians to 'watch and pray'; but Falstaff separates the two activities.
281 *Gallants*: gentlemen.

when thou hast tired thyself in base comparisons hear me speak but this.

Poins

Mark, Jack.

Prince

We two saw you four set on four, and bound them and were masters of their wealth—mark now how a plain tale shall put you down. Then did we two set on you four, and, with a word, out-faced you from your prize, and have it; yea, and can show it you here in the house. And, Falstaff, you carried your guts away as nimbly, with as quick dexterity, and roared for mercy, and still run and roared, as ever I heard bull-calf. What a slave art thou to hack thy sword as thou hast done, and then say it was in fight! What trick, what device, what starting-hole canst thou now find out, to hide thee from this open and apparent shame?

Poins

Come, let's hear, Jack, what trick hast thou now?

Falstaff

By the Lord, I knew ye as well as he that made ye. Why, hear you, my masters, was it for me to kill the heir-apparent? Should I turn upon the true prince? Why, thou knowest I am as valiant as Hercules: but beware instinct—the lion will not touch the true prince; instinct is a great matter. I was now a coward on instinct: I shall think the better of myself, and thee, during my life—I for a valiant lion, and thou for a true prince. But by the Lord, lads, I am glad you have the money. Hostess, clap to the doors! Watch tonight, pray tomorrow!—Gallants, lads, boys, hearts of gold, all the titles of good fellowship come to you! What, shall we be merry, shall we have a play extempore?

Prince

Content, and the argument shall be thy running away.

Falstaff

Ah, no more of that, Hal, and thou lovest me.

Enter Hostess

283 *shall . . . extempore*: shall we improvize a play. This was a popular form of entertainment in Elizabethan taverns; the Prince has already suggested such amusement (line 110).

285 *argument*: subject.

292 *would speak*: who wishes to speak.

294 *a royal man*: it was a favourite joke amongst the Elizabethans to make puns on 'noble' and 'royal'—the names of two coins.

296 *manner*: kind.

298 'What is an old man doing out of bed at midnight'.

301 *send . . . packing*: make him go away very quickly.

302 *fair*: well.

307 *in earnest*: seriously.

310 *swear . . . England*: swear until truth has been driven out of England.

313 *spear-grass*: grass with very sharp edges.

314 *beslubber*: smear.

316–17 *I did . . . before*: I did something that I haven't done for seven years.

Hostess

O Jesu, my lord the Prince!

Prince

How now, my lady the hostess, what say'st thou to me?

Hostess

Marry, my lord, there is a nobleman of the court at door would speak with you: he says he comes from your father.

Prince

Give him as much as will make him a royal man, and send him back again to my mother.

Falstaff

What manner of man is he?

Hostess

An old man.

Falstaff

What doth gravity out of his bed at midnight? Shall I give him his answer?

Prince

Prithee do, Jack.

Falstaff

Faith, and I'll send him packing. [*Exit*

Prince

Now, sirs: by'r Lady, you fought fair; so did you, Peto, so did you, Bardolph; you are lions too, you ran away upon instinct, you will not touch the true prince; no, fie!

Bardolph

Faith; I ran when I saw others run.

Prince

Faith, tell me now in earnest, how came Falstaff's sword so hacked?

Peto

Why, he hacked it with his dagger, and said he would swear truth out of England but he would make you believe it was done in fight, and persuaded us to do the like.

Bardolph

Yea, and to tickle our noses with spear-grass, to make them bleed, and then to beslubber our garments with it, and swear it was the blood of true men. I did that I did not this seven year

317 *devices*: schemes.

319 *taken . . . manner*: caught in the act (i.e. as he was stealing).

320 *extempore*: without any special cause (Bardolph has a very red face—like Falstaff, he is a heavy drinker).

321 *fire*: i.e. Bardolph's fiery red face.

322 *What instinct*: the Prince is still joking about the excuse that Falstaff offered for his running away (line 275).

323–4 *meteors . . . exhalations*: Bardolph refers to the spots and bumps on his face as though they were astrological phenomena (which would have some special meaning).

326 *portend*: signify.

327 Bardolph's red, spotty face must be caused by an overheated liver, the result of too much drinking; and the drinking has also caused his 'cold' (empty) purse.

328 *Choler*: quick-temper; the word is pronounced like 'collar', which suggests a pun with 'halter'.

rightly taken: properly understood ('taken').

329 If you are arrested ('taken') as you deserve to be, you will be hanged; the 'halter' is the hangman's noose.

331 *bombast*: stuffing.

334 *thy years*: your age.

335 My waist was not as round as an eagle's claw.

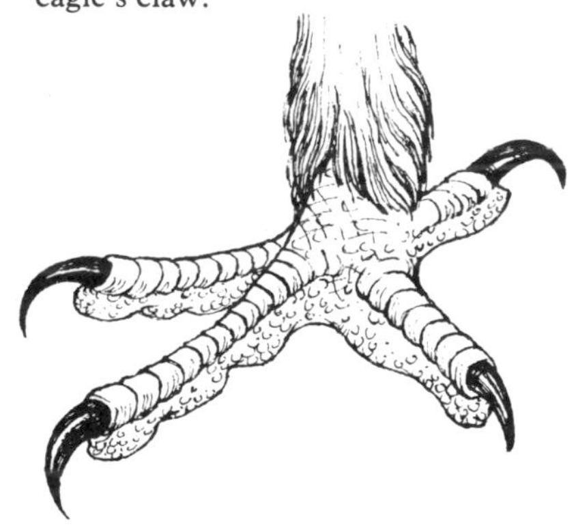

336 *alderman's thumb-ring*: rich citizens wore rings on their thumbs (which could be used for sealing documents).

before—I blushed to hear his monstrous devices.

Prince

O villain, thou stolest a cup of sack eighteen years ago, and wert taken with the manner, and ever since thou hast blushed extempore. Thou hadst fire and sword on thy side, and yet thou ran'st away—what instinct hadst thou for it?

Bardolph

My lord, do you see these meteors? Do you behold these exhalations?

Prince

I do.

Bardolph

What think you they portend?

Prince

Hot livers and cold purses.

Bardolph

Choler, my lord, if rightly taken.

Prince

No, if rightly taken, halter.

Enter Falstaff

Here comes lean Jack, here comes bare-bone. How now, my sweet creature of bombast? How long is't ago, Jack, since thou sawest thine own knee?

Falstaff

My own knee? When I was about thy years, Hal, I was not an eagle's talon in the waist; I could have crept into any alderman's thumb-ring. A plague of sighing and grief, it blows a man up like a bladder. There's villainous news abroad: here was Sir John Bracy from your father; you must to the court in the morning. That same mad fellow of the north, Percy, and he of Wales that gave Amamon the bastinado, and made Lucifer cuckold, and swore the devil his true liegeman upon the cross of a Welsh hook—what a plague call you him?

Poins

O, Glendower.

Falstaff

Owen, Owen, the same; and his son-in-law Mortimer, and old Northumberland, and that sprightly Scot of Scots, Douglas, that runs a-horseback up a hill perpendicular—

Prince

He that rides at high speed, and with his pistol kills a sparrow flying.

Falstaff

You have hit it.

Prince

So did he never the sparrow.

Falstaff

Well, that rascal hath good mettle in him; he will not run.

Prince

Why, what a rascal art thou then, to praise him so for running!

Falstaff

A-horseback, ye cuckoo! But afoot he will not budge a foot.

338 *abroad*: about, discussed publicly.
338–9 *here . . . father*: Sir John Bracy was sent here by your father.
339 *must*: must go.
341 *he of Wales*: that chap from Wales.
Amamon: the name of a devil.
342 *bastinado*: a beating on the soles of the feet.
made Lucifer cuckold: seduced Lucifer's wife; Lucifer was the name of the chief devil. It was popularly believed that a man whose wife had been seduced would grow horns on his head (the devil is often portrayed with horns).
343 *liegeman*: subject.
the cross . . . hook: the Welsh fought with long-handled axes (which did not, in fact, have cross-pieces).
348 *Scot of Scots*: most famous of all Scotsmen.
runs a-horseback: gallops on his horse.
349 *a hill perpendicular*: i.e. a hill so steep that it seems to stand at a right angle to the level ground.
352 *hit it*: got it right.
353 'Well, he never hit the sparrow.'
354–9 In these lines Falstaff and the Prince play with the different meanings of their words.
354 'He (Hotspur) is a rogue ('rascal'), but he is brave ('hath good mettle in him') and will not run away'.
rascal is a deer that will not be hunted ('run');
mettle makes a pun with 'metal': good metal does not melt ('run').
358 *cuckoo*: a small brown bird which utters only two notes.
budge: give way.

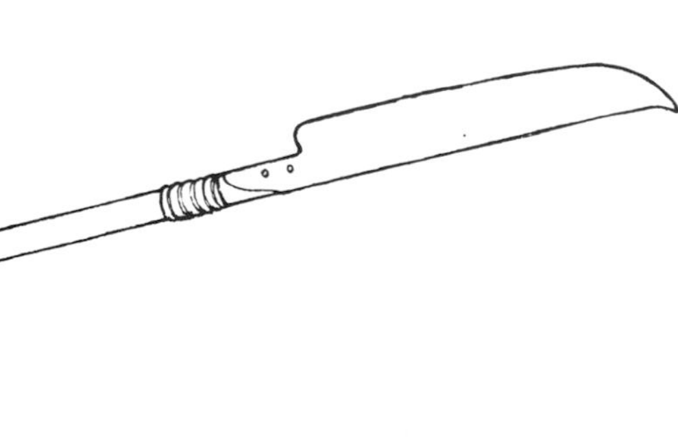

360 *on instinct*: the Prince returns again to Falstaff's own words (line 274).

361 *I grant ye*: I admit that.
is there: with the rebels.

362 *one*: a certain.
blue-caps: Scottish soldiers wore blue caps.

363 *stolen away*: gone away secretly (to join the rebels).

365 When civil war was threatened, many landlords tried to sell their property, preferring to take a low price rather than risk losing everything if the country was captured by the rebels.

366 *it is like*: probably.
come . . . June: if we have a hot summer.

367 *this . . . hold*: these civil wars continue.

367–8 It will be as easy to get a woman as it is to buy nails for mending boots (hob-nails): they will be selling themselves in hundreds.

371 *horrible afeard*: dreadfully frightened.

371–2 You are the heir to the throne, and you could not have three such terrible enemies anywhere in the world.

373 *spirit*: devil.

375 *thrill*: shiver with cold fear.

376 *Not a whit*: not in the least.

377 *chid*: scolded.

378 *if you love me*: for my sake.

378–9 *practise an answer*: prepare what you are going to say.

380 *Do . . . for*: you play the part of.
examine: question.

381 *particulars*: details.

382 *state*: throne.

385 *is taken for*: is seen to be.
joint-stool: a stool made by a joiner.

386 *leaden dagger*: cheap dagger made of lead (see p. xxviii).

387 *bald crown*: i.e. the crown of Falstaff's head.

388 *and . . . thee*: if you have any conscience (or shame) left in you.

389 *moved*: affected, made to feel ashamed.

Prince
Yes, Jack, upon instinct.

Falstaff
I grant ye, upon instinct. Well, he is there too, and one Mordake, and a thousand blue-caps more. Worcester is stolen away tonight; thy father's beard is turned white with the news; you may buy land now as cheap as stinking mackerel.

Prince
Why then, it is like, if there come a hot June, and this civil buffeting hold, we shall buy maidenheads as they buy hob-nails, by the hundreds.

Falstaff
By the mass, lad, thou sayest true; it is like we shall have good trading that way. But tell me, Hal, art not thou horrible afeard? Thou being heir apparent, could the world pick thee out three such enemies again, as that fiend Douglas, that spirit Percy, and that devil Glendower? Art thou not horribly afraid? Doth not thy blood thrill at it?

Prince
Not a whit, i'faith. I lack some of thy instinct.

Falstaff
Well, thou wilt be horribly chid tomorrow when thou comest to thy father; if thou love me practise an answer.

Prince
Do thou stand for my father and examine me upon the particulars of my life.

Falstaff
Shall I? Content! This chair shall be my state, this dagger my sceptre, and this cushion my crown.

Prince
Thy state is taken for a joint-stool, thy golden sceptre for a leaden dagger, and thy precious rich crown for a pitiful bald crown.

Falstaff
Well, and the fire of grace be not quite out of thee, now shalt thou be moved. Give me a cup of sack to

make my eyes look red, that it may be thought I have wept, for I must speak in passion; and I will do it in King Cambyses' vein.

Prince
Well, here is my leg.

Falstaff
And here is my speech. Stand aside, nobility.

Hostess
O Jesu, this is excellent sport, i'faith.

Falstaff
Weep not, sweet Queen, for trickling tears are vain.

Hostess
O the Father. How he holds his countenance!

Falstaff
For God's sake, lords, convey my tristful Queen,
For tears do stop the floodgates of her eyes.

Hostess
O Jesu, he doth it as like one of these harlotry players as ever I see!

Falstaff
Peace, good pint-pot, peace, good tickle-brain.—Harry, I do not only marvel where thou spendest thy time, but also how thou art accompanied. For though the camomile, the more it is trodden on the faster it grows, yet youth, the more it is wasted the sooner it wears. That thou art my son I have partly thy mother's word, partly my own opinion, but chiefly a villainous trick of thine eye, and a foolish hanging of thy nether lip, that doth warrant me. If then thou be son to me, here lies the point—why, being son to me, art thou so pointed at? Shall the blessed sun of heaven prove a micher, and eat blackberries? A question not to be asked. Shall the son of England prove a thief, and take purses? A question to be asked. There is a thing, Harry, which thou hast often heard of, and it is known to many in our land by the name of pitch. This pitch (as ancient writers do report) doth defile; so doth the company thou keepest. For, Harry, now I do not speak to thee in drink, but in tears; not in pleasure, but in passion; not in words only, but in woes also. And yet there is a virtuous man whom I

391 *in passion*: with powerful emotion.
392 *in . . . vein*: in the manner of *King Cambyses*—a play written more than 20 years before *Henry IV Part 1*; in lines 396 and 399–400 Shakespeare parodies the style of such old-fashioned plays.
393 *leg*: bow.
394 *nobility*: Falstaff speaks to the crowd of thieves and drinkers as though they were the king's courtiers.
397 *vain*: useless.
398 *holds his countenance*: keeps a straight (solemn) face.
399 *convey*: remove.
tristful: unhappy.
400 'Her eyes are over-flowing with tears'.
401 *as like . . . players*: just like one of those ridiculous actors.
403 *Peace*: be quiet.
pint-pot: one of the mugs in which the hostess would serve ale.
tickle-brain: strong drink, alcohol.
405 *how . . . accompanied*: what sort of friends you have.
406–7 In these lines Shakespeare parodies a popular style of writing called *euphuism* (it was first used in the novel *Euphues* by John Lyly).
camomile: a strong little herb, used on lawns, which gives a pleasant scent and grows faster when it is trodden on.
407 *wasted*: spent in riotous living.
408 *wears*: is ruined.
408–9 *have . . . word*: partly because your mother says so.
410–11 *chiefly . . . lip*: mainly because you have a certain look about your eyes, and the naughty way you pout your lower lip.
411 *warrant me*: assure me, resemble me.
413 *pointed at*: scoffed at.
414 *micher*: truant (as schoolboys played truant from school to pick blackberries).

416 *son of England*: i.e. of the King of England.
take: steal.
417–21 Falstaff's speech is rich with biblical overtones.
419 *pitch*: a dark, sticky substance made from tar—which stained anyone who touched it (see *Ecclesiasticus*, 13:1).
422 'I am speaking with such emotion because I am weeping, not because I am drunk ('in drink')'.
423 *passion*: anger.
425 *noted*: observed.
427 *manner*: kind.
428 *goodly portly*: very dignified.
a corpulent: with a good figure.
430 *carriage*: behaviour.
431 *inclining to threescore*: approaching sixty.
433 *lewdly given*: living a wicked life.
434–5 *if the tree . . . the fruit*: if the true character (i.e. the tree) can be judged from the outward appearance (the 'fruit'); Falstaff is quoting from *St Matthew*, 12:33.
436 *peremptorily . . . it*: I say with complete conviction.
437 *him keep with*: keep him as your friend.
438 *naughty varlet*: wicked lad.
439 *this month*: all this month.
440 *stand for me*: act my part.
442 *half so gravely*: with half as much dignity.
443 *word*: i.e. a choice of words.
matter: meaning.
444 *rabbit-sucker*: young rabbit.
poulter's hare: hare hung by its hind legs in a poulterer's shop.

have often noted in thy company, but I know not his name.

Prince

What manner of man, and it like your Majesty?

Falstaff

A goodly portly man, i'faith, and a corpulent; of a cheerful look, a pleasing eye, and a most noble carriage; and, as I think, his age some fifty, or—by'r Lady—inclining to threescore; and now I remember me, his name is Falstaff. If that man should be lewdly given, he deceiveth me; for, Harry, I see virtue in his looks. If then the tree may be known by the fruit, as the fruit by the tree, then peremptorily I speak it, there is virtue in that Falstaff; him keep with, the rest banish. And tell me now, thou naughty varlet, tell me where hast thou been this month?

Prince

Dost thou speak like a king? Do thou stand for me, and I'll play my father.

Falstaff

Depose me? If thou dost it half so gravely, so majestically, both in word and matter, hang me up by the heels for a rabbit-sucker, or a poulter's hare.

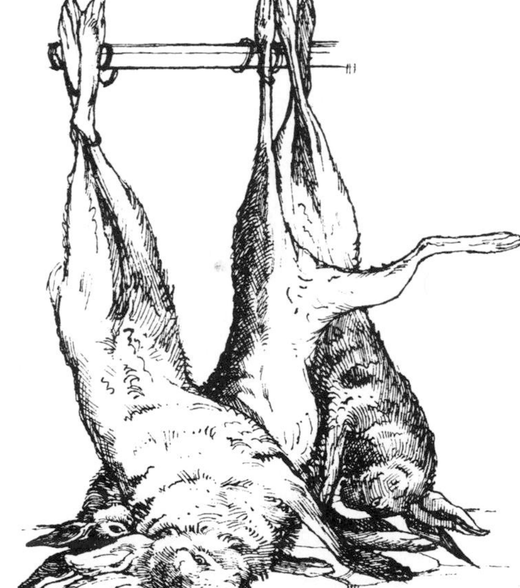

Prince
Well, here I am set.

Falstaff
And here I stand. Judge, my masters.

Prince
Now, Harry, whence come you?

Falstaff
My noble lord, from Eastcheap.

Prince
The complaints I hear of thee are grievous.

Falstaff
'Sblood, my lord, they are false! (Nay, I'll tickle ye for a young prince, i'faith.)

Prince
Swearest thou, ungracious boy? Henceforth ne'er look on me. Thou art violently carried away from grace. There is a devil haunts thee in the likeness of an old fat man; a tun of man is thy companion. Why dost thou converse with that trunk of humours, that bolting-hutch of beastliness, that swollen parcel of dropsies, that huge bombard of sack, that stuffed cloak-bag of guts, that roasted Manningtree ox with the pudding in his belly, that reverend vice, that grey iniquity, that father ruffian, that vanity in years? Wherein is he good, but to taste sack and drink it? Wherein neat and cleanly, but to carve a capon and eat it? Wherein cunning, but in craft? Wherein crafty, but in villainy? Wherein villainous, but in all things? Wherein worthy, but in nothing?

Falstaff
I would your Grace would take me with you: whom means your Grace?

Prince
That villainous abominable misleader of youth, Falstaff, that old white-bearded Satan.

Falstaff
My lord, the man I know.

Prince
I know thou dost.

Falstaff
But to say I know more harm in him than in myself were to say more than I know. That he is old, the

446 *set*: in position.
447 *Judge*: i.e. judge which is the better actor.
451 *'Sblood*: by God's blood.
451–2 *I'll . . . prince*: I'll make you laugh when I play the young prince.
453 *ungracious*: wicked, profane.
454 *violently*: dreadfully.
455 *haunts thee*: is always with you.
likeness: appearance.
456 *tun*: barrel.
457 *converse*: keep company with.
trunk of humours: body full of corruptions.
458 *bolting-hutch*: rubbish-bin (the 'bolting-hutch' was the box where the coarse flour remained after the better quality had been sifted off).
459 *dropsies*: dropsy is a disease in which the body is swollen with fluid.
bombard: leather vessel for wine.

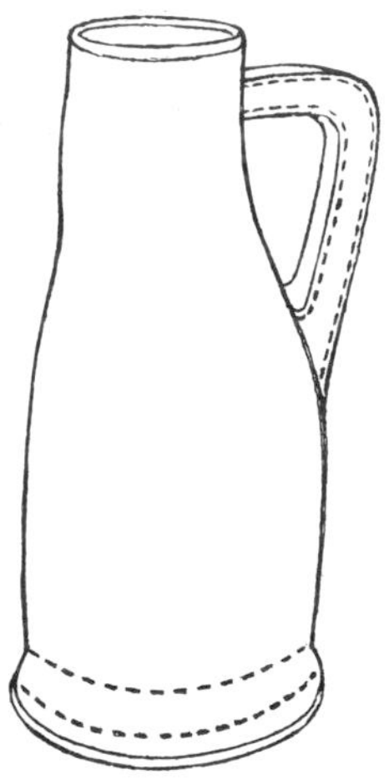

460 *cloak-bag*: portmanteau (an extra large suitcase).
460–61 *roasted . . . belly*: an ox roasted whole, stuffed with a mixture of meat and herbs (the 'pudding') was part of the entertainment at village fairs and festivals. Manningtree is in Essex—perhaps famous for fat oxen.

461–3 The following string of epithets contrasts Falstaff's age with his conduct.
reverend: respected.
vice: see p. xxviii.
grey: grey-haired.
vanity: worthlessness.
in years: aged.
463 *Wherein is he good*: what is he good for.
but: except.
464–5 *Wherein . . . cleanly*: what can he do well and properly.
465 *capon*: chicken.
466 *cunning*: knowledgeable.
craft: wickedness.
crafty: skilful.
469 *I would*: I wish.
take me with you: explain what you mean.
471 *misleader of youth*: see p. xxx.
473 *the man I know*: I know the man.
477 *witness it*: give evidence for it.
478 *saving your reverence*: with all respect (a phrase used before any unpleasant or impolite expression).
a whoremaster: one who earns his living immorally.
481 *host*: innkeeper.
482 *Pharaoh's lean kine*: the lean cows ('kine') were a sign that times of starvation were approaching; they were therefore to be hated, not loved. (*Genesis*, 41:19–21).
488 *banish not him*: do not banish him.
489–90 *banish . . . world*: if you banish fat Jack, you will banish the whole world.
493 *monstrous watch*: large company of guards.
494 *Play out*: finish.
497 *the devil . . . stick*: you are making the devil of a fuss.
500 *are come*: have come.
501–3 *Never . . . seeming so*: don't mistake the real thing for imitation—you yourself are truly royal ('essentially made'), although you do not behave in a royal manner.

more the pity: his white hairs do witness it. But that he is, saving your reverence, a whoremaster, that I utterly deny. If sack and sugar be a fault, God help the wicked! If to be old and merry be a sin, then many an old host that I know is damned. If to be fat be to be hated, then Pharaoh's lean kine are to be loved. No, my good lord; banish Peto, banish Bardolph, banish Poins—but for sweet Jack Falstaff, kind Jack Falstaff, true Jack Falstaff, valiant Jack Falstaff, and therefore more valiant, being as he is old Jack Falstaff, banish not him thy Harry's company, banish not him thy Harry's company. Banish plump Jack, and banish all the world.

Prince
I do, I will. [*A knocking is heard. Exeunt* Hostess, Francis, *and* Bardolph

Enter Bardolph, *running*

Bardolph
O my lord, my lord, the sheriff with a most monstrous watch is at the door!

Falstaff
Out, ye rogue! Play out the play! I have much to say in the behalf of that Falstaff.

Enter the Hostess

Hostess
O Jesu, my lord, my lord!

Prince
Heigh, heigh, the devil rides upon a fiddle-stick! What's the matter?

Hostess
The sheriff and all the watch are at the door; they are come to search the house. Shall I let them in?

Falstaff
Dost thou hear, Hal? Never call a true piece of gold a counterfeit: thou art essentially made without seeming so.

504 *without instinct*: i.e. without the 'instinct' which Falstaff boasted in line 275 (at last the Prince accuses Falstaff of lying and cowardice).

505 *your major*: the main part of your argument ('major' is a technical term used in logic).
so: good.

506–7 *If I . . . man*: if I do not look as fine as any man in the cart (that takes thieves to the gallows for execution).

507 *bringing up*: education.

508 *I shall . . . another*: the hangman's noose will strangle me faster than anyone else (because of his weight).

510 *arras*: in houses (and taverns) the arras was a curtain on a wooden frame between the wall and the main part of the room; in the theatre it would be the curtain concealing the acting area at the back of the stage.

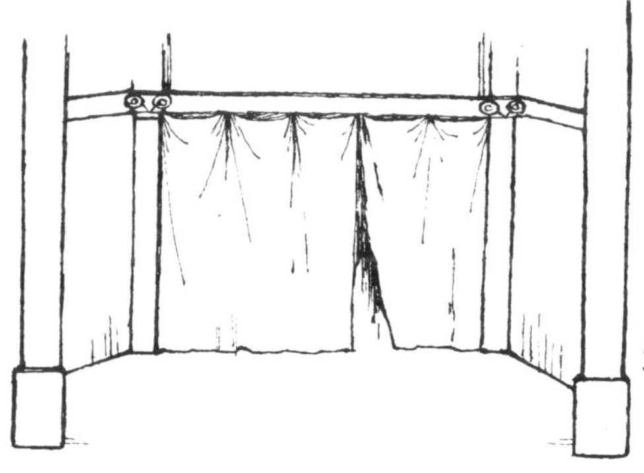

511 *above*: i.e. they could stand on the stage balcony and watch the Prince and the Sheriff from there.
true face: serious expression.

513 *their . . . out*: I have lost them (their lease has expired).

517 *hue and cry*: crowd of people chasing a thief.

523–4 He is doing something for me at this moment.

525 *engage . . . thee*: promise you.

527 *charg'd withal*: accused of.

Prince
And thou a natural coward without instinct.

Falstaff
I deny your major. If you will deny the sheriff, so; if not, let him enter. If I become not a cart as well as another man, a plague on my bringing up! I hope I shall as soon be strangled with a halter as another.

Prince
Go hide thee behind the arras, the rest walk up above. Now, my masters, for a true face, and good conscience.

Falstaff
Both which I have had, but their date is out, and therefore I'll hide me.

[*Exeunt all but the* Prince *and* Peto

Prince
Call in the sheriff.

Enter Sheriff *and the* Carrier

Now, master sheriff, what is your will with me?

Sheriff
First, pardon me, my lord. A hue and cry hath follow'd certain men unto this house.

Prince
What men?

Sheriff
One of them is well known, my gracious lord—a gross fat man—

Carrier
As fat as butter.

Prince
The man I do assure you is not here, for I myself at this time have employ'd him. And sheriff, I will engage my word to thee, that I will by tomorrow dinner-time send him to answer thee, or any man, for anything he shall be charg'd withal. And so let me entreat you leave the house.

Sheriff
I will, my lord: there are two gentlemen have in this robbery lost three hundred marks.

Prince
It may be so: if he have robb'd these men he shall be answerable. And so, farewell.

Sheriff
Good night, my noble lord.

Prince
I think it is good morrow, is it not?

Sheriff
Indeed, my lord, I think it be two o'clock.
[*Exit, with* Carrier

Prince
This oily rascal is known as well as Paul's. Go call him forth.

Peto
Falstaff! Fast asleep behind the arras, and snorting like a horse.

Prince
Hark how hard he fetches breath. Search his pockets. What has thou found?
[Peto *searches* Falstaff's *pockets and finds some papers*

Peto
Nothing but papers, my lord.

Prince
Let's see what they be. Read them.

Peto [*Reads*]

Item, a Capon	2s. 2d.
Item, Sauce	. 4d.
Item, Sack two gallons	5s. 8d.
Item, Anchovies and sack after supper	2s. 6d.
Item, Bread	. ob.

532 *answerable*: made to repay the sum.

534 *morrow*: morning.

536 *oily*: fat.
Paul's: St Paul's Cathedral—a famous London landmark.

540 *fetches*: draws.

548 *ob*: half a penny (*obolus*).

Prince

O monstrous! But one halfpennyworth of bread to this intolerable deal of sack! What there is else, keep close; we'll read it at more advantage. There let him sleep till day. I'll to the court in the morning. We must all to the wars, and thy place shall be honourable. I'll procure this fat rogue a charge of foot, and I know his death will be a march of twelve score. The money shall be paid back again with advantage. Be with me betimes in the morning; and so, good morrow, Peto.

Peto

Good morrow, good my lord. [*Exeunt*

550 *intolerable deal*: incredible amount.

551 *keep close*: hide.
at more advantage: when there is more time.

552 *I'll to*: I will go to.

553 *must all to*: must all go to.
thy place: the Prince will make sure that Peto gets a commission in the army.

555 *a charge of foot*: a whole company of infantry (foot-soldiers).

555–6 *his death . . . score*: it will kill him to walk two hundred and forty steps.

556 *The money*: i.e. that which Falstaff and the thieves had stolen.

557 *advantage*: interest; he will give the travellers some extra money (as compensation for their trouble).
betimes: early.

Act 3

Act 3 Scene 1
The rebels have now moved south; they are meeting in Wales, at the castle of Owen Glendower. Hotspur teases Glendower, refusing to believe the Welshman's claims to have magic powers. But there are serious arguments, too: they cannot agree on the division of the kingdom which they hope to win when they have fought King Henry's forces. The men are joined by their wives, and the scene ends peacefully.

1 *promises*: i.e. of support from those who sympathize with the rebels.
parties: supporters.
sure: to be trusted.

2 *induction*: the way things have started.
prosperous hope: hope that we shall do well (prosper).

6 Glendower first speaks formally ('Percy'), and then uses the more familiar nickname ('Hotspur').

7 *Lancaster*: i.e. King Henry IV.

9 *in heaven*: i.e. dead.

11 *nativity*: birth.

12 *front*: face (the sky).

13 *cressets*: torches.

16–17 There would have been the same phenomena at that time whether or not Glendower was born.

20 *was . . . mind*: did not share my opinion.

Scene 1 *A Castle in Wales*

Enter Hotspur, Worcester, Lord Mortimer, Owen Glendower

Mortimer
These promises are fair, the parties sure,
And our induction full of prosperous hope.

Hotspur
Lord Mortimer, and cousin Glendower, will you sit down?
And uncle Worcester. A plague upon it!
I have forgot the map.

Glendower No, here it is:
Sit, cousin Percy, sit, good cousin Hotspur;
For by that name as oft as Lancaster doth speak of you
His cheek looks pale, and with a rising sigh
He wisheth you in heaven.

Hotspur And you in hell,
As oft as he hears Owen Glendower spoke of.

Glendower
I cannot blame him; at my nativity
The front of heaven was full of fiery shapes,
Of burning cressets, and at my birth
The frame and huge foundation of the earth
Shak'd like a coward.

Hotspur
Why, so it would have done at the same season if your mother's cat had but kitten'd, though yourself had never been born.

Glendower
I say the earth did shake when I was born.

Hotspur
And I say the earth was not of my mind,

21 *as fearing you*: because it was afraid of you.

26 *oft*: often.
teeming: fruitful.

29 *enlargement*: freedom.

30 *beldam*: old woman.

32 *grandam*: grandmother.
distemp'rature: disorder.

33 *passion*: suffering.

33–4 *of many . . . crossings*: I do not tolerate such contradictions from many men.

39 *mark'd me*: shown that I am.

40 *courses*: events.

41 *in the roll*: on the list.

42 *clipp'd in with*: confined by.

43 *chides the banks*: restrains the shores.

44 *read to me*: taught me.

45 And show me any human being.

46 *trace me*: follow me.
tedious: difficult.
art: magic.

47 *hold me pace*: keep up with me.
deep: profound, mysterious.

48 *I'll to*: I will go to.

51 *call*: Glendower means 'conjure', 'raise up'; but Hotspur wilfully misunderstands him.
vasty deep: ocean.

If you suppose as fearing you it shook.

Glendower

The heavens were all on fire, the earth did tremble—

Hotspur

O, then the earth shook to see the heavens on fire,
And not in fear of your nativity.
Diseased nature oftentimes breaks forth
In strange eruptions; oft the teeming earth
Is with a kind of colic pinch'd and vex'd
By the imprisoning of unruly wind
Within her womb, which for enlargement striving
Shakes the old beldam earth, and topples down
Steeples and moss-grown towers. At your birth
Our grandam earth, having this distemp'rature,
In passion shook.

Glendower Cousin, of many men
I do not bear these crossings; give me leave
To tell you once again that at my birth
The front of heaven was full of fiery shapes,
The goats ran from the mountains, and the herds
Were strangely clamorous to the frighted fields.
These signs have mark'd me extraordinary,
And all the courses of my life do show
I am not in the roll of common men.
Where is he living, clipp'd in with the sea
That chides the banks of England, Scotland, Wales,
Which calls me pupil or hath read to me?
And bring him out that is but woman's son
Can trace me in the tedious ways of art,
And hold me pace in deep experiments.

Hotspur

I think there's no man speaks better Welsh: I'll to dinner.

Mortimer

Peace, cousin Percy; you will make him mad.

Glendower

I can call spirits from the vasty deep.

Hotspur

Why, so can I, or so can any man;
But will they come when you do call for them?

56 *coz*: an abbreviation (used in familiarity) of 'cousin'.

57 *telling truth*: Hotspur implies that Glendower is lying.

tell . . . devil: a proverb.

58–9 If you have the ability to bring the devil here, I am sure that I am able to make him so ashamed that he will go away.

60 *while you live*: always.

61 *unprofitable*: useless.

62–3 *made . . . power*: attacked my forces.

65 *Bootless*: unsuccessful; Hotspur makes the obvious pun.

weather-beaten: the history books describe the unusually severe weather on each of the three defeats.

67 *How . . . agues*: how does he manage not to catch a bad cold.

68–9 *divide . . . ta'en*: divide the country so that each of the three rebel leaders gets his proper share ('right').

69 *threefold order*: triple division.

ta'en: taken, already decided.

70 *The Archdeacon*: historically, the division of the kingdom was planned in the house of the Archdeacon of Bangor.

71 *limits*: regions; see map.

73 *to . . . assign'd*: allotted to my share.

75 *bound*: boundary.

77 The rest of England lying north of the river Trent.

78 Our contracts have been written in tripartite form; this legal expression meant that the three contracts were all written on a single piece of parchment (see illustration). The separate contracts were then cut off *with a jagged cut*—so that only the original three contracts could be fitted together, and any attempt at forgery could be detected.

Glendower

Why, I can teach you, cousin, to command the devil.

Hotspur

And I can teach thee, coz, to shame the devil,
By telling truth; tell truth, and shame the devil.
If thou have power to raise him, bring him hither,
And I'll be sworn I have power to shame him hence:
O, while you live, tell truth, and shame the devil!

Mortimer

Come, come, no more of this unprofitable chat.

Glendower

Three times hath Henry Bolingbroke made head
Against my power; thrice from the banks of Wye
And sandy-bottom'd Severn have I sent him
Bootless home, and weather-beaten back.

Hotspur

Home without boots, and in foul weather too!
How scapes he agues, in the devil's name?

Glendower

Come, here is the map; shall we divide our right
According to our threefold order ta'en?

Mortimer

The Archdeacon hath divided it
Into three limits very equally:
England, from Trent and Severn hitherto,
By south and east is to my part assign'd;

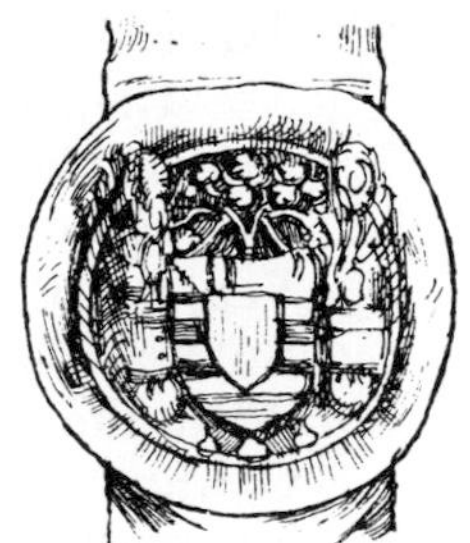

All westward, Wales beyond the Severn shore,
And all the fertile land within that bound,
To Owen Glendower; and, dear coz, to you
The remnant northward lying off from Trent.
And our indentures tripartite are drawn,
Which being sealed interchangeably,
(A business that this night may execute)
Tomorrow, cousin Percy, you and I
And my good Lord of Worcester will set forth
To meet your father and the Scottish power,
As is appointed us, at Shrewsbury.
My father Glendower is not ready yet,
Nor shall we need his help these fourteen days.
[*To* Glendower] Within that space you may have drawn together
Your tenants, friends, and neighbouring gentlemen.

Glendower

A shorter time shall send me to you, lords,
And in my conduct shall your ladies come,
From whom you now must steal and take no leave,
For there will be a world of water shed
Upon the parting of your wives and you.

Hotspur

Methinks my moiety, north from Burton here,
In quantity equals not one of yours:
See how this river comes me cranking in,
And cuts me from the best of all my land
A huge half-moon, a monstrous cantle out.
I'll have the current in this place damm'd up,
And here the smug and silver Trent shall run
In a new channel fair and evenly;

79 *sealed interchangeably*: each of the three contracts carried three wax seals; each of the three men signing the contracts would impress his own mark (often a device worn on a ring) on the wax of all three copies.
80 *that . . . execute*: that we can perform tonight.
83 *power*: army.
84 *As . . . us*: as it has been arranged for us.
86 *these fourteen days*: for another two weeks.
87 *space*: time.
90 *in my conduct*: under my protection.
91 *steal*: go secretly.
take no leave: not say goodbye.
92 *world of water*: flood of tears.
94 *Methinks :* in my opinion.
moiety: share (of the country).
95 Is not as big as either of your shares.
96 *comes . . . in*: comes winding in here.
97–8 And cuts an enormous corner ('cantle'), in the shape of a half-moon, out of the best part of my territory.
99 *in this place*: at this point (Hotspur indicates on the map how he will change the course of the river).
100 *smug*: smooth.

102 *indent*: curve.
103 *so . . . bottom*: such a fertile valley.
106 *mark*: notice.
bears his course: continues.
runs me up: flows into my territory.
107 Giving you exactly the same advantage on the opposite side.
108 *Gelding*: cutting away from.
continent: bank.
110 *charge*: i.e. of explosives.
trench him: dig a channel for him (the river).
115 *say me nay*: stop me.
120 *train'd up*: educated.
121 *framed*: fitted, set to music.
123 Added beauty to the voice (with the music of the harp).

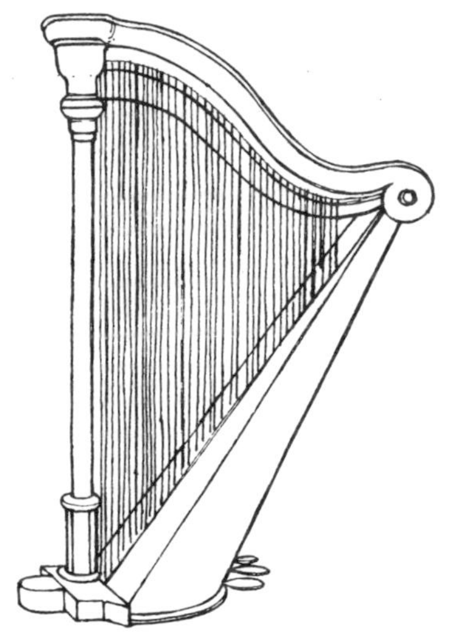

124 *A virtue*: an accomplishment.
126 *had rather*: would rather.
127 *same . . . mongers*: singers of rubbishy ballads.
128 *brazen . . . turn'd*: brass candlesticks ('cansticks') were polished by being turned on a lathe, so that metal grated on metal.
129 *dry*: without oil.
axle-tree: the rod on which a wheel turns.

It shall not wind with such a deep indent,
To rob me of so rich a bottom here.

Glendower
Not wind? It shall, it must—you see it doth.

Mortimer
Yea,
But mark how he bears his course, and runs me up
With like advantage on the other side,
Gelding the opposed continent as much
As on the other side it takes from you.

Worcester
Yea, but a little charge will trench him here,
And on this north side win this cape of land,
And then he runs straight and even.

Hotspur
I'll have it so, a little charge will do it.

Glendower
I'll not have it alter'd.

Hotspur
Will not you?

Glendower
No, nor you shall not.

Hotspur
Who shall say me nay?

Glendower
Why, that will I.

Hotspur
Let me not understand you then, speak it in Welsh.

Glendower
I can speak English, lord, as well as you,
For I was train'd up in the English court,
Where, being but young, I framed to the harp
Many an English ditty lovely well,
And gave the tongue a helpful ornament—
A virtue that was never seen in you.

Hotspur
Marry, and I am glad of it with all my heart!
I had rather be a kitten and cry 'mew'
Than one of these same metre ballad-mongers;
I had rather hear a brazen canstick turn'd,
Or a dry wheel grate on the axle-tree,

130–31 Those noises would not make me clench my teeth so much as the sound of jogging poetry.
mincing: walking in an unnatural manner.

132 It is as though an old horse ('nag') which can only walk with difficulty (shuffle) were compelled ('forc'd') to move at some uncomfortable pace ('gait').

133 *turn'd*: diverted.

136 *in . . . bargain*: when I am making a bargain.
mark ye me: take notice.

137 I'll argue over the smallest details.

138 *Are . . . drawn*: are the contracts all written out?
Shall . . . gone: isn't it time we went?

139 *may away*: can get away (i.e. they can travel by the light of the moon).

140 *haste*: hurry.
withal: at the same time.

141 *Break with*: inform.

144 *cross*: annoy.

145 *I . . . choose*: I can't help it.
sometime: sometimes.
angers: infuriates.

146 *moldwarp*: mole.

147 *Merlin*: the Welsh magician and prophet at the court of King Arthur.

149 *griffin*: a legendary beast with a lion's body and the beak of an eagle; its wings were those of an eagle, but they were clipped so that it could not fly.
moulten: moulted, shed its old feathers.

150 *couching*: a heraldic term (*couchant*) which indicated that the animal was lying down.
ramping: another heraldic term (*rampant*); the animal was rearing.

And that would set my teeth nothing on edge,
Nothing so much as mincing poetry:
'Tis like the forc'd gait of a shuffling nag.

Glendower

Come, you shall have Trent turn'd.

Hotspur

I do not care, I'll give thrice so much land
To any well-deserving friend:
But in the way of bargain, mark ye me,
I'll cavil on the ninth part of a hair.
Are the indentures drawn? Shall we be gone?

Glendower

The moon shines fair; you may away by night.
I'll haste the writer, and withal
Break with your wives of your departure hence.
I am afraid my daughter will run mad,
So much she doteth on her Mortimer. [*Exit*

Mortimer

Fie, cousin Percy, how you cross my father!

Hotspur

I cannot choose. Sometime he angers me
With telling me of the moldwarp and the ant,
Of the dreamer Merlin and his prophecies,
And of a dragon and a finless fish,
A clip-wing'd griffin and a moulten raven,
A couching lion and a ramping cat,

And such a deal of skimble-skamble stuff
As puts me from my faith. I tell you what—
He held me last night at least nine hours
In reckoning up the several devils' names
That were his lackeys. I cried 'Hum', and 'Well, go to!'
But mark'd him not a word. O, he is as tedious
As a tired horse, a railing wife;
Worse than a smoky house. I had rather live
With cheese and garlic in a windmill, far,
Than feed on cates and have him talk to me
In any summer house in Christendom.

Mortimer

In faith, he is a worthy gentleman,
Exceedingly well read, and profited
In strange concealments, valiant as a lion,
And wondrous affable, and as bountiful
As mines of India. Shall I tell you, cousin?
He holds your temper in a high respect
And curbs himself even of his natural scope
When you come 'cross his humour—faith he does!
I warrant you that man is not alive
Might so have tempted him as you have done
Without the taste of danger and reproof.
But do not use it oft, let me entreat you.

Worcester

In faith, my lord, you are too wilful-blame,
And since your coming hither have done enough
To put him quite besides his patience;
You must needs learn, lord, to amend this fault.
Though sometimes it show greatness, courage, blood—
And that's the dearest grace it renders you—
Yet oftentimes it doth present harsh rage,
Defect of manners, want of government,
Pride, haughtiness, opinion, and disdain,
The least of which haunting a nobleman
Loseth men's hearts, and leaves behind a stain
Upon the beauty of all parts besides,
Beguiling them of commendation.

Hotspur

Well, I am school'd—good manners be your speed!

151 *skimble-skamble*: rubbish; the word is Hotspur's own invention.
152 *puts . . . faith*: makes me lose my own (Christian) faith. Glendower expects Hotspur to believe so much that he finishes by believing nothing.
153 *held me*: made me listen.
154 *several*: different.
155 *lackeys*: servants.
Well, go to: well, really.
156 *mark'd . . . word*: did not believe a word he said.
157 *railing*: nagging.
159 *cheese and garlic*: very poor food.
windmill: i.e. with the constant noise of grinding machinery.
far: far (much) rather.
160 *cates*: luxury foods, delicacies.
161 *summer house*: a house in the country, built so that the owner could spend summer away from London.
Christendom: Christ's kingdom—i.e. all those parts of the world converted to Christianity.
163 *profited*: skilled.
164 *concealments*: mysteries, magic arts.
166 *mines of India*: Elizabethans were very impressed by the rich gold and jewels to be found in the newly-discovered eastern mines.
167 *temper*: character.
168 *curbs*: restrains.
natural scope: usual mood.
169 *come 'cross*: oppose.
170 *that . . . alive*: there is no man living.
171 *tempted him*: i.e. to show his violent nature.
172 *taste*: threat.
reproof: disgrace.
173 *Do . . . oft*: do not take too much advantage of Glendower's respect for you.
174 *wilful-blame*: wrong to be so obstinate.
176 To make him lose all patience.
177 *You . . . learn*: you really must learn.

178 *it*: i.e. the determined obstinacy referred to in line 174.
blood: spirit.
179 *dearest grace*: finest quality.
181 *want of government*: lack of self-control.
182 *opinion*: conceit.
183 *haunting*: affecting.
186 Making them lose the respect ('commendation') of other men.
187 *am school'd*: have been taught my lesson.
good . . . speed: I hope your good manners will be successful.
189 *spite*: irritation.
191 *she'll not*: she does not want to.
192 *she'll to*: she wants to go to.
194 *in your conduct*: under your protection.
196 *harlotry*: silly little girl (no sexual insult is intended).
do good upon: have any effect on.
197 *that pretty Welsh*: that lovely language (i.e. her tears).
198 *swelling heavens*: i.e. her eyes, swollen with crying.
199 *I . . . in*: I understand too well.
but for shame: if I were not ashamed.
200 *parley*: speech.
202 *feeling disputation*: discussion in emotions (instead of words).
203 *be a truant*: stop my lessons (as a child stays away from school).
204 *tongue*: speech.
205 *ditties . . . penn'd*: beautifully written songs.
207 To the accompaniment of enchanting notes on her lute.
208 *melt*: show signs of weakness (i.e. shed tears).
210 *wanton*: luxuriant, comfortable.
rushes: soft green plants were used as floor-covering.
213 'And send you to sleep'; in classical mythology the god of sleep was Morpheus.

Here come our wives, and let us take our leave.

Enter Glendower *with* Lady Percy *and* Lady Mortimer

Mortimer
This is the deadly spite that angers me,
My wife can speak no English, I no Welsh.

Glendower
My daughter weeps; she'll not part with you,
She'll be a soldier too, she'll to the wars.

Mortimer
Good father, tell her that she and my aunt Percy shall follow in your conduct speedily.

[Glendower *speaks in Welsh to* Lady Mortimer; *and she answers him in the same language*

Glendower
She is desperate here, a peevish, self-willed harlotry, one that no persuasion can do good upon.

[Lady Mortimer *speaks in Welsh*

Mortimer
I understand thy looks. That pretty Welsh
Which thou pourest down from these swelling heavens
I am too perfect in, and, but for shame,
In such a parley should I answer thee.

[Lady Mortimer *speaks again in Welsh*

I understand thy kisses, and thou mine,
And that's a feeling disputation;
But I will never be a truant, love,
Till I have learnt thy language, for thy tongue
Makes Welsh as sweet as ditties highly penn'd,
Sung by a fair queen in a summer's bow'r
With ravishing division to her lute.

Glendower
Nay, if you melt, then will she run mad.

[Lady Mortimer *speaks again in Welsh*

Mortimer
O, I am ignorance itself in this!

Glendower
She bids you on the wanton rushes lay you down,
And rest your gentle head upon her lap,
And she will sing the song that pleaseth you,
And on your eyelids crown the god of sleep,

214 *blood*: spirits.
heaviness: drowsiness.

215 *wake and sleep*: being awake and being asleep.

217 *the . . . team*: the sun, in classical mythology, was often portrayed as a god (Phœbus Apollo) driving a team of horses across the sky.

218 *progress*: royal journey.

220 *our . . . drawn*: our agreement (about the division of the kingdom) will be written out.

221–3 Glendower boasts that with his magic powers he can bring musicians from a great distance.

221 *and*: if.

222 *Hang in the air*: in the Elizabethan theatres, musicians were usually placed above the stage.
leagues: a 'league' was a measure of distance—about 3 miles.

223 *straight*: immediately.

224 *perfect in*: very good at.

227 Because he hears the music, Hotspur pretends to believe Glendower's boast about being able to command the devil.

228 *humorous*: temperamental.

230–31 Then you should be very musical yourself, since you are completely dominated by your different moods.

233 *brach*: hound bitch.
Irish: this may refer to the sound of the Irish language; or perhaps 'Lady' was an Irish wolf-hound.

Charming your blood with pleasing heaviness,
Making such difference 'twixt wake and sleep
As is the difference betwixt day and night,
The hour before the heavenly-harness'd team
Begins his golden progress in the east.

Mortimer

With all my heart I'll sit and hear her sing,
By that time will our book, I think, be drawn.

Glendower

Do so, and those musicians that shall play to you
Hang in the air a thousand leagues from hence,
And straight they shall be here: sit, and attend.

Hotspur

Come, Kate, thou art perfect in lying down:
Come, quick, quick, that I may lay my head in thy lap.

Lady Percy

Go, ye giddy goose. [*The music plays*

Hotspur

Now I perceive the devil understands Welsh,
And 'tis no marvel he is so humorous.
By'r Lady, he is a good musician.

Lady Percy

Then should you be nothing but musical,
For you are altogether govern'd by humours.
Lie still, ye thief, and hear the lady sing in Welsh.

Hotspur

I had rather hear Lady my brach howl in Irish.

Lady Percy

Wouldst thou have thy head broken?

Hotspur

No.

Lady Percy

Then be still.

Hotspur

Neither, 'tis a woman's fault.

Lady Percy

Now God help thee!

Hotspur

To the Welsh lady's bed.

Lady Percy

What's that?

234 Do you want me to smack your head?

236 *still*: quiet.

237 *Neither*: I won't do that, either.

a woman's fault: Hotspur must be ironic; silence is not (traditionally) a female quality.

243 *in good sooth*: indeed (a very mild expression).

245 *comfit-maker*: confectioner.

248 *sarcanet surety*: flimsy assurance ('sarcanet' was a thin silk).

249 *Finsbury*: London citizens used to walk in Finsbury Fields—a very respectable kind of public park.

250 *lady*: noblewoman (not a middle-class citizen's wife).

251 *mouth-filling*: robust.

252 *protest*: oaths, protestations.

pepper-gingerbread: a light, easily swallowed, cake.

253 *velvet-guards*: clothes trimmed with velvet, which would be worn by the respectable citizens as their best ('Sunday') clothes.

Hotspur

Peace she sings.

[*Here* Lady Mortimer *sings a Welsh song*

Come, Kate, I'll have your song too.

Lady Percy

Not mine, in good sooth.

Hotspur

Not yours, in good sooth! Heart, you swear like a
comfit-maker's wife—'Not you, in good sooth!',
and 'As true as I live!', and 'As God shall mend
me!', and 'As sure as day!'—
And givest such sarcenet surety for thy oaths
As if thou never walk'st further than Finsbury.
Swear me, Kate, like a lady as thou art,
A good mouth-filling oath, and leave 'In sooth',
And such protest of pepper-gingerbread,
To velvet-guards, and Sunday citizens.
Come, sing.

Lady Percy

I will not sing.

256–7 *'Tis . . . teacher*: singing is the quickest ('next') way to turn yourself into a tailor or a teacher of song-birds.
256 *redbreast*: a small brown bird, with red breast-feathers, which has a very sweet song.
257 *And*: if.
261 *on fire*: keen.
262 *By . . . drawn*: our contracts will be written out by now.
but seal: just sign and seal them.

Hotspur
'Tis the next way to turn tailor, or be redbreast-teacher. And the indentures be drawn, I'll away within these two hours; and so come in when ye will. [*Exit*

Glendower
Come, come, Lord Mortimer, you are as slow
As hot Lord Percy is on fire to go.
By this our book is drawn—we'll but seal,
And then to horse immediately.

Mortimer With all my heart.
[*Exeunt*

Act 3 Scene 2
King Henry has a serious talk with his son. He first recalls his own conduct when, as Henry Bolingbroke, he competed with King Richard II and won the people's respect: although Richard was the rightful king, Henry was the people's choice. Now the King believes that Prince Hal is behaving in the same way as Richard, whilst Hotspur, by contrast, wins the respect and admiration which may one day help *him* to win the crown. The Prince apologizes to his father; he explains the reason for his conduct, and promises to reform.

1 *give us leave*: please leave us alone.
2 *some private conference*: a talk together.
3 *presently*: very soon.
4 *God . . . so*: it is God's will.
5 *displeasing service*: sin.
6 *doom*: judgement.
out of my blood: from my own family.
7 *scourge*: whip, punishment.

Scene 2 *London: Westminster Palace*

Enter the King, Prince of Wales, *and others*

King
Lords, give us leave; the Prince of Wales and I
Must have some private conference: but be near at hand,
For we shall presently have need of you.
[*Exeunt* Lords
I know not whether God will have it so
For some displeasing service I have done,
That, in his secret doom, out of my blood
He'll breed revengement and a scourge for me;

8 *passages*: conduct.
9 *only mark'd*: especially chosen.
11 *mistreadings*: errors, wrongdoings.
else: is there any other explanation.
12 *inordinate*: unworthy.
13 *bare*: wretched.
lewd: low.
mean: base.
attempts: actions.
14 *rude*: rough.
15 *match'd withal*: accompanied by.
grafted to: attached to.
16 *blood*: birth, rank.
17 *hold . . . with*: be approved by.
18 *So please*: if you please.
would: wish.
19 *Quit*: clear myself.
clear excuse: good explanation.
20 *doubtless*: sure.
purge: clear.
21 *charg'd withal*: accused of now.
22–7 Prince Hal hopes that his father will make allowances for the fact that there are always rumours surrounding someone in his position.
22 *extenuation*: consideration, allowance.
23 *reproof*: disproving.
devis'd: made up, invented.
24 Which a great man is often forced to hear.
25 *smiling pickthanks*: flatterers—who think this is a way to earn the King's thanks.
newsmongers: gossips; the modern equivalent would be 'newspapermen'.
26–8 The Prince hopes that because he can prove these rumours to be false, he will be forgiven for some real faults ('some things true') which he confesses to.
true submission: sincere confession.
29 *Yet . . . wonder*: but I am still very surprised.
30 *affections*: inclinations.

But thou dost in thy passages of life
Make me believe that thou art only mark'd
For the hot vengeance and the rod of heaven
To punish my mistreadings. Tell me else,
Could such inordinate and low desires,
Such poor, such bare, such lewd, such mean attempts,
Such barren pleasures, rude society,
As thou art match'd withal, and grafted to,
Accompany the greatness of thy blood,
And hold their level with thy princely heart?

Prince

So please your Majesty, I would I could
Quit all offences with as clear excuse
As well as I am doubtless I can purge
Myself of many I am charg'd withal:
Yet such extenuation let me beg
As, in reproof of many tales devis'd,
Which oft the ear of greatness needs must hear,
By smiling pickthanks, and base newsmongers,
I may for some things true, wherein my youth
Hath faulty wander'd and irregular,
Find pardon on my true submission.

King

God pardon thee! Yet let me wonder, Harry,
At thy affections, which do hold a wing
Quite from the flight of all thy ancestors.
Thy place in Council thou hast rudely lost,
Which by thy younger brother is supply'd;
And art almost an alien to the hearts
Of all the court and princes of my blood.
The hope and expectation of thy time
Is ruin'd, and the soul of every man
Prophetically do forethink thy fall.
Had I so lavish of my presence been,
So common-hackney'd in the eyes of men,
So stale and cheap to vulgar company,
Opinion, that did help me to the crown,
Had still kept loyal to possession,
And left me in reputeless banishment,
A fellow of no mark nor likelihood.
By being seldom seen, I could not stir
But like a comet I was wonder'd at,

That men would tell their children, 'This is he!'
Others would say, 'Where, which is Bolingbroke?'
And then I stole all courtesy from heaven,
And dress'd myself in such humility
That I did pluck allegiance from men's hearts,
Loud shouts and salutations from their mouths,
Even in the presence of the crowned King.
Thus did I keep my person fresh and new;
My presence, like a robe pontifical,
Ne'er seen but wonder'd at; and so my state—
Seldom, but sumptuous—show'd like a feast,
And won by rareness such solemnity.
The skipping King, he ambled up and down,
With shallow jesters, and rash bavin wits,
Soon kindled and soon burnt, carded his state;
Mingled his royalty with cap'ring fools,

30–31 *Hold . . . Quite*: fly in a completely different direction (i.e. are quite unlike).

33 *supply'd*: taken.

34 *alien*: stranger.

35 *of my blood*: i.e. of your own family.

36–7 The hopes and expectations we had when you were young ('of thy time') have been disappointed.

38 *do*: Shakespeare uses a plural form because 'every man' implies a number.
forethink: anticipate, expect.

39 If I had been seen around so much.

40 *common-hackneyed*: ordinary, a thing to be seen every day (like a hackney—a working-horse).

41 *vulgar company*: the society of common people.

42 *Opinion*: public opinion.

43 *possession*: the man who already possessed the crown (i.e. Richard II).

44 *reputeless*: without reputation.

45 *fellow*: another ordinary man.
of no mark: with no importance.
likelihood: hope.

50 *stole . . . heaven*: assumed a heavenly graciousness (by seeming to be 'from heaven', the 'courtesy' might imply that his claim to the throne was divinely approved).

51 *dress'd . . . humility*: behaved with such humility.

56 *robe pontifical*: the vestments worn only by bishops on great festivals.

57 *state*: appearance.

58 *show'd . . . feast*: was like a festival (i.e. something very special).

59 Achieved such dignity because it was so unusual.

60 *skipping*: thoughtless (like a playful child).

61 *rash . . . wits*: bright young men ('bavin' is a wood that quickly catches fire, and is soon burnt out).

62 *carded his state*: lost his dignity (the verb *card* = to mix drinks with water, to weaken).

Had his great name profaned with their scorns,
And gave his countenance against his name
To laugh at gibing boys, and stand the push
Of every beardless vain comparative,
Grew a companion to the common streets,
Enfeoff'd himself to popularity,
That, being daily swallow'd by men's eyes,
They surfeited with honey, and began
To loathe the taste of sweetness, whereof a little
More than a little is by much too much.
So, when he had occasion to be seen,
He was but as the cuckoo is in June,
Heard, not regarded; seen, but with such eyes
As, sick and blunted with community,
Afford no extraordinary gaze,
Such as is bent on sun-like majesty
When it shines seldom in admiring eyes,
But rather drows'd and hung their eyelids down,
Slept in his face, and render'd such aspect
As cloudy men use to their adversaries,
Being with his presence glutted, gorg'd, and full.
And in that very line, Harry, standest thou,
For thou hast lost thy princely privilege
With vile participation. Not an eye
But is a-weary of thy common sight,

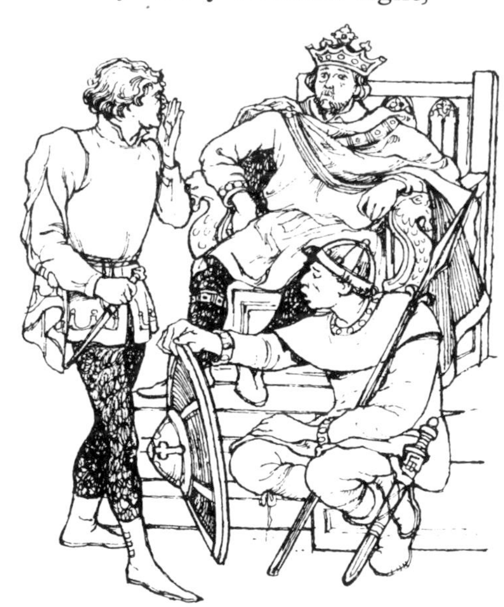

64 Allowed his royal name to be dishonoured and despised.

65 *gave his countenance*: consented.
against his name: in a manner that was most unsuitable.

66 *gibing*: insulting.
stand the push: tolerate the impudence.

67 *beardless*: young.
comparative: insulting competitor (compare *1*, 2, 78).

68 *Grew . . . to*: i.e. was frequently to be found in.

69 *Enfeoff'd*: was a slave to.

71–2 They were sick of the sight of him, as though they had eaten too much honey (were 'surfeited with honey').

74 *had occasion*: it was necessary.

75 *the cuckoo*: the call of this bird ('cuck-oo') is welcomed in April as a sign that spring has arrived; in June, however, it is tedious.

77 *blunted*: grown dull.
community: familiarity.

78 Pay no special attention.

79 *bent*: turned.
sun-like: the sun was the symbol of kingship, because it is brighter than all other stars.

81 *drows'd*: the eyes (referred to in line 76) became sleepy.

82 *face*: presence.
render'd . . . aspect: stared back at him in such a way.

83 *cloudy*: hostile.

85 *very line*: same class.

87 *With . . . participation*: by keeping such rotten company.

88 *of . . . sight*: with seeing you so often.

89 *Save*: except.

91 *tenderness*: i.e. tears.

92 *thrice*: most.

93 *Be . . . myself*: behave as I ought to do.
For . . . world: exactly.

94 *to . . . hour*: at this moment.

95 When I returned from France, landing at Ravenspurgh.

96 *even*: exactly.
Percy: i.e. Hotspur.
97 *to boot*: as well.
98–9 Hotspur's merit (worth) gives him a better claim ('interest') to the kingdom than your own, which is dependent on the vague theory ('shadow') of heredity ('succession').
100 *of no right*: with no just cause.
nor . . . right: or even the appearance of a just cause.
101 *fields*: i.e. battlefields.
harness: armour—i.e. armed men.
102 *Turns head*: opposes his forces.
the lion's . . . jaws: i.e. the King's armed forces; the lion was a symbol of royalty.
103 *no more . . . years*: no older; see p. 126.
105 *bruising arms*: hurtful war.
107–11 *whose*: i.e. those of Douglas, who had the best military reputation in Christendom until he was beaten by Hotspur.
high: brave.
108 *hot incursions*: fierce attacks.
name in arms: reputation in battle.
109 *chief majority*: greater eminence.
110 *And . . . capital*: and the chief military title.
112 *Thrice*: see p. 128.
Mars: the classical god of war.
swathling clothes: the wrappings of a new-born baby.
113 *enterprises*: actions.
114 *Discomfited*: faced in battle.
ta'en: taken, captured.
115 *Enlarged him*: set him free.
116 To increase ('fill . . . up') the calls of mighty defiance.
120 *Capitulate*: form an agreement.
are up: i.e. up in arms—ready to fight.
123 *dearest*: most loved; *and* worst.
124 *like enough*: quite likely.
vassal: servile.
125 *Base inclination*: tendency to do ignoble deeds.
start of spleen: fit of bad temper.

Save mine, which hath desir'd to see thee more,
Which now doth that I would not have it do—
Make blind itself with foolish tenderness.

Prince

I shall hereafter, my thrice gracious lord,
Be more myself.

King

For all the world
As thou art to this hour was Richard then
When I from France set foot at Ravenspurgh;
And even as I was then is Percy now.
Now by my sceptre, and my soul to boot,
He hath more worthy interest to the state
Than thou the shadow of succession.
For of no right, nor colour like to right,
He doth fill fields with harness in the realm,
Turns head against the lion's armed jaws,
And—being no more in debt to years than thou—
Leads ancient lords and reverend bishops on
To bloody battles, and to bruising arms.
What never-dying honour hath he got
Against renowned Douglas—whose high deeds,
Whose hot incursions and great name in arms,
Holds from all soldiers chief majority
And military title capital
Through all the kingdoms that acknowledge Christ.
Thrice hath this Hotspur, Mars in swathling clothes,
This infant warrior, in his enterprises
Discomfited great Douglas, ta'en him once,
Enlarged him, and made a friend of him,
To fill the mouth of deep defiance up,
And shake the peace and safety of our throne.
And what say you to this? Percy, Northumberland,
The Archbishop's Grace of York, Douglas, Mortimer,
Capitulate against us and are up.
But wherefore do I tell these news to thee?
Why, Harry, do I tell thee of my foes,
Which art my nearest and dearest enemy?
Thou that art like enough, through vassal fear,
Base inclination, and the start of spleen,

To fight against me under Percy's pay,
To dog his heels, and curtsy at his frowns,
To show how much thou art degenerate.

Prince

Do not think so, you shall not find it so;
And God forgive them that so much have sway'd
Your Majesty's good thoughts away from me!
I will redeem all this on Percy's head,
And in the closing of some glorious day
Be bold to tell you that I am your son,
When I will wear a garment all of blood,
And stain my favours in a bloody mask,
Which, wash'd away, shall scour my shame with it;
And that shall be the day, whene'er it lights,
That this same child of honour and renown,
This gallant Hotspur, this all-praised knight,
And your unthought-of Harry chance to meet.
For every honour sitting on his helm,
Would they were multitudes, and on my head
My shames redoubled! For the time will come
That I shall make this northern youth exchange
His glorious deeds for my indignities.
Percy is but my factor, good my lord,
To engross up glorious deeds on my behalf;
And I will call him to so strict account
That he shall render every glory up,
Yea, even the slightest worship of his time,
Or I will tear the reckoning from his heart.
This in the name of God I promise here,
The which if He be pleas'd I shall perform,
I do beseech your Majesty may salve
The long-grown wounds of my intemperance:
If not, the end of life cancels all bands,
And I will die a hundred thousand deaths
Ere break the smallest parcel of this vow.

126 *under Percy's pay*: on Hotspur's side, and paid by him (see p. 131).
127 *dog his heels*: follow him (as a dog walks at his master's heel).
curtsy . . . frowns: bow humbly when he looks severe.
128 *degenerate*: untrue to your royal birth.
130 *sway'd*: turned, influenced.
132 The Prince promises to rescue his lost reputation by fighting Hotspur.
133 *day*: battle.
136 *favours*: features.
138 *lights*: happens.
141 *unthought-of*: despised.
142 *helm*: helmet.
143–4 *Would . . . redoubled*: I wish that Hotspur had far more honours, and that I had even more faults to atone for.
147 *but my factor*: merely my agent; the Prince says he is using Hotspur to collect ('engross up') great deeds so that they will all become Hal's when he kills Hotspur.
149 I shall make him give such a very good account of himself (i.e. Hal will fight so fiercely).
150 *render*: surrender.
151 *the slightest . . . time*: the smallest honour he has won in all his life.

King

A hundred thousand rebels die in this!
Thou shalt have charge and sovereign trust herein.

Enter Blunt

How now, good Blunt? Thy looks are full of speed.

Blunt

So hath the business that I come to speak of.
Lord Mortimer of Scotland hath sent word
That Douglas and the English rebels met
The eleventh of this month at Shrewsbury.
A mighty and a fearful head they are,
If promises be kept on every hand,
As ever offer'd foul play in a state.

King

The Earl of Westmoreland set forth today,
With him my son, Lord John of Lancaster;
For this advertisement is five days old.
On Wednesday next, Harry, you shall set forward;
On Thursday we ourselves will march.
Our meeting is Bridgnorth; and, Harry, you
Shall march through Gloucestershire—by which account,
Our business valued, some twelve days hence
Our general forces at Bridgnorth shall meet.
Our hands are full of business; let's away:
Advantage feeds him fat while men delay.

[*Exeunt*

154 If it is God's will that I should do all this.
155 *salve*: heal.
156 The hurt that has for so long been caused by my riotous living.
157 *If not*: i.e. if it is not God's will that Prince Hal should beat Hotspur.
bands: bonds, debts.
159 *parcel*: part.
161 *charge*: command.
sovereign trust: the authority of a king.
162 *Thy . . . speed*: you look as though you are in a hurry.
163 *So . . . business*: i.e. the 'business' is also 'full of speed'.
167 *head*: force.
168 If all those who have promised support (to the rebels) keep their promises.
169 *offer'd*: threatened.
172 *advertisement*: information.
176 *by which account*: in which case.
177 *Our . . . valued*: having estimated the time that this will take.
178 *general*: entire.
179 *Our . . . business*: we have a lot to do.
180 The King's speech sounds like a proverb: his meaning is that if they waste time ('delay'), others could benefit (grow 'fat') by taking advantage.

Scene 3 *Eastcheap: the Boar's Head Tavern*

Enter Falstaff *and* Bardolph

Falstaff

Bardolph, am I not fallen away vilely since this last action? Do I not bate? Do I not dwindle? Why, my skin hangs about me like an old lady's loose gown. I am withered like an old apple-john. Well, I'll repent, and that suddenly, while I am in some liking; I shall be out of heart shortly, and then I shall have no strength to repent. And I have not forgotten what the inside of a church is made of, I

Act 3 Scene 3
Falstaff is in the tavern; he is rather bored and depressed, but he jokes with Bardolph until the Hostess joins them. They begin to quarrel and insult each other: Falstaff is angry because he has been robbed, and the Hostess complains that Falstaff owes money to her. Prince Hal returns from the interview with his father; he listens to their accusations, promises to settle all the difficulties, and finally announces that war has been declared and the fooling must stop.

1 *am . . . vilely*: haven't I lost weight terribly.

2 *action*: i.e. the robbery at Gad's Hill; Falstaff speaks as though it were a military battle.

bate: get thin.

4 *apple-john*: a kind of apple whose skin wrinkles with keeping.

5 *suddenly*: at once.

while . . . liking: while I feel like repenting; *and* while I still have some flesh left.

6 *out of heart*: lost interest; *and* in poor condition.

7 *And*: if.

9 *peppercorn*: small, dried berry.

brewer's horse: brewers were notorious for over-working and under-feeding the horses that pulled their heavy loads of barrels.

10–11 *hath . . . me*: has ruined me.

13 *there is it*: that's it (Falstaff pretends to be resigned).

14 *I was . . . given*: I lived as virtuously.

16 *diced*: gambled (throwing dice).

17 *bawdy-house*: brothel.

a quarter: usually this means 'quarter of a year'; but Falstaff is quick to change the sense.

19 *in good compass*: in good order, within bounds; the pun is inevitable.

24 *thy face*: apparently Bardolph has a big red nose (as well as spots—see 2,4,315); this is now the object of Falstaff's wit. At sea, the ships used to follow the light ('lantern') carried at the back ('in the poop') of the leading ship (the 'admiral'). In the new title for Bardolph, Falstaff parodies a popular fictional character of the time, Amadis, Knight of the Burning Sword.

am a peppercorn, a brewer's horse. The inside of a church! Company, villainous company, hath been the spoil of me.

Bardolph

Sir John, you are so fretful you cannot live long.

Falstaff

Why, there is it. Come, sing me a bawdy song, make me merry. I was as virtuously given as a gentleman need to be—virtuous enough: swore little; diced not above seven times—a week; went to a bawdy-house not above once in a quarter—of an hour; paid money that I borrowed—three or four times; lived well, and in good compass. And now I live out of all order, out of all compass.

Bardolph

Why, you are so fat, Sir John, that you must needs be out of all compass, out of all reasonable compass, Sir John.

Falstaff

Do thou amend thy face, and I'll amend my life: thou art our admiral, thou bearest the lantern in the poop, but 'tis in the nose of thee: thou art the Knight of the Burning Lamp.

Bardolph

Why, Sir John, my face does you no harm.

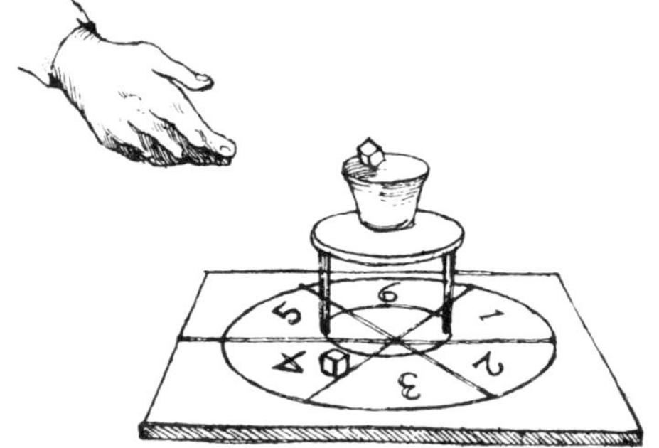

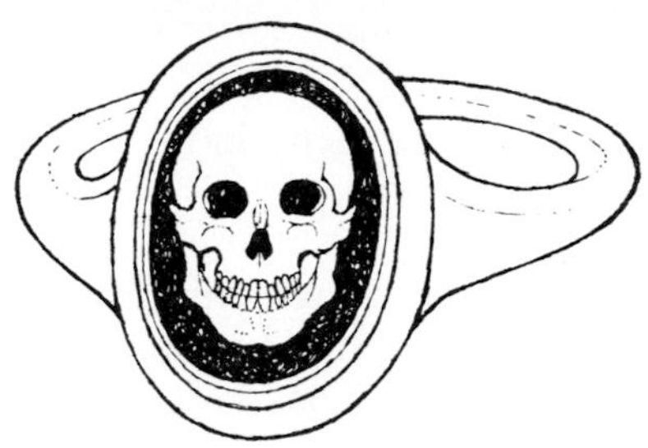

29 *I'll be sworn*: I agree.

30 *a death's-head*: a skull—or a ring with a skull, which was worn as a *memento mori*, a reminder of death.

32 *Dives*: the story of Dives, the man who lived richly ('in purple') and feasted whilst the beggar Lazarus starved, is told in St Luke's Gospel (16:19–31); Dives was condemned to burn in the fires of hell.

34 *given to virtue*: virtuous.

35 *God's angel*: angels were often said to appear in fiery flames—so Bardolph's red nose could be mistaken for an angel.

36 *given over*: committed to evil, damned.

wert: would be.

37 *but*: except.

37–8 *the son . . . darkness*: i.e. a child of the devil.

40 *ignis fatuus*: will o' the wisp (a flickering light caused by gas over marsh ground).

ball of wildfire: flaming ball of gunpowder; *or* a kind of lightning.

41 *no . . . money*: money won't buy anything.

42 *triumph*: festival (with bright lights, or a firework display).

43 *links*: flares (burning lights on sticks to show the way at night).

46 *drunk me*: drunk at my expense.

good cheap: cheaply.

47 *dearest chandler's*: the most expensive candle-maker.

48 *salamander*: a kind of lizard that was supposed to live in fire.

48–9 *any . . . years*: throughout the past thirty-two years.

52 *be heartburnt*: have indigestion.

Falstaff

No, I'll be sworn, I make as good use of it as many a man doth of a death's-head or a *memento mori*. I never see thy face but I think upon hell-fire, and Dives that lived in purple: for there he is in his robes, burning, burning. If thou wert any way given to virtue, I would swear by thy face: my oath should be 'By this fire, that's God's angel!' But thou art altogether given over; and wert indeed, but for the light in thy face, the son of utter darkness. When thou ran'st up Gad's Hill in the night to catch my horse, if I did not think thou hadst been an *ignis fatuus*, or a ball of wildfire, there's no purchase in money. O, thou art a perpetual triumph, an everlasting bonfire-light! Thou hast saved me a thousand marks in links and torches, walking with thee in the night betwixt tavern and tavern: but the sack that thou hast drunk me would have bought me lights as good cheap at the dearest chandler's in Europe. I have maintained that salamander of yours with fire any time this two and thirty years, God reward me for it!

Bardolph

'Sblood, I would my face were in your belly!

Falstaff

God-a-mercy! so should I be sure to be heart-burnt.

Enter Hostess

How now, dame Partlet the hen, have you enquired yet who picked my pocket?

Hostess

Why, Sir John, what do you think, Sir John? Do you think I keep thieves in my house? I have searched, I have inquired, so has my husband, man by man, boy by boy, servant by servant—the tithe of a hair was never lost in my house before.

Falstaff

Ye lie, hostess: Bardolph was shaved and lost many a hair, and I'll be sworn my pocket was picked. Go to, you are a woman, go.

Hostess

Who, I? No, I defy thee! God's light, I was never called so in mine own house before.

Falstaff

Go to, I know you well enough.

Hostess

No, Sir John; you do not know me, Sir John: I know you, Sir John. You owe me money, Sir John, and now you pick a quarrel to beguile me of it. I bought you a dozen of shirts to your back.

Falstaff

Dowlas, filthy dowlas. I have given them away to bakers' wives; they have made bolters of them.

Hostess

Now, as I am a true woman, holland of eight shillings an ell! You owe money here besides, Sir John, for your diet, and by-drinkings, and money lent you, four and twenty pound.

Falstaff

He had his part of it; let him pay.

Hostess

He? Alas, he is poor; he hath nothing.

Falstaff

How? Poor? Look upon his face. What call you rich? Let them coin his nose, let them coin his cheeks. I'll not pay a denier. What, will you make a younker of me? Shall I not take mine ease in mine inn but I shall have my pocket picked? I have lost a seal-ring of my grandfather's worth forty mark.

54 *dame Partlet*: a traditional name for a hen (and so for any fussy woman).

55 *picked my pocket*: stole things from my pocket.

60 *tithe*: tenth part.

63 *Go to*: don't be silly.
a woman: Falstaff does not specify the meaning of his insult.

64 *I defy thee*: I deny it (the Hostess does not understand what she is being accused of).

69 *beguile*: cheat.

70 *to your back*: to wear on your back.

71 *Dowlas*: cheap, coarse fabric.

72 *bolters*: cloths for sifting flour.

73 *holland*: the finest lawn.
of: at a cost of; the price quoted by the Hostess is exaggerated—about twice the actual amount.

74 *an ell*: about a metre.

75 *diet*: meals.
by-drinking: drinks between meals.

80 *coin*: turn into money (Bardolph's face is red and glistening—like gold).

81 *denier*: a small copper coin—quite worthless.

82–3 *will . . . me*: do you think I am some spendthrift novice ('younker').

83 *take . . . inn*: relax where I want he phrase is proverbial).

84 *but . . . have*: without having.

Hostess

O Jesu, I have heard the Prince tell him, I know not how oft, that that ring was copper!

Falstaff

How? The Prince is a jack, a sneak-up. 'Sblood, and he were here I would cudgel him like a dog if he would say so.

Enter the Prince *marching, with* Peto, *and* Falstaff *meets him, playing upon his truncheon like a fife*

How now, lad? Is the wind in that door, i'faith? Must we all march?

Bardolph

Yea, two and two, Newgate fashion.

Hostess

My lord, I pray you hear me.

Prince

What say'st thou, Mistress Quickly? How doth thy husband? I love him well, he is an honest man.

Hostess

Good my lord, hear me.

Falstaff

Prithee let her alone, and list to me.

Prince

What say'st thou, Jack?

Falstaff

The other night I fell asleep here, behind the arras, and had my pocket picked: this house is turned bawdy-house; they pick pockets.

Prince

What didst thou lose, Jack?

Falstaff

Wilt thou believe me, Hal, three or four bonds of forty pound apiece, and a seal-ring of my grandfather's.

Prince

A trifle, some eightpenny matter.

Hostess

So I told him, my lord, and I said I heard your Grace say so; and, my lord, he speaks most vilely of you, like a foul-mouthed man as he is, and said he would cudgel you.

87 *jack*: low fellow.
sneak-up: coward.

88 *cudgel*: beat.

89 *so*: i.e. that the ring was made of copper.

90 *Is . . . door*: is that the way things are (i.e. is it time for us to be soldiers).

92 *Newgate fashion*: convicts were made to walk in pairs—handcuffed together—to Newgate prison.

97 Please take no notice of her and listen to me.

103 *bonds*: papers promising to pay money to the bearer (an early form of cheque).

106 *some . . . matter*: a trivial thing.

114–115 *a stewed prune*: a bawd (stewed prunes were sold in brothels).

115 *drawn*: hunted; when 'drawn' out of its lair the fox would be especially cunning.

116–7 *Maid . . . thee*: compared to you, Maid Marian is a respectable woman. 'Maid Marian' was a character in the May Day morris dances; the part was played by a man, and was both grotesque and obscene.

117 *deputy's . . . ward*: wife of the deputy of the ward—the most responsible citizen in a section of the city.

118 *thing*: creature (the abuse is vague).

120 *to . . . on*: to be thankful to God for (once again, the abuse is vague, and the Hostess does not know how to react).

123 *setting . . . aside*: despite the fact that you are a knight (who should not insult a lady).

Prince

What! He did not?

Hostess

There's neither faith, truth, nor womanhood in me else.

Falstaff

There's no more faith in thee than in a stewed prune, nor no more truth in thee than in a drawn fox—and for womanhood, Maid Marian may be the deputy's wife of the ward to thee. Go, you thing, go!

Hostess

Say, what thing, what thing?

Falstaff

What thing? Why, a thing to thank God on.

Hostess

I am no thing to thank God on, I would thou shouldst know it! I am an honest man's wife, and setting thy knighthood aside, thou art a knave to call me so.

Falstaff

Setting thy womanhood aside, thou art a beast to say otherwise.

Hostess

Say, what beast, thou knave, thou?

Falstaff

What beast? Why, an otter.

Prince

An otter, Sir John? Why an otter?

Falstaff

Why? She's neither fish nor flesh; a man knows not where to have her.

Hostess

Thou art an unjust man in saying so. Thou or any man knows where to have me, thou knave, thou.

Prince

Thou say'st true, hostess, and he slanders thee most grossly.

Hostess

So he doth you, my lord, and said this other day you ought him a thousand pound.

Prince

Sirrah, do I owe you a thousand pound?

128 *an otter*: a small furry mammal that eats fish and lives mainly in water; scholars argued about whether it was fish or animal.

131 *where . . . her*: how to take her (i.e. understand her; *or* make sexual advances to her).
137 *ought*: owed.
141 *jack*: fellow (a term of mild abuse).
146 *as good as*: keep.
150 *lion*: Falstaff himself explains the meaning in his next line: the lion, as king of beasts, was a symbol of royalty.
154 *girdle*: belt.
158 *midriff*: stomach.
160 *embossed*: swollen.
161 *reckonings*: bills.
163 *long-winded*: sugar was given to fighting-cocks to improve their breathing (Falstaff needs it to help his drinking).
164 *injuries*: articles whose loss was an injury.
165 *stand to it*: insist that you are telling the truth.
166 *pocket up*: endure, tolerate.
168–9 *in the . . . fell*: when it was created the world was pure; even then Adam (the first man) committed a sin and lost ('fell' from) the grace of God (*Genesis* chapter 1).

Falstaff
A thousand pound, Hal? A million! Thy love is worth a million; thou owest me thy love.

Hostess
Nay, my lord, he called you jack, and said he would cudgel you.

Falstaff
Did I, Bardolph?

Bardolph
Indeed, Sir John, you said so.

Falstaff
Yea, if he said my ring was copper.

Prince
I say 'tis copper. Darest thou be as good as thy word now?

Falstaff
Why, Hal, thou knowest as thou art but man I dare, but as thou art prince, I fear thee as I fear the roaring of the lion's whelp.

Prince
And why not as the lion?

Falstaff
The King himself is to be feared as the lion: dost thou think I'll fear thee as I fear thy father? Nay, and I do, I pray God my girdle break.

Prince
O, if it should, how would thy guts fall about thy knees! But sirrah, there's no room for faith, truth, nor honesty in this bosom of thine; it is all filled up with guts and midriff. Charge an honest woman with picking thy pocket? Why, thou whoreson impudent, embossed rascal, if there were anything in thy pocket but tavern reckonings, memorandums of bawdy-houses, and one poor pennyworth of sugar-candy to make thee long-winded—if thy pocket were enriched with any other injuries but these, I am a villain: and yet you still stand to it, you will not pocket up wrong! Art thou not ashamed?

Falstaff
Dost thou hear, Hal? Thou knowest in the state of innocency Adam fell, and what should poor Jack Falstaff do in the days of villainy? Thou seest I

171–2 *more flesh . . . frailty*: there was a proverb, 'Flesh is frail'—meaning that humankind is (morally) weak and so *must* sin.

174 *by the story*: i.e. from the account Hal has already given of the contents of Falstaff's pocket.

177 *tractable*: obedient, responsive.

178 *pacified still*: always easily pacified.

179 *to*: we will turn our attention to.

180 What about the robbery? How have you explained that?

182 *beef*: ox.

be good angel: be your good angel (get you out of trouble).

184–5 *'Tis . . . labour*: it makes twice as much work (the first 'labour' was the robbery).

188 *exchequer*: government funds.

189 *with unwashed hands*: without delay (a proverbial expression).

191 *a charge of foot*: the command of an infantry regiment (foot-soldiers).

192 *I would . . . horse*: I wish it had been a cavalry regiment.

193 *one*: a man (Falstaff needs a servant).

194–5 *heinously unprovided*: terribly ill-equipped.

195–7 Falstaff welcomes the rebellion.

196 *laud*: praise.

have more flesh than another man, and therefore more frailty. You confess then, you picked my pocket?

Prince

It appears so by the story.

Falstaff

Hostess, I forgive thee! Go make ready breakfast, love thy husband, look to thy servants, cherish thy guests; thou shalt find me tractable to any honest reason. Thou seest I am pacified still—nay, prithee be gone. [*Exit* Hostess] Now, Hal, to the news at court: for the robbery, lad, how is that answered?

Prince

O my sweet beef, I must still be good angel to thee—the money is paid back again.

Falstaff

O, I do not like that paying back! 'Tis a double labour.

Prince

I am good friends with my father, and may do anything.

Falstaff

Rob me the exchequer the first thing thou dost, and do it with unwashed hands too.

Bardolph

Do, my lord.

Prince

I have procured thee, Jack, a charge of foot.

Falstaff

I would it had been of horse. Where shall I find one that can steal well? O for a fine thief of the age of two and twenty or thereabouts: I am heinously unprovided. Well, God be thanked for these rebels, they offend none but the virtuous; I laud them, I praise them.

Prince

Bardolph!

Bardolph

My lord?

Prince

Go bear this letter to Lord John of Lancaster, to

my brother John, this to my Lord of Westmoreland. [*Exit* Bardolph
Go, Peto, to horse, to horse; for thou and I have thirty miles to ride yet ere dinner-time. [*Exit* Peto
Jack, meet me tomorrow in the Temple hall at two o'clock in the afternoon: There shalt thou know thy charge, and there receive money and order for their furniture. The land is burning, Percy stands on high, and either we or they must lower lie. [*Exit*

Falstaff

Rare words! Brave world! Hostess, my breakfast, come!
O, I could wish this tavern were my drum. [*Exit*

205 *the Temple hall*: the hall of the Inner Temple (one of the Inns of Court in London).

207 *thy charge*: your regiment.
order: directions.

208 *furniture*: equipment.
The . . . burning: the country is on fire (= eager) for war.
Percy: the Percy family (i.e. the rebels); but Hal could also mean, specifically, Hotspur.

208–9 *stands on high*: has risen up.

211 *drum*: the soldiers of a regiment assembled round the regimental drum.

Act 4

Act 4 Scene 1
In the rebel camp, Hotspur is given the bad news that his father (the Earl of Northumberland) is unable to join the rebellion. At first he is angry, but he is quickly able to make the best of the situation, although Worcester is very depressed. Sir Richard Vernon brings news that now the King's forces, led by Prince Hal, are ready for the combat.

2 *fine*: refined (Hotspur is ironic).
3 *attribution*: praise.
the Douglas: the Earl of Douglas (Hotspur uses the correct form of address for the head of a Scottish family.)
4–5 No soldiers of the present time should be valued more highly throughout the world. Hotspur's metaphor is from coinage.
4 *stamp*: minting.
5 *current*: valued.
6 *defy*: despise.
7 *soothers*: flatterers.
braver: higher, more exalted.
9 *task . . . word*: put me to my word—give me a chance to show that I mean what I say.
approve: test.
10 *king of honour*: most honourable of men.
11 *potent*: powerful.
breathes . . . ground: i.e. is alive.
12 *beard*: confront, face.
13 *I . . . you*: these words are addressed to the Douglas.
16 *grievous*: seriously.
18 *justling*: unsettled, busy.
power: army.

Scene 1 *Shrewsbury: the Rebel Camp*

Enter Hotspur, Worcester, *and* Douglas

Hotspur
Well said, my noble Scot! If speaking truth
In this fine age were not thought flattery,
Such attribution should the Douglas have
As not a soldier of this season's stamp
Should go so general current through the world.
By God, I cannot flatter; I do defy
The tongues of soothers! But a braver place
In my heart's love hath no man than yourself:
Nay, task me to my word, approve me, lord.

Douglas
Thou art the king of honour:
No man so potent breathes upon the ground
But I will beard him.

Hotspur Do so, and 'tis well.

Enter a Messenger *with letters*

What letters hast thou there?—I can but thank you.

Messenger
These letters come from your father.

Hotspur
Letters from him? Why comes he not himself?

Messenger
He cannot come, my lord, he is grievous sick.

Hotspur
'Zounds, how has he the leisure to be sick
In such a justling time? Who leads his power?
Under whose government come they along?

Messenger
His letters bear his mind, not I, my lord.

Worcester
I prithee tell me, doth he keep his bed?

Messenger
He did, my lord, four days ere I set forth,
And at the time of my departure thence
He was much fear'd by his physicians.

Worcester
I would the state of time had first been whole
Ere he by sickness had been visited:
His health was never better worth than now.

Hotspur
Sick now? Droop now? This sickness doth infect
The very life-blood of our enterprise;
'Tis catching hither, even to our camp.
He writes me here that inward sickness—
And that his friends by deputation could not
So soon be drawn, nor did he think it meet
To lay so dangerous and dear a trust
On any soul remov'd but on his own.
Yet doth he give us bold advertisement
That with our small conjunction we should on,
To see how fortune is dispos'd to us;
For, as he writes, there is no quailing now,
Because the King is certainly possess'd
Of all our purposes. What say you to it?

Worcester
Your father's sickness is a maim to us.

Hotspur
A perilous gash, a very limb lopp'd off—
And yet, in faith, it is not! His present want
Seems more than we shall find it. Were it good
To set the exact wealth of all our states
All at one cast? To set so rich a main
On the nice hazard of one doubtful hour?
It were not good, for therein should we read
The very bottom and the soul of hope,
The very list, the very utmost bound
Of all our fortunes.

Douglas
Faith, and so we should, where now remains

21 *does . . . bed*: is he confined to bed?
22 *ere*: before.
24 *He*: his life (the doctors were afraid that he would die).
25 *state of time*: present situation.
whole: healthy.
26 *visited*: afflicted.
27 *better worth*: more important.
30 The infection will spread as far as the camp.
31 *writes me here*: tells me in this letter.
inward: internal.
32 *friends*: supporters.
by deputation: by means of a deputy (i.e. by someone else).
33 *drawn*: gathered together.
meet: right.
34 *dear*: important.
trust: responsibility.
35 *any . . . remov'd*: anyone not so closely concerned.
36 *advertisement*: advice.
37 *conjunction*: combined forces.
should on: should march on.
38 To see what luck we have.
39 *quailing*: hesitating.
40 *possess'd*: informed.
41 *purposes*: intentions.
42 *maim*: wound.
43 *a . . . off*: Hotspur continues the imagery of wounding by saying that the absence of his father is indeed as though a limb had been cut off.
44 *His . . . want*: the loss of him at the present time.
45 *Were it good*: would it be a good thing.
46 *set*: risk.
exact: total.
states: fortunes.
47 *cast*: throw of the dice.
main: store.
48 *nice hazard*: evenly balanced chance; 'hazard' is also the name of a gambling game played with dice.
hour: occasion.
49 *therein*: i.e. on that one occasion.
51 *list*: limit.
53 *where*: whereas.

54 *reversion*: inheritance.

54–5 *we may . . . in*: we can freely use what we have now, assured that more (soldiers) will be coming to our aid.

56 This (the knowledge that Northumberland's forces are yet to come) is a support we can retreat (retire) to.

58 *mischance*: misfortune, bad luck.
look big: threaten

59 *the maidenhead*: i.e. the beginning.

60 *would*: wish.

61 *hair*: nature.

62 *Brooks*: permits.

64 *mere*: pure, absolute.

66 *apprehension*: notion, interpretation of the situation.

67 *turn the tide*: change the opinions of.
fearful faction: timid rebellion.

68 *in*: about.

69 *off'ring*: challenging.

70 *keep . . . from*: avoid.
strict arbitrement: critical judgement.

71 *stop*: close.
loop: loop-hole.

73 *draws*: draws back.

74 *the ignorant*: i.e. those who do not know about Northumberland's sickness.

75 *strain too far*: exaggerate things.

76 *make this use*: see it this way.

77 *opinion*: prestige.

78 *a larger dare*: greater boldness.

80 *make a head*: form an army, make an attack.

82 *topsy-turvy down*: quite upside down.

83 *Yet*: at this moment.
our . . . whole: the different parts of our army are united.

84 *As . . . think*: as anyone could imagine.

87 *Pray . . . welcome*: I hope that my news is welcome.

A sweet reversion—we may boldly spend
Upon the hope of what is to come in.
A comfort of retirement lives in this.

Hotspur
A rendezvous, a home to fly unto,
If that the devil and mischance look big
Upon the maidenhead of our affairs.

Worcester
But yet I would your father had been here.
The quality and hair of our attempt
Brooks no division; it will be thought,
By some that know not why he is away,
That wisdom, loyalty, and mere dislike
Of our proceedings kept the Earl from hence.
And think how such an apprehension
May turn the tide of fearful faction,
And breed a kind of question in our cause.
For well you know we of the off'ring side
Must keep aloof from strict arbitrement,
And stop all sight-holes, every loop from whence
The eye of reason may pry in upon us.
This absence of your father's draws a curtain
That shows the ignorant a kind of fear
Before not dreamt of.

Hotspur You strain too far.
I rather of his absence make this use:
It lends a lustre and more great opinion,
A larger dare to our great enterprise,
Than if the Earl were here; for men must think,
If we without his help can make a head
To push against a kingdom, with his help
We shall o'erturn it topsy-turvy down.
Yet all goes well, yet all our joints are whole.

Douglas
As heart can think. There is not such a word
Spoke of in Scotland as this term of fear.

Enter Sir Richard Vernon

Hotspur
My cousin Vernon! Welcome, by my soul!

Vernon
Pray God my news be worth a welcome, lord.

88 *seven . . . strong*: with an army of seven thousand.

91–2 *is . . . speedily*: has already started out, or else intends to march here very soon.

93 *preparation*: forces.

96 *daff'd*: tossed (i.e. ignored what was happening or being said in the world).

97 *bid it pass*: let it [the world] go its own way.

furnish'd: prepared for battle.

98–9 They are all wearing plumes like ostriches that beat their wings with the wind, just like eagles which have recently bathed.

100 *images*: statues (which were often gilded).

103 *Wanton*: lively.

104 *beaver*: helmet.

105 *cushes*: armour to protect the thighs.

106 *feather'd Mercury*: the messenger of the classical gods had wings on his sandals and cap.

The Earl of Westmoreland, seven thousand strong,
Is marching hitherwards, with him Prince John.

Hotspur
No harm. What more?

Vernon And further, I have learn'd,
The King himself in person is set forth,
Or hitherwards intended speedily,
With strong and mighty preparation.

Hotspur
He shall be welcome too: where is his son,
The nimble-footed madcap Prince of Wales,
And his comrades that daff'd the world aside
And bid it pass?

Vernon All furnish'd, all in arms;
All plum'd like estridges that with the wind
Bated, like eagles having lately bath'd;
Glittering in golden coats like images;

107 Only a very strong and skilful man could mount a horse easily when he was wearing full armour.

109 *turn and wind*: technical terms of horsemanship; 'wind' = wheel about.
fiery: spirited.
Pegasus: a winged horse (in the classical mythology) which no mortal could ride.

110 *witch*: bewitch.

111–2 *the sun . . . agues*: it was thought that the early spring sun (in March) caused ague—whose symptoms were fever and shivering.

113 *sacrifices . . . trim*: sacrificial beasts with their decorations.

114 *the fire-ey'd maid*: the goddess of war—Bellona.

116 *the mailed Mars*: Mars (the classical god of war) in armour (mail).

118 *reprisal*: prize.
nigh: near.

119 *taste*: try, get the feel of.

122–3 *Harry . . . Meet*: one Harry (himself) will meet another (Prince Hal), with one eager horse against another.

123 *drop . . . corse*: fall lifeless.

126 *draw his power*: gather his army.
this . . . days: for another fortnight.

127 *tidings*: news.

128 *bears . . . sound*: sounds bad.

129 How big is the King's army, as a whole?

130 *Forty . . . be*: even if it were forty (thousand).

132 *The . . . us*: our own soldiers.
may serve: will be enough for.

133 *muster*: roll-call.

134 *Doomsday*: the Day of Judgement.
die all, die merrily: if we all die, we shall die happily.

As full of spirit as the month of May,
And gorgeous as the sun at midsummer;
Wanton as youthful goats, wild as young bulls.
I saw young Harry with his beaver on,
His cushes on his thighs, gallantly arm'd,
Rise from the ground like feather'd Mercury,
And vaulted with such ease into his seat
As if an angel dropp'd down from the clouds
To turn and wind a fiery Pegasus,
And witch the world with noble horsemanship.

Hotspur
No more, no more! Worse than the sun in March,
This praise doth nourish agues. Let them come!
They come like sacrifices in their trim,
And to the fire-ey'd maid of smoky war
All hot and bleeding will we offer them.
The mailed Mars shall on his altar sit
Up to the ears in blood. I am on fire
To hear this rich reprisal is so nigh,
And yet not ours! Come, let me taste my horse,
Who is to bear me like a thunderbolt
Against the bosom of the Prince of Wales.
Harry to Harry shall, hot to horse to horse,
Meet and ne'er part till one drop down a corse.
O that Glendower were come!

Vernon There is more news:
I learn'd in Worcester as I rode along
He cannot draw his power this fourteen days.

Douglas
That's the worst tidings that I hear of yet.

Worcester
Ay, by my faith, that bears a frosty sound.

Hotspur
What may the King's whole battle reach unto?

Vernon
To thirty thousand.

Hotspur Forty let it be!
My father and Glendower being both away,
The powers of us may serve so great a day.
Come, let us take a muster speedily.
Doomsday is near; die all, die merrily.

Douglas

Talk not of dying, I am out of fear
Of death or death's hand for this one half year.

[*Exeunt*

135 *I am . . . fear*: I have not been afraid.

136 *Of death . . . hand*: of dying, or of the way in which I die.

for . . . year: for the past six months.

Scene 2 *A Road near Coventry*

Enter Falstaff *and* Bardolph

Falstaff

Bardolph, get thee before to Coventry; fill me a bottle of sack. Our soldiers shall march through; we'll to Sutton Co'fil' tonight.

Bardolph

Will you give me money, captain?

Falstaff

Lay out, lay out.

Bardolph

This bottle makes an angel.

Falstaff

And if it do, take if for thy labour—and if it make twenty, take them all; I'll answer the coinage. Bid my lieutenant Peto meet me at town's end.

Bardolph

I will, captain: farewell. [*Exit*

Falstaff

If I be not ashamed of my soldiers, I am a soused gurnet; I have misused the King's press damnably. I have got, in exchange of a hundred and fifty soldiers, three hundred and odd pounds. I press me none but good householders, yeomen's sons; inquire me out contracted bachelors, such as had been asked twice on the banns—such a commodity of warm slaves as had as lief hear the devil as a drum, such as fear the report of a caliver worse than a struck fowl or a hurt wild duck. I pressed me none but such toasts-and-butter, with hearts in their bellies no bigger than pins' heads, and they have bought out their services; and now my whole charge consists of ancients, corporals, lieutenants, gentlemen of companies—slaves as ragged as Lazarus in the painted cloth, where the glutton's dogs licked his sores: and such as indeed

Act 4 Scene 2
Falstaff and his soldiers are marching to join the King's forces. But Falstaff has recruited only poor men: those who could afford the bribe have been left at home (and Falstaff has taken their money for himself).

1 *get thee before*: you go on ahead.

3 *we'll to*: we will march to.

Sutton Co'fil': Sutton Coldfield, 20 miles from Coventry (although not in the right direction for Shrewsbury—see map p. xxxiv).

5 *lay out*: use your own money (instead of the official expenses).

6 *makes*: brings the amount up to.

an angel: a gold coin bearing the image of the archangel Michael.

7 *And . . . do*: if it does.

take . . . labour: Falstaff pretends to take the literal meaning of Bardolph's words (i.e. that the bottle is *making* a coin), and offers the money as a tip.

8 *answer*: be responsible for (coining money was illegal).

9 *town's end*: outside the town.

11 *soused*: pickled; a *gurnet* was a small fish.

12 *the King's press*: officers were given a commission from the King to conscript ('press') men into their regiments.

13 *of*: for.

14 *and odd*: and a few more.

15 *press . . . but*: force into service only.

good: wealthy.

15–16 *yeomen's sons*: the sons of farmers who owned their small farms.

were never soldiers, but discarded unjust serving-men, younger sons to younger brothers, revolted tapsters, and ostlers trade-fallen, the cankers of a calm world and a long peace, ten times more dishonourable-ragged than an old fazed ancient. And such have I to fill up the rooms of them as have bought out their services, that you would think that I had a hundred and fifty tattered prodigals lately come from swine-keeping, from eating draff and husks. A mad fellow met me on the way, and told me I had unloaded all the gibbets and pressed the dead bodies. No eye hath seen such scarecrows. I'll not march through Coventry with them, that's flat. Nay, and the villains march wide betwixt the legs as if they had gyves on, for indeed I had the most of them out of prison. There's not a shirt and a half in all my company, and the half shirt is two napkins tacked together and thrown over the shoulders like a herald's coat

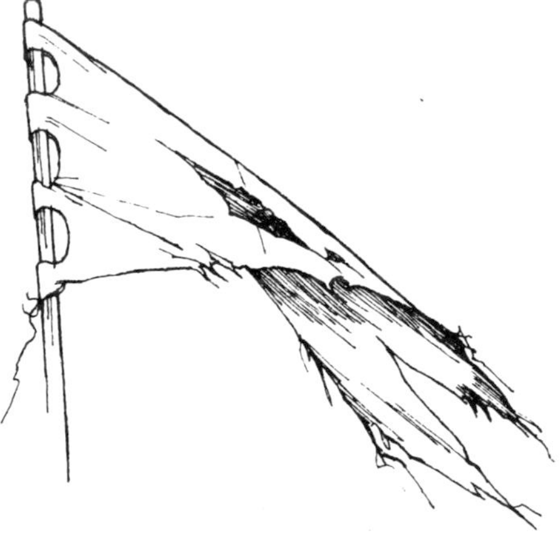

16 *inquire me out*: search out.
contracted bachelors: men engaged to be married; announcements of intended marriages were made in church (the 'banns' were 'asked') on three occasions before the wedding could take place.

18 *commodity*: collection.
warm slaves: cowards with plenty of money.
had as lief: would rather.

19 *the . . . caliver*: the bang of a gun.

20 *struck*: wounded.

21 *toasts-and-butter*: weaklings.

22 *bellies*: bodies.

23 *bought . . . services*: bought themselves out of the service (i.e. bribed Falstaff to release them).

24 *charge*: company (the soldiers he commands).
ancients: ensigns (the lowest rank of officer).

25 *gentlemen of companies*: men who were neither common soldiers nor officers.

26 *Lazarus*: the beggar in the parable of Dives (St Luke's Gospel, 16:19–31; see also *Act 3*, Scene 3, lines 32–3).
painted cloth: cloths painted with pictures were a cheap substitute for tapestry.

27 *the glutton*: i.e. Dives.

28–9 *discarded . . . men*: dishonest servants who had lost their jobs (been 'discarded').

29 *younger . . . brothers*: in English law, the eldest son inherited his father's property; his younger brother could hope for little—and the younger son of this brother would have no expectations.

29–30 *revolted tapsters*: inn-servants who have broken their apprenticeships—as Hal teasingly suggests to Francis in *Act 2* Scene 4.

30 *trade-fallen*: unemployed because trade is poor.

cankers: parasites.

30–31 *a calm . . . peace*: the Elizabethans believed that war was useful in creating jobs for men who could find no employment in a time of peace.

32 *dishonourable-ragged*: ragged in a dishonourable way.

fazed: tattered.

ancient: ensign—the flag carried into battle.

33 *fill . . . rooms*: take the places.

36–7 *prodigals . . . husks*: the parable of the Prodigal Son is told in St Luke's Gospel (15:16): the son wasted his inheritance, and then found a job guarding pigs; he was so hungry that he ate the food of the swine ('draff and husks').

38–9 *unloaded . . . bodies*: taken the bodies from the gallows and conscripted them into his regiment.

41 *flat*: certain.

41–2 *march . . . gyves on*: march with their legs wide apart, as though they were in chains ('gyves') (i.e. like convicts chained together).

43 *had*: got.

45 *tacked*: roughly stitched.

46 *a herald's coat*: a tabard.

48 *my host*: the inn-keeper.

49 *that's all one*: that doesn't matter.

50 *linen . . . hedge*: Elizabethan housewives spread their washing on the hedges to dry (and Falstaff will encourage his men to steal).

51 *blown . . . quilt*: Hal makes two puns: 'blown' = out of breath *and* swollen; 'Jack' is *both* a familiar form of 'John' *and* the word for a soldier's padded (quilted) jacket.

52 *wag*: joker.

54 *cry you mercy*: beg your pardon.

55 *had . . . Shrewsbury*: would have been at Shrewsbury by this time.

without sleeves; and the shirt to say the truth stolen from my host at Saint Albans, or the red-nose innkeeper of Daventry. But that's all one, they'll find linen enough on every hedge.

Enter the Prince *and the* Lord of Westmoreland

Prince

How now, blown Jack? How now, quilt?

Falstaff

What, Hal! How now, mad wag? What a devil dost thou in Warwickshire? My good Lord of Westmoreland, I cry you mercy; I thought your honour had already been at Shrewsbury.

Westmoreland

Faith, Sir John, 'tis more than time that I were

57 *powers*: soldiers.

58 *looks for*: is expecting.

59 *away all night*: march throughout the night.

60 *never fear me*: don't worry about me.

vigilant: alert and ready.

62–3 *I think . . . butter*: I think you must certainly have been stealing cream—that is what has made you so fat (butter is made from cream).

64 *come after*: are following.

67 *toss*: i.e. on the pikes of the enemies.

food for powder: cannon-fodder (good enough to be shot at).

68 *they'll . . . better*: their dead bodies can be thrown into a pit as well as those of better men.

69 *mortal men*: human beings who have got to die some time.

71 *bare*: ragged; *and* thin.

72 *had*: got.

73 *bareness*: thinness.

75–6 *three . . . ribs*: fat on the ribs as thick as three fingers.

77 *in the field*: prepared for battle.

78 *is . . . encamped*: has the King set up his camp.

81–3 *To . . . guest*: a proverbial saying.

81 *fray*: fight.

83 *dull*: unwitting.

keen: eager.

there, and you too, but my powers are there already; the King I can tell you looks for us all; we must away all night.

Falstaff

Tut, never fear me: I am as vigilant as a cat to steal cream.

Prince

I think, to steal cream indeed, for thy theft hath already made thee butter. But tell me, Jack, whose fellows are these that come after?

Falstaff

Mine, Hal, mine.

Prince

I did never see such pitiful rascals.

Falstaff

Tut, tut, good enough to toss, food for powder, food for powder; they'll fill a pit as well as better. Tush, man, mortal men, mortal men.

Westmoreland

Ay, but, Sir John, methinks they are exceeding poor and bare, too beggarly.

Falstaff

Faith, for their poverty I know not where they had that; and for their bareness I am sure they never learned that of me.

Prince

No, I'll be sworn, unless you call three fingers in the ribs bare. But sirrah, make haste; Percy is already in the field. [*Exit*

Falstaff

What, is the King encamped?

Westmoreland

He is, Sir John; I fear we shall stay too long. [*Exit*

Falstaff

Well,
To the latter end of a fray, and the beginning of a feast
Fits a dull fighter and a keen guest. [*Exit*

Act 4 Scene 3
Hotspur is eager to start fighting at once, but his friends try to dissuade him. Their discussion is interrupted by Sir Walter Blunt, who brings a message of peace from the King. Hotspur does not want peace, and he recites the list of the rebels' grievances and the King's broken promises; but he agrees to wait until morning before sending his reply to the King.

2 *You . . . advantage*: Douglas argues that a delay will be an advantage to the King.
whit: bit.

3 *Looks . . . supply*: isn't he expecting reinforcements (extra troops).

6 *counsel*: advise.

9 *maintain . . . life*: prove my courage by giving up my life.

10 *well-respected*: well-considered.
bid me on: tells me to go out and fight.

11 *I . . . with*: take as little notice of.

17 *leading*: experience.

19 *Drag . . . expedition*: prevent us from moving fast.
horse: cavalry.

24 *not . . . himself*: not one of the horses has a fraction of its usual strength.

Scene 3 *Shrewsbury: the Rebel Camp*

Enter Hotspur, Worcester, Douglas, Vernon

Hotspur
We'll fight with him tonight.
Worcester It may not be.
Douglas
You give him then advantage.
Vernon Not a whit.
Hotspur
Why say you so? Looks he not for supply?
Vernon
So do we.
Hotspur His is certain, ours is doubtful.
Worcester
Good cousin, be advis'd, stir not tonight.
Vernon
Do not, my lord.
Douglas You do not counsel well.
You speak it out of fear and cold heart.
Vernon
Do me no slander, Douglas; by my life—
And I dare well maintain it with my life—
If well-respected honour bid me on,
I hold as little counsel with weak fear
As you, my lord, or any Scot that this day lives;
Let it be seen tomorrow in the battle
Which of us fears.
Douglas Yea, or tonight.
Vernon Content.
Hotspur
Tonight, say I.
Vernon
Come, come, it may not be. I wonder much,
Being men of such great leading as you are,
That you foresee not what impediments
Drag back our expedition: certain horse
Of my cousin Vernon's are not yet come up;
Your uncle Worcester's horse came but today,
And now their pride and mettle is asleep,
Their courage with hard labour tame and dull,
That not a horse is half the half himself.

26 *journey-bated*: tired with travelling.
brought low: in poor condition.
27 *full of rest*: well rested.
29 *stay . . . in*: wait until everyone has arrived.
29sd *sounds a parley*: calls to summon them to a discussion.
31 If you will agree to listen and take notice of what I say.
33 *of our determination*: on our side.
35 Are reluctant to praise you and give you the honour ('good name') that you deserve.
36 *of our quality*: on our side.
37 *stand against*: oppose.
38 *defend*: forbid.
still: always.

Hotspur
So are the horses of the enemy
In general journey-bated and brought low.
The better part of ours are full of rest.
Worcester
The number of the King exceedeth ours.
For God's sake, cousin, stay till all come in.
[*The trumpet sounds a parley*

Enter Sir Walter Blunt

Blunt
I come with gracious offers from the King,
If you vouchsafe me hearing and respect.
Hotspur
Welcome, Sir Walter Blunt: and would to God

39 *out of limit*: beyond the bounds of your allegiance.
true rule: proper conduct.
41 *to my charge*: let me say what I have been commanded to say.
42 *griefs*: grievances.
whereupon: for what reason.
43 *conjure*: call up (as though by magic).
the . . . peace: the hearts of peace-loving citizens.
44 *duteous land*: law-abiding nation.
46 *your good deserts*: the good deeds you have done which should be rewarded.
47 And he admits that there are very many of these (the 'good deserts').
49 *your . . . interest*: all that you want—and more.
50 *absolute*: unconditional.
50–51 *these . . . suggestion*: those who have been led astray through your influence.
52 *kind*: Hotspur is sarcastic.
52–3 *well . . . pay*: we know how the King makes promises which he never keeps.
55 *royalty*: the title of 'king', the crown.
56 *he was . . . strong*: he had no more than 26 supporters.
57 *sick*: poor.
regard: opinion.
58 *unminded*: ignored.
61 *came . . . Lancaster*: see p. v.
but: only.
62 *sue his livery*: ask for the deliverance of his lands.
63 *terms of zeal*: declarations of sincerity.
64 *in . . . mov'd*: out of the kindness of his heart and because he was sorry for him.
65 Promised to give him help, and did help him.
67 *lean to him*: take his side (against Richard II).
68 *The more and less*: both high and low (the nobles and the common people).
with cap and knee: taking off their hats and bowing (in sign of respect).

You were of our determination!
Some of us love you well, and even those some
Envy your great deservings and good name,
Because you are not of our quality,
But stand against us like an enemy.

Blunt

And God defend but still I should stand so,
So long as out of limit and true rule
You stand against anointed majesty.
But to my charge. The King hath sent to know
The nature of your griefs, and whereupon
You conjure from the breast of civil peace
Such bold hostility, teaching his duteous land
Audacious cruelty. If that the King
Have any way your good deserts forgot,
Which he confesseth to be manifold,
He bids you name your griefs, and with all speed
You shall have your desires with interest,
And pardon absolute for yourself and these
Herein misled by your suggestion.

Hotspur

The King is kind, and well we know the King
Knows at what time to promise, when to pay.
My father, and my uncle, and myself
Did give him that same royalty he wears;
And when he was not six and twenty strong,
Sick in the world's regard, wretched and low,
A poor unminded outlaw sneaking home,
My father gave him welcome to the shore;
And when he heard him swear and vow to God
He came but to be Duke of Lancaster,
To sue his livery, and beg his peace,
With tears of innocency and terms of zeal,
My father, in kind heart and pity mov'd,
Swore him assistance, and perform'd it too.
Now when the lords and barons of the realm
Perceiv'd Northumberland did lean to him,
The more and less came in with cap and knee,
Met him in boroughs, cities, villages,

70 *Attended*: waited for.
in lanes: in rows (so Bolingbroke could walk between them).
71 *proffer'd . . . oaths*: swore oaths of allegiance.
72 *Gave . . . pages*: i.e. the noblemen sent their sons to attend Bolingbroke as pageboys (a sign of their allegiance).
73 *Even . . . heels*: close behind him.
golden: richly dressed; *and* promising success.
74 *presently*: immediately.
as . . . itself: as he began to recognize his power.
75 *Steps . . . higher*: climb a bit above.
76 *blood*: spirit.
poor: humble.
77 *naked*: barren.
78 *forsooth*: indeed.
79 *certain*: particular.
strait: strict.
81 *Cries out upon*: exposes.
82 *by this face*: with this appearance.
83 *This . . . justice*: pretending to be concerned with justice.
84 *angle for*: fish for, try to catch.
87 *In deputation*: as substitutes to rule for him (see p. iv).
88 *was personal in*: went himself to.
92 *in the neck of*: immediately after.
task'd: taxed.
93 *suffer'd*: allowed.
March: the Earl of March (Mortimer).
94 *if . . . plac'd*: if everyone had his proper title.
95 *his king*: see p. 126.
engag'd: held prisoner.
96 To be kept there, unredeemed, because no ransom was paid.
97 *Disgrac'd*: discredited.
happy: splendid.
98 *intelligence*: secret information (provided by spies).
99 *Rates*: dismissed with abuse.
103 *head of safety*: army in self-defence.
withal: also.
103–4 *to pry . . . title*: to investigate his claim to the throne.

Attended him on bridges, stood in lanes,
Laid gifts before him, proffer'd him their oaths,
Gave him their heirs as pages, follow'd him
Even at the heels in golden multitudes.
He presently, as greatness knows itself,
Steps me a little higher than his vow
Made to my father while his blood was poor
Upon the naked shore at Ravenspurgh;
And now, forsooth, takes on him to reform
Some certain edicts and some strait decrees
That lie too heavy on the commonwealth;
Cries out upon abuses, seems to weep
Over his country's wrongs; and by this face,
This seeming brow of justice, did he win
The hearts of all that he did angle for;
Proceeded further—cut me off the heads
Of all the favourites that the absent King
In deputation left behind him here,
When he was personal in the Irish war.

Blunt

Tut, I came not to hear this.

Hotspur

Then to the point.
In short time after, he depos'd the King;
Soon after that depriv'd him of his life;
And in the neck of that, task'd the whole state;
To make that worse, suffer'd his kinsman March
(Who is, if every owner were well plac'd,
Indeed his king) to be engag'd in Wales,
There without ransom to lie forfeited;
Disgrac'd me in my happy victories,
Sought to entrap me by intelligence,
Rated mine uncle from the Council-board;
In rage dismiss'd my father from the court;
Broke oath on oath, committed wrong on wrong,
And in conclusion drove us to seek out
This head of safety, and withal to pry
Into his title—the which we find
Too indirect for long continuance.

Blunt

Shall I return this answer to the King?

Hotspur

Not so, Sir Walter. We'll withdraw awhile.
Go to the King, and let there be impawn'd

105 *too indirect*: not in a sufficiently straight line of descent (see p. vi); *and* morally doubtful (see p. v).

for . . . continuance: to last long.

108–9 *let . . . again*: let someone (from the King's army) remain with us as a pledge ('be impawn'd' as 'surety') that my uncle shall return safely.

110 *mine uncle*: i.e. Worcester.

111 *Bring . . . purposes*: go to the King and tell him our intentions.

112 *I would*: I wish.

Some surety for a safe return again,
And in the morning early shall mine uncle
Bring him our purposes—and so, farewell.

Blunt
I would you would accept of grace and love.

Hotspur
And may be so we shall.

Blunt Pray God you do. [*Exeunt*

Act 4 Scene 4
The Archbishop of York (who supports the rebels against the King) is sending letters to his friends, asking for assistance. He explains that the rebels are not as powerful as they had hoped to be, and he is afraid that they will be defeated by the King's army.

1 *Hie*: hurry.

sealed brief: letter with the Archbishop's seal.

2 *winged haste*: as fast as if you could fly.

the Lord Marshal: Thomas Mowbray, Duke of Norfolk.

3 *my cousin Scroop*: several members of the Scroop family supported the rebels' cause; the Archbishop himself was Lord Scroop.

4 *directed*: addressed.

5 *How . . . import*: how important they are.

7 *tenor*: purpose.

10 *bide the touch*: be tested.

12 *quick-raised power*: an army which has been very quickly formed.

13 *Lord Harry*: Hotspur (Lord Harry Percy).

15 Whose army was the largest.

17 *rated sinew*: valuable source of strength.

18 *comes not in*: will not be joining the rebels.

o'er-rul'd by prophecies: deterred by evil omens.

Scene 4 *York: the Archbishop's Palace*

Enter the Archbishop of York *and* Sir Michael

Archbishop
Hie, good Sir Michael, bear this sealed brief
With winged haste to the Lord Marshal;
This to my cousin Scroop; and all the rest
To whom they are directed. If you knew
How much they do import, you would make haste.

Sir Michael
My good lord,
I guess their tenor.

Archbishop Like enough you do.
Tomorrow, good Sir Michael, is a day
Wherein the fortune of ten thousand men
Must bide the touch; for, sir, at Shrewsbury,
As I am truly given to understand,
The King with mighty and quick-raised power
Meets with Lord Harry: and I fear, Sir Michael,
What with the sickness of Northumberland,
Whose power was in the first proportion,
And what with Owen Glendower's absence thence,
Who with them was a rated sinew too,
And comes not in, o'er-rul'd by prophecies,

I fear the power of Percy is too weak
To wage an instant trial with the King.

Sir Michael

Why, my good lord, you need not fear,
There is Douglas, and Lord Mortimer.

Archbishop

No, Mortimer is not there.

Sir Mortimer

But there is Mordake, Vernon, Lord Harry Percy,
And there is my Lord of Worcester, and a head
Of gallant warriors, noble gentlemen.

Archbishop

And so there is; but yet the King hath drawn
The special head of all the land together:
The Prince of Wales, Lord John of Lancaster,
The noble Westmoreland, and warlike Blunt,
And many mo corrivals and dear men
Of estimation and command in arms.

Sir Michael

Doubt not, my lord, they shall be well oppos'd.

Archbishop

I hope no less, yet needful 'tis to fear;
And to prevent the worst, Sir Michael, speed.
For if Lord Percy thrive not, ere the King
Dismiss his power he means to visit us,
For he hath heard of our confederacy,
And 'tis but wisdom to make strong against him:
Therefore make haste. I must go write again
To other friends; and so, farewell, Sir Michael.

[*Exeunt*

20 *wage*: fight.
instant: immediate.

25 *head*: army.

27–8 *drawn . . . together*: assembled the finest army of the country.

31 *mo*: more.
corrivals: partners.
dear: noble.

32 *estimation*: high reputation.
command in arms: experienced warriors.

33 *they . . . oppos'd*: their opponents will fight well.

34 *needful 'tis*: it is necessary.

36 *thrive not*: does not conquer.
ere: before.

38 *our confederacy*: our plotting with the rebels.

39 *make strong*: defend ourselves strongly.

Act 5

Act 5 Scene 1
The King's army has gathered at Shrewsbury. The Earl of Worcester comes from the rebel camp and reminds the King of the rebels' grievances. The Prince of Wales sends a challenge to Hotspur, offering to fight him in single combat rather than risk the lives of thousands of men in a full battle. The King offers peace and forgiveness if the rebels will yield. The scene ends with the parting of Hal and Falstaff, and Falstaff's meditation on the subject of honour.

1–3 *How . . . distemp'rature*: in England, a red sky at sunrise is often a sign that the day will be wet or stormy.

2 *yon*: yonder.

3 *distemp'rature*: disorder.

The southern wind: the south wind brings stormy weather in England.

4 *play . . . purposes*: blows like a trumpet to announce the coming events (as a herald would do).

his: i.e. the sun's.

10 *upon such terms*: in such a relationship (i.e. as enemies).

12 *doff*: throw off.

easy: comfortable.

15 *unknit*: untangle.

16 *churlish*: brutal.

all-abhorred: utterly hateful, hated by everyone.

17 The King compares the rebels to stars, which should each move in a fixed orbit ('obedient orb').

19 *exhal'd*: displaced.

20 *prodigy of fear*: fearful monster.

21 Of trouble that has exploded now and will affect future generations.

Scene 1 *Shrewsbury: the King's Camp*

Enter the King, Prince of Wales, Lord John of Lancaster, Sir Walter Blunt, Falstaff

King
How bloodily the sun begins to peer
Above yon bulky hill! The day looks pale
At his distemp'rature.

Prince The southern wind
Doth play the trumpet to his purposes,
And by his hollow whistling in the leaves
Foretells a tempest and a blust'ring day.

King
Then with the losers let it sympathize,
For nothing can seem foul to those that win.
[*The trumpet sounds*

Enter Worcester *and* Vernon

How now, my Lord of Worcester! 'Tis not well
That you and I should meet upon such terms
As now we meet. You have deceiv'd our trust,
And made us doff our easy robes of peace
To crush our old limbs in ungentle steel:
This is not well, my lord, this is not well.
What say you to it? Will you again unknit
This churlish knot of all-abhorred war,
And move in that obedient orb again
Where you did give a fair and natural light,
And be no more an exhal'd meteor,
A prodigy of fear, and a portent
Of broached mischief to the unborn times?

Worcester
Hear me, my liege:

For mine own part, I could be well content
To entertain the lag-end of my life
With quiet hours. For I protest
I have not sought the day of this dislike.

King

You have not sought it? How comes it, then?

Falstaff

Rebellion lay in his way, and he found it.

Prince

Peace, chewet, peace!

Worcester

It pleas'd your Majesty to turn your looks
Of favour from myself and all our house;
And yet I must remember you, my lord,
We were the first and dearest of your friends:
For you my staff of office did I break
In Richard's time, and posted day and night
To meet you on the way, and kiss your hand,
When yet you were, in place and in account,
Nothing so strong and fortunate as I.
It was myself, my brother, and his son,
That brought you home, and boldly did outdare
The dangers of the time. You swore to us,
And you did swear that oath at Doncaster,
That you did nothing purpose 'gainst the state,
Nor claim no further than your new-fall'n right—
The seat of Gaunt, dukedom of Lancaster.
To this we swore our aid. But in short space
It rain'd down fortune show'ring on your head,
And such a flood of greatness fell on you,
What with our help, what with the absent King,
What with the injuries of a wanton time,
The seeming sufferances that you had borne,
And the contrarious winds that held the King
So long in his unlucky Irish wars
That all in England did repute him dead:
And from this swarm of fair advantages
You took occasion to be quickly woo'd
To gripe the general sway into your hand;
Forgot your oath to us at Doncaster;
And being fed by us, you us'd us so
As that ungentle gull, the cuckoo's bird,
Useth the sparrow—did oppress our nest,

24 *lag-end*: last days.

26 *I . . . sought*: I did not want.
dislike: enmity.

29 *chewet*: jackdaw (= chatterbox).

32 *remember*: remind.

34–5 *For you . . . time*: when Worcester joined the rebels, he gave up the stewardship of Richard II's household and broke the white rod (which was the symbol of this office).

35 *posted*: galloped.

36 *kiss your hand*: as a sign of allegiance.

37–8 When you were still very much inferior to me.

37 *yet*: still, as yet.
place: status, position.
account: public opinion.

38 *Nothing*: nothing like.

43 *did . . . 'gainst*: had no hostile intentions against.

44 *further*: more.
new-fall'n right: what had recently become your right (by the death of his father, John of Gaunt).

45 *seat*: property.

46 *space*: time.

49 *the absent king*: Richard II was not in England when Bolingbroke returned from exile.

50 *injuries*: abuses.
wanton: badly governed.

51 *seeming sufferances*: apparent hardships.

52 *contrarious*: contrary.

54 *repute*: believe.

56 *woo'd*: persuaded.

57 *gripe*: grab.
general sway: rule of the whole kingdom.

59–61 *you . . . sparrow*: you made use of us in the same way that the young cuckoo—a wretched nestling ('gull')—makes use of the sparrow. (The cuckoo does not build a nest, but lays its eggs in the nests of smaller birds, such as the sparrow; eventually the young cuckoo pushes the sparrow's own young out of the nest—or it might even eat them.)

63 *our love*: we who loved you.
durst: dare.
64 *swallowing*: being swallowed.
66 *head*: army.
67 *Whereby*: because of this (i.e. Bolingbroke's behaviour as a 'cuckoo's bird').
opposed: in conflict with each other.
by such means: for such reasons.
68 *forg'd*: created (Worcester speaks as though the King had himself made the weapons—swords—with which they now fight.)
69 *unkind*: discourteous; *also* unnatural.
dangerous countenance: threatening appearance.
70 *troth*: trust.
71 *younger*: earlier (i.e. the plan to recover his own property).
72 *articulate*: announced.
73 *market crosses*: the stone cross in the centre of the market-place was the general meeting-point for citizens, where they would hear most of the news and official announcements.
74 *face*: decorate.
75 *colour*: excuse (as well as the word's usual sense).
76 *fickle changelings*: those who easily change their allegiances.
poor discontents: wretches who are never satisfied with anything.
77 *gape*: stand open-mouthed.
rub the elbow: hug themselves with delight (it was believed that joy made the elbows itch).
78 *hurlyburly innovation*: a revolution which will turn things upside down.
79 *want*: lack.
80 *water-colours*: i.e. weak excuses ('water-colours' are paints that can easily be washed away).
impaint: paint.
his: its.
81 *moody*: sullen.
82 *pellmell*: riotous.
85 *they . . . trial*: the armies engage in battle.

Grew by our feeding to so great a bulk
That even our love durst not come near your sight
For fear of swallowing; but with nimble wing
We were enforc'd for safety sake to fly
Out of your sight, and raise this present head;
Whereby we stand opposed by such means
As you yourself have forg'd against yourself
By unkind usage, dangerous countenance,
And violation of all faith and troth
Sworn to us in your younger enterprise.

King

These things, indeed, you have articulate,
Proclaim'd at market crosses, read in churches,
To face the garment of rebellion
With some fine colour that may please the eye
Of fickle changelings and poor discontents,
Which gape and rub the elbow at the news
Of hurlyburly innovation;
And never yet did insurrection want
Such water-colours to impaint his cause,
Nor moody beggars, starving for a time
Of pellmell havoc and confusion.

Prince

In both your armies there is many a soul
Shall pay full dearly for this encounter,
If once they join in trial. Tell your nephew,

87 *hopes*: i.e. of salvation after death.
88 If we forget this responsibility ('set off his head') for the present business.
89 *braver*: finer.
90 *active-valiant*: valiant in action (i.e. courageous in war).
valiant-young: valiant (courageous) in his youth.
92 *latter*: modern.
93 *I . . . shame*: I am ashamed to have to say this.
94 I have been absent from the heroic world of chivalry (as a schoolboy is absent from school—playing 'truant').
95 *account me*: consider me (i.e. as a 'truant').
96 Yet let me say this in front of His Majesty the King, my father.
97 *odds*: advantages.
98 *estimation*: reputation.
100 *Try fortune*: risk my chances.
101–3 The King would have confidence in his son, but he can see too many political difficulties in such a single combat.
102 *Albeit*: yet on the other hand.
considerations infinite: an infinite number of considerations.
103 *make against it*: make it undesirable.
104 *even . . . love*: we love even those.
105 Who are misguided enough to fight on your relation's side ('cousin' here has its vague, non-specific, meaning of 'relative').
106 *will they take*: if they will accept.
grace: pardon.
107 *yea*: indeed.
111 *dread correction*: dreadful punishment.
wait on us: are in my power.
112 *do their office*: be used appropriately.
114 We are making a fair offer; think about it carefully.
117 Think they can fight against the whole world.

The Prince of Wales doth join with all the world
In praise of Henry Percy: by my hopes,
This present enterprise set off his head,
I do not think a braver gentleman,
More active-valiant or more valiant-young,
More daring or more bold, is now alive
To grace this latter age with noble deeds.
For my part (I may speak it to my shame),
I have a truant been to chivalry,
And so I hear he doth account me too;
Yet this before my father's majesty—
I am content that he shall take the odds
Of his great name and estimation,
And will, to save the blood on either side,
Try fortune with him in a single fight.

King

And, Prince of Wales, so dare we venture thee,
Albeit considerations infinite
Do make against it. No, good Worcester, no!
We love our people well—even those we love
That are misled upon your cousin's part—
And will they take the offer of our grace,
Both he, and they, and you, yea, every man
Shall be my friend again, and I'll be his:
So tell your cousin, and bring me word
What he will do. But if he will not yield,
Rebuke and dread correction wait on us,
And they shall do their office. So, be gone;
We will not now be troubled with reply:
We offer fair; take it advisedly.

[*Exit* Worcester, *with* Vernon

Prince

It will not be accepted, on my life:
The Douglas and the Hotspur both together
Are confident against the world in arms.

118 *charge*: regiment.
119 *on their answer*: as soon as they reply.
set on: attack.
120 *as*: to the extent that.
121 *bestride*: stand over (i.e. protect).
122 *so*: that will please me.
a point of friendship: your duty as my friend.
123 *Colossus*: the gigantic statue that once stood on the harbour walls at Rhodes.
126 *thou . . . death*: a proverbial saying (with the sense of 'you must die some day').
127 *'Tis . . . yet*: it is not yet time to pay the debt (Falstaff picks up the metaphor of 'owest').
128 *forward with*: prompt to pay.
129 *calls not*: is making no demands.
130 *pricks*: urges, spurs.
130–31 *prick me off*: kills me (by pricking—or stabbing—with a sword).
131–2 *set to a leg*: set (mend) a broken leg.
132 *grief*: pain.
135–6 *A trim reckoning*: a fine summing-up.
136–7 *a-Wednesday*: last Wednesday.
138 *'Tis insensible*: it cannot be perceived by any of the five senses.
140 *Detraction*: slander.
suffer: allow.
140–41 *I'll none of it*: I won't have anything to do with it.
141 *a mere scutcheon*: nothing more than the drapery at a funeral (the churches were hung with special heraldic banners).
142 *catechism*: a form of teaching by oral questions and answers; it was used particularly for religious instruction.

King
Hence, therefore, every leader to his charge;
For on their answer will we set on them,
And God befriend us as our cause is just!
[*Exeunt all but the* Prince *and* Falstaff

Falstaff
Hal, if thou see me down in the battle and bestride me, so; 'tis a point of friendship.

Prince
Nothing but a Colossus can do thee that friendship. Say thy prayers, and farewell.

Falstaff
I would 'twere bed-time, Hal, and all well.

Prince
Why, thou owest God a death. [*Exit*

Falstaff
'Tis not due yet: I would be loath to pay him before his day—what need I be so forward with him that calls not on me? Well, 'tis no matter, honour pricks me on. Yea, but how if honour prick me off when I come on, how then? Can honour set to a leg? No. Or an arm? Or take away the grief of a wound? No. Honour hath no skill in surgery then? No. What is honour? A word. What is in that word 'honour'? What is that honour? Air. A trim reckoning! Who hath it? He that died a-Wednesday. Doth he feel it? Doth he hear it? No. 'Tis insensible, then? Yea, to the dead. But will it not live with the living? No. Why? Detraction will not suffer it. Therefore I'll none of it. Honour is a mere scutcheon—and so ends my catechism. [*Exit*

Act 5 Scene 2
Worcester has returned to the rebel camp, but he is unwilling to tell Hotspur that the King has made an offer of peace. War is declared.

3 *undone*: ruined.
5 *keep . . . us*: be friends with us as he promised.
7 *this offence*: i.e. the rebellion.
8 *Supposition*: suspicion; Worcester imagines a monster with many eyes, watching the rebels for the rest of their lives.
10 *lock'd up*: kept in a cage.
11 *a wild . . . ancestor*: the habit of his wild ancestors.
12 *or . . . or . . .*: whether . . . or . . .
13 Our appearances will be misinterpreted and wrongly reported.
14 *at a stall*: kept in the stable (i.e. being fattened for the butcher).
15 *still*: always.
16 *may . . . forgot*: may well be forgotten.
18 *an adopted name*: a nickname (i.e. 'Hotspur').
of privilege: which gives him the privilege of being hot-tempered.
19 *hare-brain'd*: rash, thoughtless.
spleen: impulsiveness.
20 *live*: lie; Worcester believes that he and Northumberland will be blamed for Hotspur's faults.
21 *train him on*: lead him on, encourage him.
22 *corruption*: wickedness.
ta'en: caught (like an infection).
23 *spring*: source.
25 *In any case*: whatever happens.
26 *Deliver . . . will*: give them whatever message you like.

28 *Deliver up*: release (apparently the Earl of Westmoreland had been kept as the hostage demanded in *4*, 3,109).
30 *bid you battle*: challenge you to fight.
presently: immediately.

Scene 2 *Shrewsbury: the Rebel Camp*

Enter Worcester *and* Sir Richard Vernon

Worcester
O no, my nephew must not know, Sir Richard,
The liberal and kind offer of the King.

Vernon
'Twere best he did.

Worcester
Then are we all undone.
It is not possible, it cannot be,
The King should keep his word in loving us;
He will suspect us still, and find a time
To punish this offence in other faults:
Supposition all our lives shall be stuck full of eyes,
For treason is but trusted like the fox,
Who, never so tame, so cherish'd and lock'd up,
Will have a wild trick of his ancestors.
Look how we can, or sad or merrily,
Interpretation will misquote our looks,
And we shall feed like oxen at a stall,
The better cherish'd still the nearer death.
My nephew's trespass may be well forgot,
It hath the excuse of youth and heat of blood,
And an adopted name of privilege—
A hare-brain'd Hotspur, govern'd by a spleen.
All his offences live upon my head
And on his father's. We did train him on,
And, his corruption being a ta'en from us,
We as the spring of all shall pay for all.
Therefore, good cousin, let not Harry know
In any case the offer of the King.

Vernon
Deliver what you will; I'll say 'tis so.
Here comes your cousin.

Enter Hotspur *and* Douglas

Hotspur
My uncle is return'd;
Deliver up my Lord of Westmoreland.
Uncle, what news?

Worcester
The King will bid you battle presently.

Douglas
Defy him by the Lord of Westmoreland.

Hotspur
Lord Douglas, go you and tell him so.

Douglas
Marry, and shall, and very willingly. [*Exit*

Worcester
There is no seeming mercy in the King.

Hotspur
Did you beg any? God forbid!

Worcester
I told him gently of our grievances,
Of his oath-breaking—which he mended thus,
By now forswearing that he is forsworn.
He calls us rebels, traitors, and will scourge
With haughty arms this hateful name in us.

Enter Douglas

Douglas
Arm, gentlemen, to arms! for I have thrown
A brave defiance in King Henry's teeth,
And Westmoreland that was engag'd did bear it,
Which cannot choose but bring him quickly on.

Worcester
The Prince of Wales stepp'd forth before the King,
And nephew, challeng'd you to single fight.

Hotspur
O, would the quarrel lay upon our heads,
And that no man might draw short breath today
But I and Harry Monmouth! Tell me, tell me,
How show'd his tasking? Seem'd it in contempt?

Vernon
No, by my soul, I never in my life
Did hear a challenge urg'd more modestly,
Unless a brother should a brother dare
To gentle exercise and proof of arms.
He gave you all the duties of a man,
Trimm'd up your praises with a princely tongue,
Spoke your deservings like a chronicle,
Making you ever better than his praise
By still dispraising praise valu'd with you;
And, which became him like a prince indeed,

31 *Defy him*: return his challenge.

34 *no seeming mercy*: apparently no forgiveness.

37 *mended*: corrected (the tone is sarcastic).

38 By swearing falsely *now* that he ever swore false in the past.

43 *engag'd*: held as hostage.

44 Which can only make him advance quickly.

47 *would*: I wish.
lay . . . heads: was our responsibility.

48 *draw short breath*: pant (with fighting).

50 *How show'd*: how did it look.
tasking: challenge.

52 *urg'd*: presented.

54 *proof of arms*: test of skill with weapons.

55 *all . . . man*: all that is due to a man.

56 *Trimm'd up*: elaborated, gave a good description of.

57 Described your merits as though he were writing your life-story ('chronicle' = history book).

58–9 Always saying that he knew no words good enough to praise you properly.

58 *ever*: always.

59 *still*: constantly.
praise: i.e. words of praise.
valu'd: compared.

60 *became him*: showed him that he was.

61 He gave an account ('cital') of himself, blushing with shame.

62 *chid*: reproached.
truant: disobedient (see the Prince's words in 5, 1,94).

63–4 Vernon thinks that the Prince showed the ability to teach and the ability to learn, both at the same time.

63 *master'd*: was in possession.

64 *instantly*: simultaneously.

65 *There . . . pause*: he stopped there (i.e. did not say any more).

66 *outlive*: survives.
envy: hostility, warfare.

67 *owe*: own, possess.

68 *misconstru'd . . . wantonness*: misunderstood because of his wild behaviour.

69–70 *thou . . . follies*: you have fallen in love with his crazy ways.

70–71 *Never . . . liberty*: I have never heard of a king's son who was so irresponsible.

72 *be . . . will*: whatever he is like.
ere: before.

74 So that he will not be so great when I have finished with him.
courtesy: Hotspur is ironic—the 'courtesy' of his 'soldier's arm' will (he threatens) kill Prince Hal.

76–8 You should think about what you have to do rather than listen to me, because I can't speak well enough to inspire you with my words of persuasion.

77 *gift of tongue*: eloquence.

78 *lift . . . up*: excite you.

82–4 *To spend . . . hour*: if there were only one hour to live, it would be too long if we were to spend that hour in a dishonourable way.

83 *a dial's point*: the hand of a clock.

87 *for*: as for.

87–8 *the arms . . . just*: it is right to make war (bear arms) when there is a good reason ('intent') for fighting.

89 *apace*: fast.

90 *cuts . . . tale*: shortens my speech.

91 *I profess not talking*: I don't claim to be a good speaker.

He made a blushing cital of himself,
And chid his truant youth with such a grace
As if he master'd there a double spirit
Of teaching and of learning instantly.
There did he pause. But let me tell the world—
If he outlive the envy of this day,
England did never owe so sweet a hope
So much misconstru'd in his wantonness.

Hotspur

Cousin, I think thou art enamoured
On his follies. Never did I hear
Of any prince so wild a liberty.
But be he as he will, yet once ere night
I will embrace him with a soldier's arm,
That he shall shrink under my courtesy.
Arm, arm with speed! And fellows, soldiers, friends,
Better consider what you have to do
Than I, that have not well the gift of tongue,
Can lift your blood up with persuasion.

Enter a Messenger

Messenger

My lord, here are letters for you.

Hotspur

I cannot read them now.
O gentlemen, the time of life is short!
To spend that shortness basely were too long
If life did ride upon a dial's point,
Still ending at the arrival of an hour.
And if we live, we live to tread on kings;
If die, brave death when princes die with us!
Now, for our consciences, the arms are fair
When the intent of bearing them is just.

Enter another Messenger

Messenger

My lord, prepare, the King comes on apace.

Hotspur

I thank him that he cuts me from my tale,
For I profess not talking: only this—
Let each man do his best; and here draw I

93 *temper*: steel (tempering is a process in the hardening of steel).
94 *withal*: with.
96 *Esperance! Percy!* the battle-cry of the Percy family; the final *e* of 'Esperance' (= Good Hope, Good Luck) is pronounced.
set on: start fighting.
97 *lofty . . . war*: i.e. the martial trumpets.
98 *by*: to the sound of.
99 *heaven to earth*: the odds are as high as heaven is from earth.

A sword whose temper I intend to stain
With the best blood that I can meet withal
In the adventure of this perilous day.
Now, Esperance! Percy! and set on.
Sound all the lofty instruments of war,
And by that music let us all embrace,
For, heaven to earth, some of us never shall
A second time do such a courtesy.
[*Here they embrace; the trumpets sound, exeunt*

Act 5 Scene 3
The fighting has begun. We learn that several noblemen are disguised to look like the King; and we see how one of these is killed. Prince Hal is looking for Hotspur, but Falstaff claims that he has killed him.

2 *crossest*: oppose.
3 *Upon my head*: by killing me.
4 *haunt*: follow.
7–8 Looking like you has today been very expensive for the Earl of Stafford; Douglas believes that Blunt really is the King.
9 *him*: i.e. his life.

Scene 3 *Shrewsbury: the Field of Battle*

Enter the King *with his army. Alarum to the battle. Then enter (on opposite sides)* Douglas, *and* Sir Walter Blunt (*disguised as the* King

Blunt
What is thy name that in the battle thus
Thou crossest me? What honour dost thou seek
Upon my head?
Douglas Know then my name is Douglas,
And I do haunt thee in the battle thus
Because some tell me that thou art a king.
Blunt
They tell thee true.
Douglas
The Lord of Stafford dear today hath bought
Thy likeness, for instead of thee, King Harry,
This sword hath ended him: so shall it thee
Unless thou yield thee as my prisoner.
Blunt
I was not born a yielder, thou proud Scot,
And thou shalt find a king that will revenge
Lord Stafford's death.
[*They fight.* Douglas *kills* Blunt

Enter Hotspur

Hotspur
O Douglas, hadst thou fought at Holmedon thus

15 I would never have beaten the Scots (Douglas and Hotspur were on opposite sides at the Battle of Holmedon—see *1*, 1,55).

16 *breathless*: i.e. lifeless.

19 *full*: very.

21 *Semblably furnish'd*: dressed in the same way.

22 May the name of 'fool' accompany your soul, wherever it has gone (to heaven or hell); Douglas speaks to Blunt's body.

23 Pretending to be someone else (the King) has cost you too much.

25 *many*: i.e. many men.
coats: sleeveless tunics ('surcoats') with heraldic devices, worn over the armour so that the wearer could be easily identified.

29 *stand . . . day*: have a very good chance of victory.

30 *scape shot-free*: escape without being wounded; *and* avoid paying the bill.

31 *shot*: bullets—or arrows.
scoring: a pun on 'hitting' *and* 'charging the bill'.
pate: head.

32 *Soft*: look at this.

32–3 *there's . . . you*: Falstaff recalls his 'catechism' on honour in *Act 5*, Scene 1.

33 *Here's no vanity*: this (the dead body) is the real thing.

34–5 *molten*: melted.
God . . . me: God save me from gunshot (made of lead).

36 *bowels*: i.e. body.
led: sent (Falstaff would not have marched with his soldiers).

37 *peppered*: massacred (Falstaff can now keep the money which should have been the soldiers' pay).
not: no more than.

38–9 *they . . . life*: they will have to sit at the entrance to the town and beg for the rest of their lives; (the soldiers are badly wounded).

42 *vaunting*: boastful.

I never had triumph'd upon a Scot.

Douglas
All's done, all's won: here breathless lies the King.

Hotspur
Where?

Douglas
Here.

Hotspur
This, Douglas? No, I know this face full well,
A gallant knight he was, his name was Blunt,
Semblably furnish'd like the King himself.

Douglas
A fool go with thy soul, whither it goes!
A borrow'd title hast thou bought too dear.
Why didst thou tell me that thou wert a king?

Hotspur
The King hath many marching in his coats.

Douglas
Now, by my sword, I will kill all his coats;
I'll murder all his wardrobe, piece by piece,
Until I meet the King.

Hotspur Up and away!
Our soldiers stand full fairly for the day. [*Exeunt*

Alarum. Enter Falstaff

Falstaff
Though I could scape shot-free at London, I fear the shot here; here's no scoring but upon the pate. Soft! who are you? Sir Walter Blunt—there's honour for you! Here's no vanity! I am as hot as molten lead, and as heavy too—God keep lead out of me, I need no more weight than mine own bowels. I have led my ragamuffins where they are peppered; there's not three of my hundred and fifty left alive, and they are for the town's end, to beg during life. But who comes here?

Enter the Prince

Prince
What, stands thou idle here? Lend me thy sword.
Many a nobleman lies stark and stiff
Under the hoofs of vaunting enemies,

Whose deaths are yet unrevenged. I prithee lend me thy sword.

Falstaff

O Hal, I prithee give me leave to breathe awhile—Turk Gregory never did such deeds in arms as I have done this day; I have paid Percy, I have made him sure.

Prince

He is indeed, and living to kill thee: I prithee lend me thy sword.

Falstaff

Nay, before God, Hal, if Percy be alive thou gets not my sword; but take my pistol if thou wilt.

Prince

Give it me: what, is it in the case?

Falstaff

Ay, Hal, 'tis hot, 'tis hot; there's that will sack a city.

[The Prince *draws it out, and finds it to be a bottle of sack*

44 *breathe awhile*: get my breath back, have a short rest.

45 *Turk Gregory*: the name of 'Turk' was applied to any particularly cruel man; and by 'Gregory' Falstaff probably refers to Pope Gregory XIII, who was associated with the vicious Massacre of St Bartholomew's Day in 1572.

in arms: in fighting.

46 *paid*: killed.

Percy: i.e. Hotspur.

47 *made him sure*: made certain that he is dead.

48 *He is indeed*: Hal pretends to think that 'sure' = 'safe'.

52 *case*: holster (instead of being ready for shooting).

53 *'tis hot*: i.e. after shooting (Falstaff pretends that he has put away his pistol until it cools).

53–4 *there's . . . city*: there is enough to conquer a whole city. Falstaff makes a pun on 'sack' = 'conquer' and 'sack'—the drink his holster contains.

55 *dally*: fool around.
56 *pierce*: the word was pronounced as 'perse'; Falstaff makes a pun with 'Percy'.
57 *so*: that will be fine.
if he . . . in his: if he does not come in my way, and if I get in his way.
58 *carbonado*: grilled steak (which was slashed with a knife before being cooked).
59–61 If I can save my life, that will be good; and if I can't save it, then I shall get honour without making an effort—and that's all there is to it.

Prince
What, is it a time to jest and dally now?
[*He throws the bottle at* Falstaff. *Exit*

Falstaff
Well, if Percy be alive, I'll pierce him. If he do come in my way, so: if he do not, if I come in his willingly, let him make a carbonado of me. I like not such grinning honour as Sir Walter hath. Give me life—which if I can save, so: if not, honour comes unlooked for, and there's an end. [*Exit*

Act 5 Scene 4
The battle continues, Prince Hal is slightly wounded, but he refuses to stop fighting and he is able to save his father's life when the King is in danger. At last the Prince encounters Hotspur.

1 *withdraw thyself*: go back to your tent.
4–5 *make up . . . friends*: go up to the front of the battle, or else your supporters will think you have retreated and be worried.
5 *retirement*: withdrawal, retreat.
amaze: distress, worry.
12 *stain'd*: dishonoured (by being defeated); *and* bloodstained.
nobility: noble men.
13 *rebels' arms*: the fighting rebels.
14 *breathe*: rest.

Scene 4 *The Battlefield*

Alarum. Excursions. Enter the King, *the* Prince, Lord John of Lancaster, Earl of Westmoreland

King
I prithee, Harry, withdraw thyself, thou bleed'st too much.
Lord John of Lancaster, go you with him.

Lancaster
Not I, my lord, unless I did bleed too.

Prince
I beseech your Majesty, make up,
Lest your retirement do amaze your friends.

King
I will do so. My Lord of Westmoreland,
Lead him to his tent.

Westmoreland
Come, my lord, I'll lead you to your tent.

Prince
Lead me, my lord? I do not need your help;
And God forbid a shallow scratch should drive
The Prince of Wales from such a field as this,
Where stain'd nobility lies trodden on,
And rebels' arms triumph in massacres!

Lancaster
We breathe too long: come, cousin Westmoreland,
Our duty this way lies: for God's sake, come.
[*Exeunt* Lancaster *and* Westmoreland

17 *lord . . . spirit*: possessed such courage.
18–19 Until today I loved you because you were my brother, but now I have very great respect for you.
20 *at the point*: i.e. the point of his sword.
21 *lustier maintenance*: greater tenacity.
look for: expect to see.
22 *ungrown*: inexperienced.
23 *Lends mettle*: inspires.

Prince
By God, thou hast deceiv'd me, Lancaster,
I did not think thee lord of such a spirit.
Before, I lov'd thee as a brother, John,
But now I do respect thee as my soul.

King
I saw him hold Lord Percy at the point
With lustier maintenance than I did look for
Of such an ungrown warrior.

Prince O, this boy
Lends mettle to us all! [*Exit the* Prince

24 *Hydra*: a snake (in classical mythology) which grew two new heads each time a head was cut off.

26 *wear those colours*: are disguised in the King's surcoats (see nóte to 5, 3,25).

29 *shadows*: imitators (the word is often used by Shakespeare to refer to actors).

30 *very*: real.
two boys: i.e. his sons, Prince Hal and Lord John.

32 *fall'st*: has found me.

33 *assay*: tackle you myself.

35 *bearest thee*: behave.

36 *mine*: i.e. my victim (or conquest).

38 *like*: likely.

40 *Shirley*, *Stafford*, *Blunt*: the noblemen killed by Douglas.

43 *Cheerly*: don't worry, cheer up.

44 *succour*: assistance, reinforcements.

45 *I'll to*: I will go to.
straight: immediately.

46 *breathe*: rest.

47 *opinion*: reputation.

48 *mak'st . . . of*: have some care for.

51 *hearken'd for*: was looking forward to.

52 *let alone*: not interfered with.

53 *insulting*: conquering.

54 *as . . . end*: killed you as quickly.

Enter Douglas

Douglas
Another king! They grow like Hydra's heads!
I am the Douglas, fatal to all those
That wear those colours on them. What art thou
That counterfeit'st the person of a king?

King
The King himself, who, Douglas, grieves at heart
So many of his shadows thou hast met,
And not the very King. I have two boys
Seek Percy and thyself about the field;
But seeing thou fall'st on me so luckily
I will assay thee, and defend thyself.

Douglas
I fear thou art another counterfeit,
And yet, in faith, thou bearest thee like a king;
But mine I am sure thou art, who'er thou be,
And thus I win thee.
[*They fight; the* King *is in danger*

Enter Prince of Wales

Prince
Hold up thy head, vile Scot, or thou art like
Never to hold it up again! The spirits
Of valiant Shirley, Stafford, Blunt are in my arms.
It is the Prince of Wales that threatens thee,
Who never promiseth but he means to pay.
[*They fight:* Douglas *flies*
Cheerly, my lord. How fares your grace?
Sir Nicholas Gawsey hath for succour sent,
And so hath Clifton—I'll to Clifton straight.

King
Stay and breathe a while:
Thou hast redeem'd thy lost opinion,
And show'd thou mak'st some tender of my life,
In this fair rescue thou has brought to me.

Prince
O God, they did me too much injury
That ever said I hearken'd for your death.
If it were so, I might have let alone
The insulting hand of Douglas over you,
Which would have been as speedy in your end

As all the poisonous potions in the world,
And sav'd the treacherous labour of your son.

King

Make up to Clifton; I'll to Sir Nicholas Gawsey.
[*Exit* King Henry

Enter Hotspur

Hotspur

If I mistake not, thou art Harry Monmouth.

Prince

Thou speak'st as if I would deny my name.

Hotspur

My name is Harry Percy.

Prince Why then I see
A very valiant rebel of that name.
I am the Prince of Wales, and think not, Percy,
To share with me in glory any more:
Two stars keep not their motion in one sphere,
Nor can one England brook a double reign
Of Harry Percy and the Prince of Wales.

Hotspur

Nor shall it, Harry, for the hour is come
To end the one of us; and would to God
Thy name in arms were now as great as mine!

Prince

I'll make it greater ere I part from thee,
And all the budding honours on thy crest
I'll crop to make a garland for my head.

Hotspur

I can no longer brook thy vanities. [*They fight*

Enter Falstaff

Falstaff

Well said, Hal! To it, Hal! Nay, you shall find no boy's play here, I can tell you.

Enter Douglas*; he fights with* Falstaff, *who falls down as if he were dead. Exit* Douglas. *The* Prince *mortally wounds* Hotspur

Hotspur

O Harry, thou hast robb'd me of my youth!
I better brook the loss of brittle life

56 And saved your son from having to do a treacherous job.

57 *Make up*: go to help.

61 *rebel*: when Hal speaks this word, it is a term of insult—with the sense, almost, of 'coward' (so that 'valiant rebel' is a paradox).

64 In the Ptolemaic system of the universe, the earth is at the centre and the planets ('stars') circle around ('keep their motion'), each one in its own orbit or 'sphere'.

65 *brook*: tolerate.

68 *the one of us*: the life of one of us.
would: I wish.

69 *name in arms*: reputation for fighting.

71 *crest*: helmet; in *3*, 2,142 Hal speaks of the 'honour sitting on his (Hotspur's) helm'.

73 *brook*: endure.
vanities: boasting.

74–5 *you . . . here*: this isn't child's play, you know (Falstaff speaks to Hotspur).

78 *proud*: glorious.
won of me: won from me.

79–80 *thought's . . . life*: i.e. 'life' controls 'thought' as a master controls a slave.

80 *life . . . fool*: life is made a fool by time—because it is restricted to a certain time.

81–2 *time . . . stop*; even time, that commands ('takes survey of') all the world, will end.

82 *prophesy*: the Elizabethans believed that prophecies were often spoken by dying men.

Than those proud titles thou hast won of me;
They wound my thoughts worse than thy sword
my flesh:
But thought's the slave of life; and life, time's fool;
And time, that takes survey of all the world,
Must have a stop. O, I could prophesy,
But that the earthy and cold hand of death
Lies on my tongue. No, Percy, thou art dust,
And food for— [*Dies*

87 Hal compares Hotspur's misdirected ambition to badly-woven ('Ill-weav'd') cloth which has shrunk because it was not well made.

89 *bound*: limit.

92 *stout*: brave.

93–4 If I thought you could ('wert sensible of') tell what I am doing, I would not make such an emotional expression of my feelings.

95 *my favours*: the plumes from his helmet (Hal covers Hotspur's face).

96 *in thy behalf*: on your behalf.

99–100 May your shame (for his part in the rebellion) be buried with you, and not mentioned in your epitaph.

104 *heavy*: sorrowful (and a reference to Falstaff's weight).
miss: loss.

105 *vanity*: frivolity, foolishness.

107 *dearer*: more valuable.

108 *Embowell'd*: disembowelled: the human intestines were removed before the body was embalmed—and the entrails of a hunted deer were taken out before the meat was 'powdered' with spices to preserve it.

109 *in blood*: in the bloodshed of battle; the phrase 'in blood' was also used to describe a live deer in good condition (as Falstaff is in fact).

111 *powder*: preserve with spices.

113 *termagant*: bloodthirsty.
had paid me: would have killed me.
scot . . . too: Falstaff refers to the phrase 'to pay scot and lot' (= to pay completely), making word-play out of the double meanings of both 'pay' and 'scot'.

Prince

For worms, brave Percy. Fare thee well, great heart!
Ill-weav'd ambition, how much art thou shrunk!
When that this body did contain a spirit,
A kingdom for it was too small a bound;
But now two paces of the vilest earth
Is room enough. This earth that bears thee dead
Bears not alive so stout a gentleman.
If thou wert sensible of courtesy
I should not make so dear a show of zeal.
But let my favours hide thy mangled face;
And even in thy behalf I'll thank myself
For doing these fair rites of tenderness.
Adieu, and take thy praise with thee to heaven!
Thy ignominy sleep with thee in the grave,
But not remember'd in thy epitaph!
[*He sees* Falstaff *on the ground*
What, old acquaintance, could not all this flesh
Keep in a little life? Poor Jack, farewell!
I could have better spar'd a better man.
O, I should have a heavy miss of thee
If I were much in love with vanity!
Death hath not struck so fat a deer today,
Though many dearer, in this bloody fray.
Embowell'd will I see thee by and by,
Till then in blood by noble Percy lie. [*Exit*

Falstaff *rises up*

Falstaff

Embowelled? If thou embowel me today, I'll give you leave to powder me and eat me too tomorrow. 'Sblood, 'twas time to counterfeit, or that hot termagant Scot had paid me, scot and lot too.

Counterfeit? I lie, I am no counterfeit: to die is to be a counterfeit, for he is but the counterfeit of a man, who hath not the life of a man: but to counterfeit dying, when a man thereby liveth, is to be no counterfeit, but the true and perfect image of life indeed. The better part of valour is discretion, in the which better part I have saved my life. 'Zounds, I am afraid of this gunpowder Percy, though he be dead! How if he should counterfeit too, and rise? By my faith, I am afraid he would prove the better counterfeit; therefore I'll make him sure, yea, and I'll swear I killed him. Why may not he rise as well as I? Nothing confutes me but eyes, and nobody sees me: therefore, sirrah [*stabs him*], with a new wound in your thigh, come you along with me.

[*He takes up Hotspur on his back*

Enter Prince *and* Lord John of Lancaster

Prince
Come, brother John, full bravely hast thou flesh'd
Thy maiden sword.

Lancaster But soft, whom have we here?
Did you not tell me this fat man was dead?

Prince
I did, I saw him dead,
Breathless and bleeding on the ground. Art thou alive?
Or is it fantasy that plays upon our eyesight?
I prithee speak—we will not trust our eyes
Without our ears: thou art not what thou seem'st.

Falstaff
No, that's certain, I am not a double-man: but if I be not Jack Falstaff, then am I a jack: there is Percy [*throws the body down*]! If your father will do me any honour, so: if not, let him kill the next Percy himself. I look to be either earl or duke, I can assure you.

Prince
Why, Percy I kill'd myself; and saw thee dead.

Falstaff
Didst thou? Lord, Lord, how this world is given

117 *thereby*: as a result (Falstaff is alive now only because he pretended to be dead in his fight with Douglas).

119 *The better . . . discretion*: a proverbial saying, meaning that commonsense should accompany bravery; but Falstaff seems to imply that the two are separate—and that his 'discretion' (i.e. in pretending to be dead) was better than the 'valour' of continuing to fight.

121 *gunpowder*: explosive, dangerous.

122 *how if*: what would happen if.

124–5 *make him sure*: make certain he is dead.

126–7 *Nothing . . . eyes*: I could only be called a liar by someone who can see what I am doing.

130 *full*: very.
flesh'd: used for the first time.

131 *maiden*: new, never used.
soft: wait.

134 *Breathless*: not breathing.

135 *fantasy that plays*: imagination playing tricks.

138 *double-man*: deceiver; *and* ghost (also, Falstaff appears to be two men because he is carrying the body of Hotspur).

139 *a jack*: a rascal.

141 *do me*: reward me with, recognize what I have done.
so: good.

142 *look to be*: expect to be made.

146 *I grant you*: I agree that.
147–8 *at an instant*: at the same time.
148–9 *a long . . . clock*: a whole hour—as I could tell the time from Shrewsbury town clock.
150–51 *bear . . . heads*: be responsible for their own fault (in not giving Falstaff his proper reward).
151 *I'll take . . . death*: a very solemn oath.
158 *a lie*: i.e. one told by Falstaff.
do thee grace: do you any good.
159 I'll improve your story by telling it in the finest language ('terms') I know.
160 *The trumpet . . . retreat*: i.e. the trumpet of the rebels gives the signal for withdrawal.
the day is ours: we have won the battle.
161 *let us . . . field*: let us go to the highest part of the battlefield.
163 After the hunt, the hounds were said to 'follow' and be given 'reward' (the parts of the deer not preserved and eaten as venison).
164 *grow great*: i.e. be made a nobleman (earl or duke) as a reward for the service he claims to have done.
165 *purge*: repent; *and* go on a diet—to lose weight.
leave sack: stop drinking.
cleanly: decently.

to lying! I grant you I was down, and out of breath, and so was he; but we rose both at an instant, and fought a long hour by Shrewsbury clock. If I may be believed, so: if not, let them that should reward valour bear the sin upon their own heads. I'll take it upon my death, I gave him this wound in the thigh; if the man were alive, and would deny it, 'zounds, I would make him eat a piece of my sword.

Lancaster
This is the strangest tale that ever I heard.

Prince
This is the strangest fellow, brother John.
Come, bring your luggage nobly on your back.
[*Aside to* Falstaff] For my part, if a lie may do thee grace,
I'll gild it with the happiest terms I have.
[*A retreat is sounded*
The trumpet sounds retreat, the day is ours.
Come, brother, let us to the highest of the field,
To see what friends are living, who are dead.
[*Exeunt* Prince of Wales *and* Lancaster

Falstaff
I'll follow, as they say, for reward. He that rewards me, God reward him! If I do grow great, I'll grow less, for I'll purge, and leave sack, and live cleanly as a nobleman should do.
[*Exit, bearing off the body*

Act 5 Scene 5
The King holds a victory conference. Worcester and Vernon are sentenced to death, but Douglas is released; then Henry IV gives directions for an attack on the remaining rebels.

1 This is the way that rebellion is always ('ever') kept in control.
rebuke: check.
2 *Ill-spirited*: evil-minded.
grace: favour.
3 *terms*: expressions.
4 *turn . . . contrary*: misrepresent our offers.

Scene 5 *The Battlefield*

The trumpets sound. Enter the King, Prince of Wales, Lord John of Lancaster, Earl of Westmoreland, *with* Worcester *and* Vernon *prisoners*

King
Thus ever did rebellion find rebuke.
Ill-spirited Worcester, did not we send grace,
Pardon, and terms of love to all of you?
And wouldst thou turn our offers contrary?

5 Abuse the nature of the trust that Hotspur ('thy kinsman') put in you.
6 *upon our party*: on our side.
7 *A noble earl*: the Earl of Stafford was killed in this battle.
9 *truly*: honestly.
9–10 *borne . . . intelligence*: carried true information between our two armies.
11 I did what I thought would be the safest.
14 *to the death*: to be executed.
15 *pause upon*: decide later what to do with them.
16 *field*: battle.
18 *quite turn'd from him*: had completely left him.
20 *Upon . . . fear*: running away in fear.
22 *took*: captured.
26 *honourable bounty*: noble act.
27–8 *deliver . . . pleasure*: release him to do whatever he wants.
28 *ransomless*: without having to pay a ransom.
29 The courage he has shown in fighting in this battle against us ('upon our crests').
30 *high*: noble.
31 Even when they are done by those who are fighting against us.
32 *high courtesy*: great generosity.
33 *give away*: i.e. by releasing Douglas.
34 *this remains*: this is what is left to do.
power: army.
36 *bend you*: direct yourselves.
dearest: best.
38 *busily in arms*: busy preparing to fight.

Misuse the tenor of thy kinsman's trust?
Three knights upon our party slain today,
A noble earl and many a creature else,
Had been alive this hour,
If like a Christian thou hadst truly borne
Betwixt our armies true intelligence.

Worcester

What I have done my safety urg'd me to;
And I embrace this fortune patiently,
Since not to be avoided it falls on me.

King

Bear Worcester to the death, and Vernon too:
Other offenders we will pause upon.
[*Exeunt* Worcester *and* Vernon, *guarded*
How goes the field?

Prince

The noble Scot, Lord Douglas, when he saw
The fortune of the day quite turn'd from him,
The noble Percy slain, and all his men
Upon the foot of fear, fled with the rest,
And falling from a hill, he was so bruis'd
That the pursuers took him. At my tent
The Douglas is; and I beseech your Grace
I may dispose of him.

King With all my heart.

Prince

Then, brother John of Lancaster, to you
This honourable bounty shall belong;
Go to the Douglas and deliver him
Up to his pleasure, ransomless and free:
His valours shown upon our crests today
Have taught us how to cherish such high deeds,
Even in the bosom of our adversaries.

Lancaster

I thank your Grace for this high courtesy,
Which I shall give away immediately.

King

Then this remains, that we divide our power:
You, son John, and my cousin Westmoreland,
Towards York shall bend you with your dearest speed
To meet Northumberland and the prelate Scroop,
Who, as we hear, are busily in arms.

Myself and you, son Harry, will towards Wales,
To fight with Glendower and the Earl of March.
Rebellion in this land shall lose his sway,
Meeting the check of such another day;
And since this business so fair is done,
Let us not leave till all our own be won. [*Exeunt*

39 *will*: will march.

41 *lose his sway*: have no more power.

42 If it is controlled by another battle like this one.

43 *fair*: successfully.

44 *leave*: stop.
till . . . won: until we have completely finished the job.

An Historical Appendix

Henry IV, Part 1 is not a history lesson. Shakespeare did not intend to teach his audience the facts about the rebellion against King Henry IV in 1402. His play is based on historical truth: but it is not historically accurate. The dramatist omits to mention much that a historian would consider important; he adds much that is pure invention (the character of Falstaff, and all the scenes in which he appears); and he alters some historical facts to suit his dramatic purposes.

The greatest alteration affects the person of Hotspur, 'Young Harry Percy', who is constantly contrasted with King Henry's son, his own 'young Harry'. The King even wishes

> that it could be prov'd
> That some night-tripping fairy had exchang'd
> In cradle-clothes our children where they lay.

Shakespeare clearly intends us to think that the two 'children' are of the same age. But the real Hotspur was born in 1364; and Prince Hal was born in 1387. At the battle of Shrewsbury in 1402 the young Prince of Wales (aged fifteen) fought bravely; but it was not he who killed the famous Hotspur.

Another character who was not—historically—what he seems to be is the Earl of March, Edmund Mortimer. In *Act 1*, Scene 3 King Henry speaks scornfully of 'the foolish Mortimer' who apparently 'betray'd The lives of those that he did lead to fight' against the Welsh, and who then married the daughter of 'that great magician, damn'd Glendower'. The King refuses to pay a ransom for Mortimer, and Worcester explains the reason for Henry's hatred and fear: Mortimer was the true heir to the throne of England, 'the next of blood' to Richard II.

The first family tree—'The Plantagenets'—shows Edmund Mortimer, son of Roger Mortimer, whose descent from Lionel Duke of Clarence gave him the right to the throne after the death of Richard II (who had no children). As the son of Roger Mortimer, he took the title 'Earl of March' after his father's death in 1398. But he was born in 1391; and so he was only eleven years old at the time Shakespeare's play opens.

The second family tree, however, solves the problem: there were two historical figures with the same name: one was the child heir to the throne, who did become Earl of March; and the other was his uncle, the 'revolted Mortimer' who appears in the play with his Welsh wife. Perhaps Shakespeare himself was confused?

Modern historians also accuse Shakespeare of confusing two *rebellions*; it now appears that the 'indenture tripartite' which is so important to the rebels (*Act 3*, Scene 1) belongs to the year 1405—two years after the death of Hotspur at Shrewsbury (when Shakespeare's play ends). For this confusion, however, Shakespeare is not to blame: his authority was the sixteenth-century historian, Raphael Holinshed, whose work *The Chronicles of England, Scotland, and Ireland* was the chief (but not the only) source for this play.

Shakespeare never worried about the minor details which are often so important to a modern director (especially those in charge of television drama) who is keen to give his production 'period' accuracy. In the play *Julius Caesar*, for instance, Shakespeare's ancient Romans tell the time by clocks, and cover their heads with hats, just as the Elizabethans did. In *1 Henry IV* there are similar anachronisms. Prince Hal describes the Earl of Douglas as 'He rides at high speed, and with his pistol kills a sparrow flying'. In fact the pistol was not invented until the sixteenth century in Italy. But what Prince Hal is doing is showing respect for Douglas' skill, and at the same time showing scorn for the energy wasted on such a trivial achievement. It is more important that we should appreciate Hal's attitude than that we should object to a fourteenth-century Scottish Earl using a sixteenth-century Italian pistol: the fact is irrelevant.

Selections from *The Chronicles of England, Scotland, and Ireland*

By Raphael Holinshed

The Percys' Rebellion

Owen Glendower, according to his accustomed manner robbing and spoiling within the English borders, caused all the forces of the shire of Hereford to assemble together against them, under the conduct of Edmund Mortimer, Earl of March. But coming to try the matter by battle . . . the English power was discomfited, the Earl taken prisoner, and above a thousand of his people slain in the place. The shameful villainy used by the Welshwomen towards the dead carcasses was such as honest ears would be ashamed to hear . . .

The King was not hasty to purchase the deliverance of the Earl March, because his title to the crown was well enough known, and therefore suffered him to remain in miserable prison, wishing both the Earl and his lineage out of this life . . .

About the mid of August the King, to chastise the presumptuous attempts of the Welshmen, went with a great power of men into Wales to pursue the captain of the Welsh rebel Owen Glendower, but in effect he lost his labour, for Owen conveyed himself out of the way, into his known lurking places; and (as was thought) through art magic he caused such foul weather of winds, tempest, rain, snow, and hail, to be raised for the annoyance of the King's army, that the like had not been heard of—in such sort that the King was constrained to return home . . .

Archibald, Earl Douglas . . . procured a commission to invade England . . . [but] at a place called Holmedon they were so fiercely assailed by the English, under the leading of the Lord Percy, surnamed Henry Hotspur . . . that with violence of the English shot they were quite vanquished and put to flight, on the Rood day in harvest, with a great slaughter made by the Englishmen . . .

Henry Earl of Northumberland, with his brother Thomas Earl of Worcester and his son the Lord Henry Percy (surnamed Hotspur) which were to King Henry in the beginning of his reign both faithful friends and earnest aiders, began now to envy his wealth and felicity; and especially they were grieved because the King demanded of the Earl and his son such Scottish prisoners as were taken at Holmedon . . .

[Hotspur and his father] came to the King unto Windsor . . . and there required of him, that either by ransom or otherwise he would cause to be delivered out of prison Edmund Mortimer Earl of March, their cousin . . . The King began not a little to muse at this request, and not without cause; for indeed it touched him somewhat near, sith this Edmund . . . at King Richard's going into Ireland was proclaimed heir apparent to the crown and realm . . . The King, when he had studied on the matter, made answer . . . he would neither ransom him nor redeem him . . .

[In great anger, Hotspur and his father departed], minding nothing more than to depose King Henry from the high type of his royalty, and to place in his seat their cousin Edmund Earl of March, whom they did not only deliver out of captivity, but also (to the high displeasure of King Henry) entered in league with the foresaid Owen Glendower. Herewith, they by their deputies, in the house of the Archdeacon of Bangor, divided the realm amongst them, causing a tripartite indenture to be made and sealed with all their seals, by the covenants whereof all England from Severn and Trent, south and eastward, was assigned to the Earl of March; all Wales and the lands beyond Severn, westward, were appointed to Owen Glendower; and all the remnant, from Trent northward, to the Lord Percy.

This was done (as some have said) through a foolish credit given to a vain prophecy, as though King Henry was the moldwarp, cursed of God's own mouth, and they three were the dragon, the lion, and the wolf—which should divide this realm between them . . .

King Henry . . . gathered a great army to go again into Wales; . . . Northumberland and his son . . . raised all the power they could make, and sent to the Scots, which before were taken prisoners at Holmedon, for aid of men . . .

The Percies, to make their part seem good, devised certain articles, by the advice of Richard Scroope, Archbishop of York, brother to the Lord Scroope whom King Henry had caused to be beheaded at Bristow. These articles being showed to divers noblemen and other states of the realm moved them to favour their purpose, insomuch that many of them did not only promise to the Percies' aid and succour by words, but also by their writings and seals confirmed the same. Howbeit when the matter came to trial, the most part of the confederates abandoned them, and at the day of conflict left them alone . . .

The Earl of Northumberland himself was not with them; but being sick, had promised upon his amendment to repair unto them (as some write) with all convenient speed . . .

King Henry, advertized of the proceedings of the Percies, forthwith gathered about him such power as he might . . . [and] passed forward with such speed that he was in sight of his enemies, lying in camp near to Shrewsbury, before they were in doubt of any such thing; for the Percies thought that he would have stayed at Burton-upon-Trent . . .

Forthwith the Lord Percy (as captain of high courage) began to exhort the captains and soldiers to prepare themselves to battle, sith the matter was grown to that point that by no means it could be avoided; so that (said he) this day shall either bring us all to advancement and honour, or else, if it shall chance us to be overcome, shall deliver us from the King's spiteful malice and cruel disdain. For playing the men (as we ought to do) better it is to die in battle for the commonwealth's cause, than through cowardlike fear to prolong life, which after shall be taken from us by sentence of the enemy . . .

Now when the two armies were encamped, the one against the other, the Earl of Worcester and the Lord Percy with their complices sent the articles . . . to King Henry, under their hands and seals; which articles in effect charged him with manifest perjury in that (contrary to his oath received . . . at Doncaster, when he first entered the realm after his exile) he had taken upon him the crown and royal dignity, imprisoned King Richard, caused him to resign his title, and finally to be murdered . . .

King Henry . . . answered . . . that he was ready with dint of sword and fierce battle to prove their quarrel false . . . [but] next day, in the morning . . . the abbot of Shrewsbury and one of the clerks of the privy seal were sent from the King unto the Percies, to offer them pardon if they would come to any reasonable agreement. By their persuasions, the Lord Henry Percy began to give ear unto the King's offers, and so sent with them his uncle, the Earl of Worcester, to declare unto the King the causes of those troubles, and to require some effectual reformation in the same.

It was reported for a truth, that now when the King had condescended unto all that was reasonable at his hands to be required, and seemed to humble himself more than was meet for his estate, the Earl of Worcester (upon his return to his nephew) made relation clean contrary to that the King had said, in such sort that he set his nephew's heart more in displeasure towards the

King than ever it was before, driving him by that means to fight, whether he would or not.

Then suddenly blew the trumpets—the King's part crying 'Saint George!' upon them, the adversaries cried '*Esperance Percy!*' And so the two armies furiously joined . . .

The prince that day holp his father like a lusty young gentleman; for although he was hurt in the face with an arrow, so that divers noblemen that were about him would have conveyed him forth of the field, yet he would not suffer them so to do, lest his departure from amongst his men might haply have stricken some fear into their hearts; and so, without regard of his hurt, he continued with his men and never ceased either to fight where the battle was most hot, or to encourage his men where it seemed most need . . .

At length the King . . . adventured so far that (as some write) the Earl Douglas strake him down, and at that instant slew Sir Walter Blunt and three others apparelled in the King's suit and clothing, saying 'I marvel to see so many kings thus suddenly arise, one in the neck of another'. The King indeed was raised, and did that day many a noble feat of arms, for (as it is written) he slew that day with his own hands six and thirty persons of his enemies. The other on his part, encouraged by his doings, fought valiantly, and slew the Lord Percy, called Sir Henry Hotspur . . .

To conclude, the King's enemies were vanquished and put to flight; in which flight the Earl of Douglas . . . was taken—and for his valiantness of the King frankly and freely delivered.

Henry IV and the Prince of Wales

The Lord Henry, Prince of Wales, eldest son to King Henry, got knowledge that certain of his father's servants were busy to give information against him, whereby discord might arise betwixt him and his father; for they put into the King's head not only what evil rule (according to the course of youth) the prince kept, to the offence of many, but also what great resort of people came to his house, so that the court was nothing furnished with such a train as daily followed the Prince. These tales brought no small suspicion into the King's head, lest his son would presume to usurp the crown (he being yet alive); through which suspicious jealousy it was perceived that he favoured not his son as in times past he had done.

The Prince . . . wrote his letters into every part of the realm, to reprove all such slanderous devices of those that sought his discredit. And to clear himself the better . . . he came to the court . . . [which] was then at Westminster . . . He . . . was straight admitted to the presence of the King . . . [and] kneeling down before his father, said:

> 'Most redoubted and sovereign lord and father, I am at this time come to your presence as your liege man, and as your natural son, in all things to be at your commandment. And where I understand you have in suspicion my demeanour against your grace, you know very well that if I knew any man within this realm of whom you should stand in fear, my duty were to punish that person, thereby to remove that grief from your heart. Then how much more ought I to suffer death, to ease your grace of that grief which you have of me . . . And therefore I beseech you . . . to ease your heart of all such suspicion as you have of me, and to dispatch me here, before your knees, with this same dagger . . .'

The King, moved herewith, cast from him the dagger, and, embracing the Prince, kissed him and (with shedding tears) confessed that indeed he had him partly in suspicion—though now (as he perceived) not with just cause; and therefore from henceforth no misreport should cause him to have him in mistrust . . .

So by his great wisdom was the wrongful suspicion which his father had conceived against him removed, and he restored to his favour . . .

Indeed he was youthfully given, grown to audacity, and had chosen him companions agreeable to his age, with whom he spent the time in such recreations, exercises, and delights as he fancied. But yet it should seem (by the report of some writers) that his behaviour was not offensive or at least tending to the damage of anybody, sith he had a care to avoid doing of wrong, and to tedder his affections within the tract of virtue, whereby he opened unto himself a ready passage of good liking among the prudent sort, and was beloved of such as could discern his disposition, which was in no degree so excessive as that he deserved in such vehement manner to be suspected. In whose dispraise I find little, but to his praise very much.

Classwork and Examinations

The works of Shakespeare are studied all over the world, and this classroom edition is being used in many different countries. Teaching methods vary from school to school, and there are many different ways of examining a student's work. Some teachers and examiners expect detailed knowledge of Shakespeare's text; others ask for imaginative involvement with his characters and their situations; and there are some teachers who want their students to share in the theatrical experience of directing and performing a play. Most people use a variety of methods. This section of the book offers a few suggestions for approaches to *Henry IV Part I* which could be used in schools and colleges to help with students' understanding and *enjoyment* of the play.

A Discussion
B Character Study
C Activities
D Context Questions
E Comprehension Questions
F Essays
G Projects

A Discussion

Talking about the play—about the issues it raises and the characters who are involved—is one of the most rewarding and pleasurable aspects of the study of Shakespeare. It makes sense to discuss each scene as it is read, sharing impressions — and perhaps correcting misapprehensions. It can be useful to compare aspects of this play with other fictions—plays, novels, films—or with modern life.

Suggestions

A1 A great deal of necessary information is presented in the play's first scene. How would you stage this scene so that a modern audience would be sure to understand everything?

A2 In this play the characters are much concerned with 'honour'. What do *you* understand by 'honour', and how important is it to you?

A3 Comparing himself with Richard II, King Henry warns his son about the dangers of over-familiarity:

> The skipping King, he ambled up and down,
> With shallow jesters, and rash bavin wits,
> Soon kindled and soon burnt, carded his state;
> Mingled his royalty with cap'ring fools . . .
>
> (*3*, 2, 60ff.)

How accessible do you think the monarch/president/prime minister ought to be?

A4 Discuss the different roles characters construct for themselves in this play.

A5 How are the different plots of *Henry IV Part I* related to each other?

B Character Study

Shakespeare is famous for his creation of characters who seem like real people. We can judge their actions and we can try to understand their thoughts and feelings—just as we criticize and try to understand the people we know. As the play progresses, we learn to like or dislike, love or hate, them—just as though they lived in *our* world. Characters can be studied *from the outside*, by observing what they do, and listening sensitively to what they say. This is the scholar's method: the scholar—or any reader—has access to the whole play, and can see the function of every character within the whole scheme of that play. Another approach works *from the inside*, taking a single character and looking at the action and the other characters from his/her point of view. This is an actor's technique when creating a character—who can have only a partial view of what is going on—for performance; and it asks for a student's inventive imagination. The two methods—both useful in different ways—are really complementary to each other.

Suggestions

a) from 'outside' the character

B1 At a very early point in the play (*1*, 1, 77–87), King Henry makes a comparison between his son, Prince Hal, and Henry Percy—Hotspur:

a) develop this comparison.
b) consider whether Hotspur is indeed such a paragon ('the theme of honour's tongue') as the King believes.
c) examine the extent to which 'riot and dishonour stain the brow' of the King's own son.

B2 Make a careful study of Prince Hal's soliloquy at the end of *Act 1*, Scene 2 ('I know you all . . .', lines 197–219), and consider how it affects your understanding of the Prince's character and your response to his personality.

B3 Trace the development in the character of Prince Hal from his first appearance (*Act 1*, Scene 1) in London until he leaves the play (*Act 5*, Scene 5) to march to Wales with his father.

B4 Describe the character of King Henry IV.

B5 Does your attitude to Falstaff change during the course of the play?

B6 Examine the relationship between the Earl of Northumberland and his son, Hotspur.

B7 How 'honourable' are the rebels?

b) from 'inside' a character

B8 In the character of Prince Hal, give an account—either in a private diary, or in a 'memoir' for official publication—of your relationship with Falstaff.

B9 As Falstaff, give a *sober* account of your friendship with Prince Hal.

B10 How would Poins describe, to complete strangers, the plotting and acting of the robbery at Gadshill?

B11 In Worcester's diary, record your impressions of Hotspur at the end of *Act 1*, Scene 3.

B12 In the diary of Lady Mortimer write (in English or in Welsh) your impressions of the people you have met in *Act 3*, Scene 1.

B13 As Lady Percy (Kate), write to your best friend, describing your husband and confiding your suspicions and fears for his safety after he has gone off (at the end of *Act 3*, Scene 1) to the battle of Shrewsbury.

B14 How would Francis the Drawer recount— either to his mates in the Boar's Head, or to inquisitive twentieth-century journalists—the behaviour of the Prince of Wales?

B15 Being a knight, Falstaff would be attended by a page. Write the page's account (in a letter home) of the battle of Shrewsbury.

C Activities

These can involve two or more students, preferably working *away from* the desk or study-table and using gesture and position ('body-language') as well as speech. They can help students to develop a sense of drama and the dramatic aspects of Shakespeare's play—which was written to be *performed*, not studied in a classroom.

Suggestions

C1 Act the play—or at least some part of it.

C2 Present the first scene as a press conference, with reporters from all the media and representatives of all political views—e.g. Welsh Nationalist, Royalist.

C3 Transpose the carriers' scene—*Act 2*, Scene 1—to a modern transport café.

C4 Report the Gadshill robbery as a news item in all the media—at first of only local interest until the personalities are identified.

C5 All the media are covering the Shrewsbury battlefront. Give full coverage (with signing for the deaf) from all of them. Be sure to highlight the fate of Falstaff's 'ragamuffins' and the confrontation between Prince Hal and Hotspur.

C6 Using your own words act out the scenes between
- a) Henry IV and the rebels in *Act 1*, Scene 3.
- b) Henry IV and Prince Hal in *Act 3*, Scene 2.
- c) The Archbishop of York and Sir Michael in *Act 4*, Scene 4.
- d) Hotspur and Lady Percy in *Act 3*, Scene 1.

D Context Questions

In written examinations, these questions present you with short passages from the play, and ask you to explain them. They are intended to test your knowledge of the play and your understanding of its words. Usually you have to make a choice of passages: there may be five on the paper, and you are asked to choose three. Be very sure that you know exactly how many passages you must choose. Study the ones offered to you, and select those you feel most certain of. Make your answers accurate and concise—don't waste time writing more than the examiner is asking for.

D1 And then I stole all courtesy from heaven,
And dress'd myself in such humility
That I did pluck allegiance from men's hearts,
Loud shouts and salutations from their mouths,
Even in the presence of the crowned King.

(i) Who speaks these words, and to whom are they addressed?
(ii) What has he just said about his own behaviour? With what has he contrasted it?
(iii) With what else does he go on to contrast his own behaviour?

D2 He never did fall off, my sovereign liege,
But by the chance of war: to prove that true
Needs no more but one tongue for all those wounds,
Those mouthed wounds, which valiantly he took.

(i) Who is speaking, and to whom does he refer?
(ii) Where, and from whom, did the subject of the passage receive the wounds?
(iii) What answer is given to the speaker at the end of his speech?

D3 All furnish'd, all in arms;
All plum'd like estridges that with the wind
Bated, like eagles lately bath'd;
Glittering in golden coats like images;
As full of spirit as the month of May,
And gorgeous as the sun at midsummer.

(i) Who is the speaker, and to whom is he speaking?
(ii) What is he describing?
(iii) How are his words received?

D4 Wherein is he good, but to taste sack and drink it? wherein neat and cleanly, but to carve a capon and eat it? wherein cunning, but in craft? wherein crafty, but in villainy? wherein villainous, but in all things? wherein worthy, but in nothing?

(i) Who speaks these words, and to whom does he refer?
(ii) To whom is he speaking, and why?
(iii) What does the speaker intend to do to the character he is describing?

D5 I know not whether God will have it so
For some displeasing service I have done,
That, in his secret doom, out of my blood
He'll breed revengement and a scourge for me.

(i) Who is the speaker, and to whom is he speaking?
(ii) What was the 'displeasing service', and how might God be punishing him?
(iii) What reply is made to this accusation?

E Comprehension Questions

These also present passages from the play and ask questions about them, and again you often have a choice of passages. But the extracts are much longer than those presented as context questions. A detailed knowledge of the language of the play is asked for here, and you must be able to express unusual or archaic phrases in your own words; you may also be asked to comment critically on the effectiveness of Shakespeare's language.

E1 Cousin, of many men
I do not bear these crossings; give me leave
To tell you once again that at my birth
The front of heaven was full of fiery shapes,
The goats ran from the mountains, and the herds
Were strangely clamorous to the frighted fields.
These signs have mark'd me extraordinary,
And all the courses of my life do show
I am not in the common roll of men.
Where is he living, clipp'd in with the sea
That chides the banks of England, Scotland, Wales,

Which calls me pupil or hath read to me?
And bring him out that is but woman's son
Can trace me in the tedious ways of art,
And hold me pace in deep experiments.

(i) Name the speaker and the person he calls 'Cousin'; on what occasion are they met?
(ii) Explain the meaning of 'crossings' (line 2); 'clipp'd in' (line 10); and 'read to' (line 12).
(iii) In your own words express the meaning of lines 13–15 ('And bring . . . experiments').
(iv) What do these lines show of the speaker's character?

E2 Why, hear you my masters, was it for me to kill the heir-apparent? should I turn upon the true prince? Why, thou knowest I am as valiant as Hercules: but beware instinct—the lion will not touch the true prince; instinct is a great matter: I was now a coward on instinct: I shall think the better of myself, and thee, during my life—I for a valiant lion, and thou for a true prince. But by the Lord, lads, I am glad you have the money.

(i) Give the exact context of this speech.
(ii) What is meant by 'was it for me' (line 1); 'during my life' (line 6)?
(iii) Who was 'Hercules' (line 3)?
(iv) What does this speech reveal about the character of Falstaff?

E3 My blood hath been too cold and temperate,
Unapt to stir at these indignities,
And you have found me—for accordingly
You tread upon my patience: but be sure
I will from henceforth rather be myself,
Mighty and to be fear'd, than my condition,
Which hath been smooth as oil, soft as young down,
And therefore lost that title of respect
Which the proud soul ne'er pays but to the proud.

(i) Give the precise location of this speech, identifying the speaker and the person (or persons) spoken to.
(ii) What is the meaning of 'you have found me' (line 3); 'young down' (line 7); 'title of respect' (line 8)?

(iii) Express in your own words the meaning of lines 5–6 ('I will . . . condition').
(iv) Does the King seem 'cold and temperate' in this play?

F Essays

These will usually give you a specific topic to discuss, or perhaps a question that must be answered, in writing, *with a reasoned argument*. They *never* want you to tell the story of the play—so don't! Your examiner—or teacher—has read the play and does not need to be reminded of it. Relevant quotations will always help you to make your points more strongly.

F1 Cite examples of the range of language that Shakespeare uses in *Henry IV Part I* (formal verse, informal verse, prose, etc.) and describe the effects achieved by each.

F2 Compare the two fathers (Henry IV and Northumberland) and their treatment of their sons (Hal and Hotspur).

F3 Discuss the various types of 'corruption' that you find in *Henry IV Part I*.

F4 How important are lies and the ability to lie convincingly in *Henry IV Part I*?

F5 Discuss the humour of *Henry IV Part I*.

F6 'Shakespeare engages our sympathy for the rebels, even though we never lose sight of the disloyalty of their actions.' Discuss.

F7 'The ending of the play actually resolves very little.' Discuss.

F8 'This play is not about King Henry IV, but about the future King Henry V.' Discuss.

F9 'The rebels are *characters* too: they are all individuals.' Give an account of any TWO of the rebel leaders, showing how they are distinguished from each other.

G Projects

In some schools, students are asked to do more 'free-ranging' work, which takes them outside the text—but which should always be relevant to the play. Such Projects may demand skills other than reading and writing; design and artwork, for instance, may be involved. Sometimes a 'portfolio' of work is assembled over a considerable period of time; and this can be presented to the examiner as part of the student's work for assessment.

The availability of resources will, obviously, do much to determine the nature of the Projects; but this is something that only the local teachers will understand. However, there is always help to be found in libraries, museums, and art galleries.

Suggested Topics

G1 Falstaff in performance.

G2 Falstaff as inspiration.

G3 Shakespeare's use of his sources.

G4 Shakespeare's theatre.

G5 Political uprisings as a theme in literature.

Background

England c. *1592*

When Shakespeare was writing *Henry IV Part I*, most people believed that the sun went round the earth. They were taught that this was a divinely ordered scheme of things, and that—in England—God had instituted a Church and ordained a Monarchy for the right government of the land and the populace.

'The past is a foreign country; they do things differently there.'

L.P. Hartley

Government

For most of Shakespeare's life, the reigning monarch of England was Queen Elizabeth I. With her counsellors and ministers, she governed the nation (population about five million) from London, although not more than half a million people inhabited the capital city. In the rest of the country, law and order were maintained by the land-owners and enforced by their deputies. The average man had no vote—and his wife had no rights at all.

Religion

At this time, England was a Christian country. All children were baptized, soon after they were born, into the Church of England; they were taught the essentials of the Christian faith, and instructed in their duty to God and to humankind. Marriages were performed, and funerals conducted, only by the licensed clergy and in accordance with the Church's rites and ceremonies. Attendance at divine service was compulsory; absences (without good—medical—reason) could be punished by fines. By such means, the authorities were able to keep some check on the populace—recording births, marriages, and deaths; being alert to any religious nonconformity, which could be politically dangerous; and ensuring a minimum of orthodox instruction through the official 'Homilies' which were regularly preached from the pulpits of all parish churches throughout the realm. Following Henry VIII's break away from the Church of Rome, all people in England were able to hear the church services *in their own language*. The Book of Common Prayer was used in every church, and an English translation of the Bible was read aloud in public. The Christian religion had never been so well taught before!

Education

School education reinforced the Church's teaching. From the age of four, boys might attend the 'petty school' (French '*petite école*') to learn the rudiments of reading and writing along with a few prayers; some schools also included work with numbers. At the age of seven, the boy was ready for the grammar school (if his father was willing and able to pay the fees).

A thorough grounding in Latin grammar was followed by translation work and the study of Roman authors, paying attention as much to style as to matter. The arts of fine writing were thus inculcated from early youth. A very few students proceeded to university; these were either clever scholarship boys, or else the sons of noblemen. Girls stayed at home, and acquired domestic and social skills—cooking, sewing, perhaps even music. The lucky ones might learn to read and write.

Language

At the start of the sixteenth century the English had a very poor opinion of their own language: there was little serious writing in English, and hardly any literature. Latin was the language of international scholarship, and Englishmen admired the eloquence of the Romans. They made many translations, and in this way they extended the resources of their own language, increasing its vocabulary and stretching its grammatical structures. French, Italian, and Spanish works were also translated, and for the first time, there were English versions of the Bible. By the end of the century, English was a language to be proud of: it was rich in synonyms, capable of infinite variety and subtlety, and ready for all kinds of word-play—especially the *puns*, for which Shakespeare's English is renowned.

Drama

The great art-form of the Elizabethan age was its drama. The Elizabethans inherited a tradition of play-acting from the Middle Ages, and they reinforced this by reading and translating the

Roman playwrights. At the beginning of the sixteenth century, plays were performed by groups of actors, all-male companies (boys acted the female roles) who travelled from town to town, setting up their stages in open places (such as inn-yards) or, with the permission of the owner, in the hall of some noble house. The touring companies continued, in the provinces, into the seventeenth century; but in London, in 1576, a new building was erected for the performance of plays. This was the Theatre, the first purpose-built playhouse in England. Other playhouses followed, (including Shakespeare's own theatre, the Globe) and the English drama reached new heights of eloquence.

There were those who disapproved, of course. The theatres, which brought large crowds together, could encourage the spread of disease—and dangerous ideas. During the summer, when the plague was at its worst, the playhouses were closed. A political censorship was imposed, more or less severe at different times. The Puritan faction tried to close down the theatres, but—partly because there was royal favour for the drama, and partly because the buildings were outside the city limits—they did not succeed until 1642.

Theatre

From contemporary comments and sketches—most particularly a drawing by a Dutch visitor, Johannes de Witt—it is possible to form some idea of the typical Elizabethan playhouse for which most of Shakespeare's plays were written. Hexagonal in shape, it had three roofed galleries encircling an open courtyard. The plain, high stage projected into the yard, where it was surrounded by the audience of standing 'groundlings'. At the back were two doors for the actors' entrances and exits; and above these doors was a balcony—useful for a musicians' gallery or for the acting of scenes '*above*'. Over the stage was a thatched roof, supported on two pillars, forming a canopy—which seems to have been painted with the sun, moon, and stars for the 'heavens'. Underneath was space (concealed by curtaining) which could be used by characters ascending and descending through a trap-door in the stage. Costumes and properties were kept backstage, in the 'tiring house'. The actors dressed lavishly, often wearing the secondhand clothes bestowed by rich patrons. Stage properties were important for defining a location, but the dramatist's own words were needed to explain the time of day, since all performances took place in the early afternoon.

Selected Further Reading

Bevington, David (ed.), *Henry IV, Parts 1 and 2: Critical Essays*, (New York and London, 1986).

Hunter, G.K. (ed.), *'Henry IV, Parts 1 and 2': A Casebook*, (London, 1970).

Reese, M.M., *The Cease of Majesty*, (London, 1961).

Ribner, Irving, *The English History Play in the Age of Shakespeare*, (Princeton, NJ, 1957; rev. edn., 1965).

Tillyard, E.M.W., *The Elizabethan World Picture*, (London, 1943).

Tillyard, E.M.W., *Shakespeare's History Plays*, (London, 1944).

Traversi, Derek A., *Shakespeare: From 'Richard II' to 'Henry V'*, (Stanford, Calif., 1957).

Vickers, Brian, *The Artistry of Shakespeare's Prose*, (London, 1968).

Background Reading

Blake, N.F., *Shakespeare's Language: an Introduction*, (Methuen, 1983).

Muir, K., and Schoenbaum, S., *A New Companion to Shakespeare Studies*, (Cambridge, 1971).

Schoenbaum, S., *William Shakespeare: A Documentary Life*, (Oxford, 1975).

Thomson, Peter, *Shakespeare's Theatre*, (Routledge and Kegan Paul, 1983).

William Shakespeare, 1564–1616

Elizabeth I was Queen of England when Shakespeare was born in 1564. He was the son of a tradesman who made and sold gloves in the small town of Stratford-upon-Avon, and he was educated at the grammar school in that town. Shakespeare did not go to university when he left school, but worked, perhaps in his father's business. When he was eighteen he married Anne Hathaway, who became the mother of his daughter, Susanna, in 1583, and of twins in 1585.

There is nothing exciting, or even unusual, in this story; and from 1585 until 1592 there are no documents that can tell us anything at all about Shakespeare. But we have learned that in 1592 he was known in London, and that he had become both an actor and a playwright.

We do not know when Shakespeare wrote his first play, and indeed we are not sure of the order in which he wrote his works. If you look on page 148 at the list of his writings and their approximate dates, you will see how he started by writing plays on subjects taken from the history of England. No doubt this was partly because he was always an intensely patriotic man—but he was also a very shrewd business-man. He could see that the theatre audiences enjoyed being shown their own history, and it was certain that he would make a profit from this kind of drama.

The plays in the next group are mainly comedies, with romantic love stories of young people who fall in love with one another and, at the end of the play, marry and live happily ever after.

At the end of the sixteenth century the happiness disappears, and Shakespeare's plays become melancholy, bitter, and tragic. This change may have been caused by some sadness in the writer's life (one of his twins died in 1596). Shakespeare, however, was not the only writer whose works at this time were very serious. The whole of England was facing a crisis. Queen Elizabeth I was growing old. She was greatly loved, and the people were sad to think she must soon die; they were also afraid, for the Queen had never married, and so there was no child to succeed her.

When James I came to the throne in 1603, Shakespeare

continued to write serious drama—the great tragedies and the plays based on Roman history (such as *Julius Caesar*) for which he is most famous. Finally, before he retired from the theatre, he wrote another set of comedies. These all have the same theme: they tell of happiness which is lost, and then found again.

Shakespeare returned from London to Stratford, his home town. He was rich and successful, and he owned one of the biggest houses in the town. He died in 1616.

Shakespeare also wrote two long poems, and a collection of sonnets. The sonnets describe two love-affairs, but we do not know who the lovers were. Although there are many public documents concerned with his career as a writer and a business-man, Shakespeare has hidden his personal life from us. A nineteenth-century poet, Matthew Arnold, addressed Shakespeare in a poem and wrote 'We ask and ask—Thou smilest, and art still'.

There is not even a trustworthy portrait of the world's greatest dramatist.

Approximate order of composition of Shakespeare's works

Period	Comedies	History plays	Tragedies	Poems
I	Comedy of Errors	Henry VI, part 1	Titus Andronicus	
	Taming of the Shrew	Henry VI, part 2		
1594	Two Gentlemen of Verona	Henry VI, part 3		
		Richard III		Venus and Adonis
	Love's Labour's Lost	King John		Rape of Lucrece
II	Midsummer Night's Dream	Richard II	Romeo and Juliet	Sonnets
	Merchant of Venice	Henry IV, part 1		
1599	Merry Wives of Windsor	Henry IV, part 2		
	Much Ado About Nothing			
	As You Like It	Henry V		
III	Twelfth Night		Julius Caesar	
	Troilus and Cressida		Hamlet	
1608	Measure for Measure		Othello	
	All's Well That Ends Well		Timon of Athens	
			King Lear	
			Macbeth	
			Antony and Cleopatra	
			Coriolanus	
IV	Pericles			
	Cymbeline			
1613	The Winter's Tale			
	The Tempest	Henry VIII		